Neural Network Projects
with Python

The ultimate guide to using Python to explore the true power
of neural networks through six projects

James Loy

BIRMINGHAM - MUMBAI

Neural Network Projects with Python

Commissioning Editor: Pravin Dhandre
Acquisition Editor: Nelson Morris
Content Development Editor: Pratik Andrade
Technical Editor: Jovita Alva
Copy Editor: Safis Editing
Project Coordinator: Namrata Swetta
Proofreader: Safis Editing
Indexer: Rekha Nair
Graphics: Jisha Chirayil
Production Coordinator: Arvindkumar Gupta

First published: February 2019

Production reference: 1270219

Published by Packt Publishing Ltd.
Livery Place
35 Livery Street
Birmingham
B3 2PB, UK.

ISBN 978-1-78913-890-0

www.packtpub.com

To my wife Agnes Lim - my partner, soulmate, and cheerleader.
Without her, this book would not have been possible.

- James Loy

`mapt.io`

Mapt is an online digital library that gives you full access to over 5,000 books and videos, as well as industry leading tools to help you plan your personal development and advance your career. For more information, please visit our website.

Why subscribe?

- Spend less time learning and more time coding with practical eBooks and Videos from over 4,000 industry professionals

- Improve your learning with Skill Plans built especially for you

- Get a free eBook or video every month

- Mapt is fully searchable

- Copy and paste, print, and bookmark content

Packt.com

Did you know that Packt offers eBook versions of every book published, with PDF and ePub files available? You can upgrade to the eBook version at `www.packt.com` and as a print book customer, you are entitled to a discount on the eBook copy. Get in touch with us at `customercare@packtpub.com` for more details.

At `www.packt.com`, you can also read a collection of free technical articles, sign up for a range of free newsletters, and receive exclusive discounts and offers on Packt books and eBooks.

Contributors

About the author

James Loy has more than five years, expert experience in data science in the finance and healthcare industries. He has worked with the largest bank in Singapore to drive innovation and improve customer loyalty through predictive analytics. He has also experience in the healthcare sector, where he applied data analytics to improve decision-making in hospitals. He has a master's degree in computer science from Georgia Tech, with a specialization in machine learning.

His research interest includes deep learning and applied machine learning, as well as developing computer-vision-based AI agents for automation in industry. He writes on *Towards Data Science*, a popular machine learning website with more than 3 million views per month.

About the reviewer

Mike Thompson has worked as a software engineer in a variety of roles involving data engineering, service development, and distributed systems design over the past 8 years.

Mike worked for Bungie and helped ship game titles in the Destiny franchise. His credits include Destiny in 2014 and Destiny 2 in 2017, including many expansions in between for both titles. His contributions were integral to scaling Bungie's backend data infrastructure and allowing millions of players to enjoy the Destiny games.

Mike now works for ProbablyMonsters, a growing family of game studios, where he focuses on data services and infrastructure, along with many other duties that are required to get a new business off the ground.

Packt is searching for authors like you

If you're interested in becoming an author for Packt, please visit authors.packtpub.com and apply today. We have worked with thousands of developers and tech professionals, just like you, to help them share their insight with the global tech community. You can make a general application, apply for a specific hot topic that we are recruiting an author for, or submit your own idea.

Table of Contents

Preface

Machine learning and **artificial intelligence (AI)** have become ubiquitous in our everyday lives. Wherever we go, whatever we do, we are constantly interacting with AI in one way or another. And neural networks and deep learning are driving these AI advances. Powered by neural networks, AI systems are now able to achieve human-like performance in many areas.

This book provides you with the opportunity to create six different neural network projects from scratch. Through these projects, you will have the opportunity to create some of the AI systems that we commonly see today, including face recognition, sentiment analysis, and medical diagnosis. In each project, we'll provide a problem statement, the specific neural network architecture to be used to tackle that problem, the reasoning for the choice of neural network used, and the Python code to implement the given solution from scratch.

By the end of the book, you will be well versed in the different neural network architectures, having created cutting edge AI projects in Python that will immediately strengthen your machine learning portfolio.

Who this book is for

This book is perfect for data scientists, machine learning engineers, and deep learning enthusiasts who wish to create practical neural network projects in Python. Readers should have some basic knowledge with regard to Python and machine learning to follow the exercises in this book.

What this book covers

Chapter 1, *Machine Learning and Neural Networks 101*, covers the basics of machine learning and neural networks. The first chapter aims to solidify your understanding of machine learning and neural networks. To do that, we'll create our own neural network from scratch in Python, without any machine learning libraries.

Chapter 2, *Predicting Diabetes with Multilayer Perceptrons*, kick-starts our first neural network project. Using a basic neural network known as a multilayer perceptron, we'll build a classifier that can predict whether a patient is at risk of diabetes.

Chapter 3, *Predicting Taxi Fares with Deep Feedforward Nets,* makes use of a deep feedforward neural network in a regression problem. In particular, we'll use a neural network to predict taxi fares in New York City.

Chapter 4, *Cats Versus Dogs – Image Classification Using CNNs,* uses a **convolutional neural network (CNN)** for an image classification problem. We'll use the CNN to predict whether an image includes a cat or a dog.

Chapter 5, *Removing Noise from Images Using Autoencoders,* leverages on autoencoders for noise removal in images. The images come from office documents corrupted by coffee stains and other artifacts. We'll use autoencoders to remove these artifacts from the images, restoring them to their original state.

Chapter 6, *Sentiment Analysis on Movie Reviews Using LSTM,* uses a **long short-term memory (LSTM)** neural network to analyze and classify the sentiment of movie reviews posted online. We'll create an LSTM neural network that is able to discern the sentiment of written English sentences.

Chapter 7, *Implementing a Face Recognition System with Neural Networks,* uses a Siamese neural network to build a facial recognition system that can recognize our own faces, using the webcam in our laptop.

Chapter 8, *What's Next?,* summarizes everything that we have learned in this book. We'll peer ahead into the future and see what machine learning and AI will look like in the next few years.

To get the most out of this book

You should have some basic familiarity with programming in Python in order to get the most out of this book. Nevertheless, the book will take you through every step in the project and explain the code as much as possible.

In terms of hardware, you should be running the code on a fairly modern computer with at least 8 GB of RAM and 15 GB of hard disk space (for the datasets). Training deep neural networks requires strong computational resources, and can be sped up significantly if you have a dedicated GPU. However, it is perfectly fine to run the code without a GPU, as well (such as on a laptop). Throughout the book, we will alert you if certain code will take some time to run if you do not have a GPU.

At the start of each chapter, we will inform you of the necessary Python libraries required for the project. To simplify the set-up process, we have provided an `environment.yml` file together with the code. The `environment.yml` file allows you to easily set up a virtual environment with the specific Python version and the requisite libraries installed in it. This way, you can be assured that your code will be running in a standardized virtual environment that we have designed. Detailed instructions will be provided in `Chapter 1`, *Machine Learning and Neural Networks 101*, under the *Setting up your computer for machine learning* section, as well as at the start of each chapter.

Download the example code files

You can download the example code files for this book from your account at `www.packt.com`. If you purchased this book elsewhere, you can visit `www.packt.com/support` and register to have the files emailed directly to you.

You can download the code files by following these steps:

1. Log in or register at `www.packt.com`.
2. Select the **SUPPORT** tab.
3. Click on **Code Downloads & Errata**.
4. Enter the name of the book in the **Search** box and follow the onscreen instructions.

Once the file is downloaded, please make sure that you unzip or extract the folder using the latest version of:

- WinRAR/7-Zip for Windows
- Zipeg/iZip/UnRarX for Mac
- 7-Zip/PeaZip for Linux

The code bundle for the book is also hosted on GitHub at `https://github.com/PacktPublishing/Neural-Network-Projects-with-Python`. In case there's an update to the code, it will be updated on the existing GitHub repository.

We also have other code bundles from our rich catalog of books and videos available at `https://github.com/PacktPublishing/`. Check them out!

Download the color images

We also provide a PDF file that has color images of the screenshots/diagrams used in this book. You can download it here: http://www.packtpub.com/sites/default/files/downloads/9781789138900_ColorImages.pdf.

Conventions used

There are a number of text conventions used throughout this book.

CodeInText: Indicates code words in text, database table names, folder names, filenames, file extensions, pathnames, dummy URLs, user input, and Twitter handles. Here is an example: "We apply the detect_faces function that we defined earlier on these images."

A block of code is set as follows:

```
def detect_faces(img, draw_box=True):
  # convert image to grayscale
  grayscale_img = cv2.cvtColor(img, cv2.COLOR_BGR2GRAY)
```

Any command-line input or output is written as follows:

```
$ cd Neural-Network-Projects-with-Python
```

Bold: Indicates a new term, an important word, or words that you see on screen. For example, words in menus or dialog boxes appear in the text like this.

Warnings or important notes appear like this.

Tips and tricks appear like this.

Get in touch

Feedback from our readers is always welcome.

General feedback: If you have questions about any aspect of this book, mention the book title in the subject of your message and email us at customercare@packtpub.com.

Errata: Although we have taken every care to ensure the accuracy of our content, mistakes do happen. If you have found a mistake in this book, we would be grateful if you would report this to us. Please visit www.packt.com/submit-errata, selecting your book, clicking on the Errata Submission Form link, and entering the details.

Piracy: If you come across any illegal copies of our works in any form on the Internet, we would be grateful if you would provide us with the location address or website name. Please contact us at copyright@packt.com with a link to the material.

If you are interested in becoming an author: If there is a topic that you have expertise in and you are interested in either writing or contributing to a book, please visit authors.packtpub.com.

Reviews

Please leave a review. Once you have read and used this book, why not leave a review on the site that you purchased it from? Potential readers can then see and use your unbiased opinion to make purchase decisions, we at Packt can understand what you think about our products, and our authors can see your feedback on their book. Thank you!

For more information about Packt, please visit packt.com.

Machine Learning and Neural Networks 101

1

Artificial intelligence (AI) has captured much of our attention in recent years. From face recognition security systems in our smartphones to booking an Uber ride through Alexa, AI has become ubiquitous in our everyday lives. Still, we are constantly being reminded that the full potential of AI has not yet been realized, and that AI will become an even bigger transformative factor in our lives.

When we look at the horizon, we can see the relentless progression of AI with its promise to better our everyday lives. Powered by AI, self-driving cars are becoming less science fiction, and more of a reality. Self-driving cars aim to reduce traffic accidents by eliminating human error, ultimately improving our lives. Similarly, the usage of AI in healthcare promises to improve outcomes. Notably, the UK's National Health Service has announced an ambitious AI project to diagnose early-stage cancer, which can potentially save thousands of lives.

The transformative nature of AI has led experts to call it the fourth industrial revolution. AI is the catalyst that will shape modern industries, and having knowledge of AI is essential in this new world. By the end of this book, you will have a better understanding of the algorithms that power AI, and will have developed real-life projects using these cutting-edge algorithms.

In this chapter, we will cover the following topics:

- A primer on machine learning and neural networks
- Setting up your computer for machine learning
- Executing your machine learning projects from start to finish using the machine learning workflow

- Creating your own neural network from scratch in Python without using a machine learning library
- Using pandas for data analysis in Python
- Leveraging machine learning libraries such as Keras to build powerful neural networks

What is machine learning?

Although machine learning and AI are often used interchangeably, there are subtle differences that set them apart. The term AI was first coined in the 1950s, and it refers to the capability of a machine to imitate intelligent human behavior. To that end, researchers and computer scientists have pursued several approaches. Early efforts in AI were centered around an approach known as symbolic AI. Symbolic AI attempts to express human knowledge in a declarative form that computers could process. The height of symbolic AI resulted in the expert system, a computer system that emulated human decision making.

However, one major drawback of symbolic AI is that it relied on the domain knowledge of human experts, and required those rules and knowledge to be hardcoded for problem-solving. AI as a scientific field went through a period of drought (known as the AI winter), when scientists became increasingly disillusioned by the limitations of AI.

While symbolic AI took center stage in the 1950s, a subfield of AI known as machine learning was quietly bubbling in the background.

Machine learning refers to algorithms that computers use to learn from data, allowing it to make predictions on future, unseen data.

However, early AI researchers did not pay much attention to machine learning, as computers back then were neither powerful enough nor had the capability to store the huge amount of data that machine learning algorithms require. As it turns out, machine learning would not be left in the cold for long. In the late 2000s, AI enjoyed a resurgence, with machine learning largely propelling its growth. The key reason for this resurgence was the maturation of computer systems that could collect and store a massive amount of data (big data), along with processors that are fast enough to run the machine learning algorithms. Thus, the AI summer began.

Machine learning algorithms

Now that we have talked about what machine learning is, we need to understand how machine learning algorithms work. Machine learning algorithms can be broadly classified into two categories:

- **Supervised learning**: Using labeled training data, the algorithm learns the rule for mapping the input variables into the target variable. For example, a supervised learning algorithm learns to predict whether there will be rain (the target variable) from input variables such as the temperature, time, season, atmospheric pressure, and so on.
- **Unsupervised learning**: Using unlabeled training data, the algorithm learns associative rules for the data. The most common use case for unsupervised learning algorithms is in clustering analysis, where the algorithm learns hidden patterns and groups in data that are not explicitly labeled.

In this book, we will focus on supervised learning algorithms. As a concrete example of a supervised learning algorithm, let's consider the following problem. You are an animal lover and a machine learning enthusiast and you wish to build a machine learning algorithm using supervised learning to predict whether an animal is a friend (a friendly puppy) or a foe (a dangerous bear). For simplicity, let's assume that you have collected two measurements from different breeds of dogs and bears—their **Weight** and their **Speed**. After collecting the data (known as the training dataset), you plot them out on a graph, along with their labels (**Friend or Foe**):

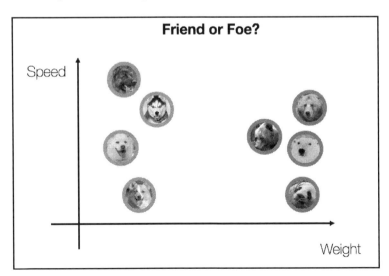

Immediately, we can see that dogs tend to weigh less, and are generally faster, while bears are heavier and generally slower. If we draw a line (known as a decision boundary) between the dogs and the bears, we can use that line to make future predictions. Whenever we receive the measurements for a new animal, we can just see if it falls to the left or to the right of the line. Friends are to the left, and foes are to the right.

But this is a trivial dataset. What if we collect hundreds of different measurements? Then the graph would be more than 100-dimensional, and it would be impossible for a human being to draw a dividing line. However, such a task is not a problem for machine learning.

In this example, the task of the machine learning algorithm is to learn the optimal decision boundary separating the datasets. Ideally, we want the algorithm to produce a **Decision Boundary** that completely separates the two classes of data (although this is not always possible, depending on the dataset):

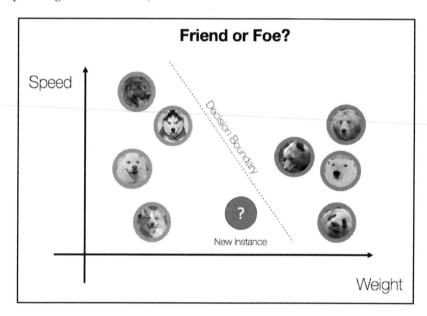

With this **Decision Boundary**, we can then make predictions on future, unseen data. If the **New Instance** lies to the left of the **Decision Boundary**, then we classify it as a friend. Vice versa, if the new instance lies to the right of the **Decision Boundary**, then we classify it as a foe.

In this trivial example, we have used only two input variables and two classes. However, we can generalize the problem to include multiple input variables with multiple classes.

Naturally, our choice of machine learning algorithm affects the kind of decision boundary produced. Some of the more popular supervised machine learning algorithms are as follows:

- Neural networks
- Linear regression
- Logistic regression
- **Support vector machines (SVMs)**
- Decision trees

The nature of the dataset (such as an image dataset or a numerical dataset) and the underlying problem that we are trying to solve should dictate the machine learning algorithm used. In this book, we will focus on neural networks.

The machine learning workflow

We have discussed what machine learning is. But how exactly do you *do* machine learning? At a high level, machine learning projects are all about taking in raw data as input and churning out **Predictions** as **Output**. To do that, there are several important intermediate steps that must be accomplished. This machine learning workflow can be summarized by the following diagram:

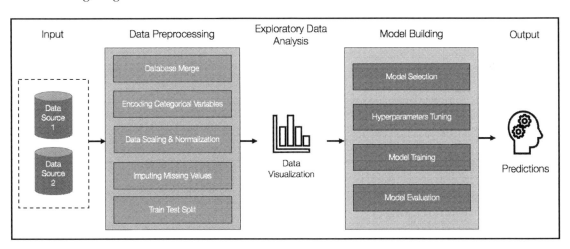

The **Input** to our machine learning workflow will always be data. Data can come from different sources, with different data formats. For example, if we are working on a computer vision-based project, then our data will likely be images. For most other machine learning projects, the data will be presented in a tabular form, similar to spreadsheets. In some machine learning projects, data collection will be a significant first step. In this book, we will assume that the data will be provided to us, allowing us to focus on the machine learning aspect.

The next step is to preprocess the data. Raw data is often messy, error-prone, and unsuitable for machine learning algorithms. Hence, we need to preprocess the data before we feed it to our models. In cases where data is provided from multiple sources, we need to merge the data into a single dataset. Machine learning models also require a numeric dataset for training purposes. If there are any categorical variables in the raw dataset (that is, gender, country, day of week, and so on), we need to encode those variables as numeric variables. We will see how we can do so later on in the chapter. Data scaling and normalization is also required for certain machine learning algorithms. The intuition behind this is that if the magnitude of certain variables is much greater than other variables, then certain machine learning algorithms will mistakenly place more emphasis on those dominating variables.

Real-world datasets are often messy. You will find that the data is incomplete and contains missing data in several rows and columns. There are several ways to deal with missing data, each with its own advantages and disadvantages. The easiest way is to simply discard rows and columns with missing data. However, this may not be practical, as we may end up discarding a significant percentage of our data. We can also replace the missing variables with the mean of the variables (if the variables happen to be numeric). This approach is more ideal than discarding data, as it preserves our dataset. However, replacing missing values with the mean tends to affect the distribution of the data, which may negatively impact our machine learning models. One other method is to predict what the missing values are, based on other values that are present. However, we have to be careful as doing this may introduce significant bias into our dataset.

Lastly, in **Data Preprocessing**, we need to split the dataset into a training and testing dataset. Our machine learning models will be trained and fitted only on the training set. Once we are satisfied with the performance of our model, we will then evaluate our model using the testing dataset. Note that our model should never be trained on the testing set. This ensures that the evaluation of model performance is unbiased, and will reflect its real-world performance.

Once **Data Preprocessing** has been completed, we will move on to **Exploratory Data Analysis (EDA)**. EDA is the process of uncovering insights from your data using data visualization. EDA allows us to construct new features (known as feature engineering) and inject domain knowledge into our machine learning models.

Finally, we get to the heart of machine learning. After **Data Preprocessing** and EDA have been completed, we move on to **Model Building**. As mentioned in the earlier section, there are several machine learning algorithms at our disposal, and the nature of the problem should dictate the type of machine learning algorithm used. In this book, we will focus on neural networks. In **Model Building**, **Hyperparameter Tuning** is an essential step, and the right hyperparameters can drastically improve the performance of our model. In a later section, we will look at some of the hyperparameters in a neural network. Once the model has been trained, we are finally ready to evaluate our model using the testing set.

As we can see, the machine learning workflow consists of many intermediate steps, each of which are crucial to the overall performance of our model. The major advantage of using Python for machine learning is that the entire machine learning workflow can be executed end-to-end entirely in Python, using just a handful of open source libraries. In this book, you will gain experience using Python in each step of the machine learning workflow, as you create sophisticated neural network projects from scratch.

Setting up your computer for machine learning

Before we dive deeper into neural networks and machine learning, let's make sure that you have set up your computer properly, so that you can run the code in this book smoothly.

In this book, we will use the Python programming language for each neural network project. Along with Python itself, we also require several Python libraries, such as Keras, pandas, NumPy, and many more. There are several ways to install Python and the required libraries, but the easiest way by far is to use Anaconda.

Anaconda is a free and open source distribution of Python and its libraries. Anaconda provides a handy package manager that allows us to easily install Python and all other libraries that we require. To install Anaconda, simply head to the website at `https://www.anaconda.com/distribution/` and download the Anaconda installer (select the Python 3.x installer).

Besides Anaconda, we also require Git. Git is essential for machine learning and software engineering in general. Git allows us to easily download code from GitHub, which is probably the most widely used software hosting service. To install Git, head to the Git website at `https://git-scm.com/book/en/v2/Getting-Started-Installing-Git`. You can simply download and run the appropriate installer for your OS.

Once Anaconda and Git are installed, we are ready to download the code for this book. The code that you see in this book can be found in our accompanying GitHub repository.

To download the code, simply run the following command from a command line (use Terminal if you're using macOS/Linux, and if you're using Windows, use the Anaconda Command Prompt):

```
$ git clone
https://github.com/PacktPublishing/Neural-Network-Projects-with-Python
```

The `git clone` command will download all the Python code in this book to your computer.

Once that's done, run the following command to move into the folder that you just downloaded:

```
$ cd Neural-Network-Projects-with-Python
```

Within the folder, you will find a file titled `environment.yml`. With this file, we can install Python and all the required libraries into a virtual environment. You can think of a virtual environment as an isolated, sandboxed environment where we can install a fresh copy of Python and all the required libraries. The `environment.yml` file contains instructions for Anaconda to install a specific version of each library into a virtual environment. This ensures that the Python code will be executed in a standardized environment that we have designed.

To install the required dependencies using Anaconda and the `environment.yml` file, simply execute the following command from a command line:

```
$ conda env create -f environment.yml
```

Just like that, Anaconda will install all required packages into a `neural-network-projects-python` virtual environment. To enter this virtual environment, we execute this next command:

```
$ conda activate neural-network-projects-python
```

That's it! We are now in a virtual environment with all dependencies installed. To execute a Python file in this virtual environment, we can run something like this:

```
$ python Chapter01\keras_chapter1.py
```

To leave the virtual environment, we can run the following command:

```
$ conda deactivate
```

Just note that you should be within the virtual environment (by running `conda activate neural-network-projects-python` first) whenever you run any Python code provided by us.

Now that we've set up our computer, let's return back to neural networks. We'll look at the theory behind neural networks, and how to program one from scratch in Python.

Neural networks

Neural networks are a class of machine learning algorithms that are loosely inspired by neurons in the human brain. However, without delving too much into brain analogies, I find it easier to simply describe neural networks as a mathematical function that maps a given input to the desired output. To understand what that means, let's take a look at a single layer neural network (known as a perceptron).

A **Perceptron** can be illustrated with the following diagram:

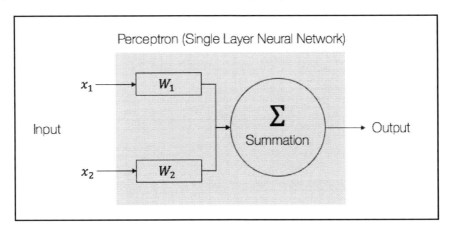

At its core, the **Perceptron** is simply a mathematical function that takes in a set of inputs, performs some mathematical computation, and outputs the result of the computation. In this case, that mathematical function is simply this:

$$y = \sum (w_i * x_i)$$

w_i refers to the weights of the **Perceptron**. We will explain what the weights in a neural network refers to in the next few sections. For now, we just need to keep in mind that neural networks are simply mathematical functions that map a given input to a desired output.

Why neural networks?

Before we dive into creating our own neural network, it is worth understanding why neural networks have gained such an important foothold in machine learning and AI.

The first reason is that neural networks are universal function approximators. What that means is that given any arbitrary function that we are trying to model, no matter how complex, neural networks are always able to represent that function. This has a profound implication on neural networks and AI in general. Assuming that any problem in the world can be described by a mathematical function (no matter how complex), we can use neural networks to represent that function, effectively modeling anything in the world. A caveat to this is that while scientists have proved the universality of neural networks, a large and complex neural network may never be trained and generalized correctly.

The second reason is that the architecture of neural networks are highly scalable and flexible. As we will see in the next section, we can easily stack layers in each neural network, increasing the complexity of the neural network. Perhaps more interestingly, the capabilities of neural networks are only limited by our own imagination. Through creative neural network architecture design, machine learning engineers have learned how to use neural networks to predict time series data (known as **recurrent neural networks (RNNs)**), which are used in areas such as speech recognition. In recent years, scientists have also shown that by pitting two neural networks against each other in a contest (known as a **generative adversarial network (GAN)**), we can generate photorealistic images that are indistinguishable to the human eye.

The basic architecture of neural networks

In this section, we will look at the basic architecture of neural networks, the building blocks on which all complex neural networks are based. We will also code up our own basic neural network from scratch in Python, without any machine learning libraries. This exercise will help you gain an intuitive understanding of the inner workings of neural networks.

Neural networks consist of the following components:

- An input layer, x
- An arbitrary amount of hidden layers
- An output layer, $\hat{y}$
- A set of weights and biases between each layer, W and b
- A choice of activation function for each hidden layer, σ

The following diagram shows the architecture of a two-layer neural network (note that the input layer is typically excluded when counting the number of layers in a neural network):

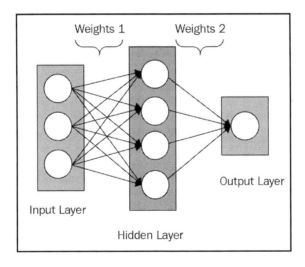

Training a neural network from scratch in Python

Now that we understand the basic architecture of a neural network, let's create our own neural network from scratch in Python.

First, let's create a `NeuralNetwork` class in Python:

```python
import numpy as np

class NeuralNetwork:
    def __init__(self, x, y):
        self.input    = x
        self.weights1 = np.random.rand(self.input.shape[1],4)
        self.weights2 = np.random.rand(4,1)
        self.y        = y
        self.output = np.zeros(self.y.shape)
```

 Notice that in the preceding code, we initialize the weights (`self.weights1` and `self.weights2`) as a NumPy array with random values. NumPy arrays are used to represent multidimensional arrays in Python. The exact dimensions of our weights are specified in the parameters of the `np.random.rand()` function. For the dimensions of the first weight array, we use a variable (`self.input.shape[1]`) to create an array of variable dimensions, depending on the size of our input.

The output, $\hat{y}$, of a simple two-layer neural network is as follows:

$$\hat{y} = \sigma(W_2\sigma(W_1x + b_1) + b_2)$$

You might notice that in the preceding equation, the weights, W, and the biases, b, are the only variables that affects the output, $\hat{y}$.

Naturally, the right values for the weights and biases determine the strength of the predictions. The process of fine-tuning the weights and biases from the input data is known as training the neural network.

Each iteration of the training process consists of the following steps:

1. Calculating the predicted output $\hat{y}$, known as **Feedforward**
2. Updating the weights and biases, known as **Backpropagation**

The following sequential graph illustrates the process:

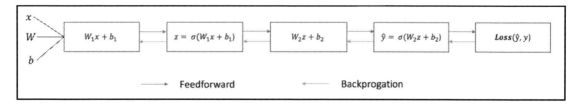

Feedforward

As we've seen in the preceding sequential graph, feedforward is just simple calculus, and for a basic two-layer neural network, the output of the neural network is as follows:

$$\hat{y} = \sigma(W_2 \sigma(W_1 x + b_1) + b_2)$$

Let's add a `feedforward` function in our Python code to do exactly that. Note that for simplicity, we have assumed the biases to be `0`:

```python
import numpy as np

def sigmoid(x):
    return 1.0/(1 + np.exp(-x))

class NeuralNetwork:
    def __init__(self, x, y):
        self.input    = x
        self.weights1 = np.random.rand(self.input.shape[1],4)
        self.weights2 = np.random.rand(4,1)
        self.y        = y
        self.output   = np.zeros(self.y.shape)

    def feedforward(self):
        self.layer1 = sigmoid(np.dot(self.input, self.weights1))
        self.output = sigmoid(np.dot(self.layer1, self.weights2))
```

However, we still need a way to evaluate the accuracy of our predictions (that is, how far off our predictions are). The `loss` function allows us to do exactly that.

The loss function

There are many available `loss` functions, and the nature of our problem should dictate our choice of `loss` function. For now, we'll use a simple *Sum-of-Squares Error* as our `loss` function:

$$Sum - of - Squares\ Error = \sum_{i=1}^{n}(y - \hat{y})^2$$

The *sum-of-squares error* is simply the sum of the difference between each predicted value and the actual value. The difference is squared so that we measure the absolute value of the difference.

Our goal in training is to find the best set of weights and biases that minimizes the `loss` function.

Backpropagation

Now that we've measured the error of our prediction (loss), we need to find a way to propagate the error back, and to update our weights and biases.

In order to know the appropriate amount to adjust the weights and biases by, we need to know the derivative of the `loss` function with respect to the weights and biases.

Recall from calculus that the derivative of a function is simply the slope of the function:

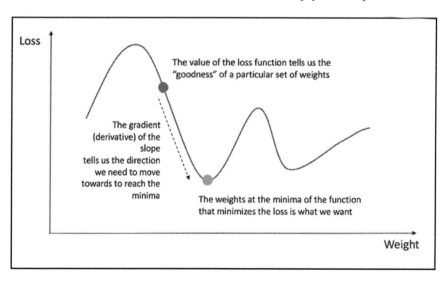

If we have the derivative, we can simply update the weights and biases by increasing/reducing with it (refer to the preceding diagram). This is known as **gradient descent**.

However, we can't directly calculate the derivative of the `loss` function with respect to the weights and biases because the equation of the `loss` function does not contain the weights and biases. We need the chain rule to help us calculate it. At this point, we are not going to delve into the chain rule because the math behind it can be rather complicated. Furthermore, machine learning libraries such as Keras takes care of gradient descent for us without requiring us to work out the chain rule from scratch. The key idea that we need to know is that once we have the derivative (slope) of the `loss` function with respect to the weights, we can adjust the weights accordingly.

Now let's add the `backprop` function into our Python code:

```python
import numpy as np

def sigmoid(x):
    return 1.0/(1 + np.exp(-x))

def sigmoid_derivative(x):
    return x * (1.0 - x)

class NeuralNetwork:
    def __init__(self, x, y):
        self.input    = x
        self.weights1 = np.random.rand(self.input.shape[1],4)
        self.weights2 = np.random.rand(4,1)
        self.y        = y
        self.output = np.zeros(self.y.shape)

    def feedforward(self):
        self.layer1 = sigmoid(np.dot(self.input, self.weights1))
        self.output = sigmoid(np.dot(self.layer1, self.weights2))

    def backprop(self):
        # application of the chain rule to find the derivation of the
        # loss function with respect to weights2 and weights1
        d_weights2 = np.dot(self.layer1.T, (2*(self.y - self.output) *
                    sigmoid_derivative(self.output)))
        d_weights1 = np.dot(self.input.T, (np.dot(2*(self.y - self.output)
                    * sigmoid_derivative(self.output), self.weights2.T) *
                    sigmoid_derivative(self.layer1)))

        self.weights1 += d_weights1
        self.weights2 += d_weights2
```

```
if __name__ == "__main__":
    X = np.array([[0,0,1],
                  [0,1,1],
                  [1,0,1],
                  [1,1,1]])
    y = np.array([[0],[1],[1],[0]])
    nn = NeuralNetwork(X,y)

    for i in range(1500):
        nn.feedforward()
        nn.backprop()

print(nn.output)
```

 Notice that in the preceding code, we used a `sigmoid` function in the feedforward function. The `sigmoid` function is an activation function to *squash* the values between 0 and 1. This is important because we need our predictions to be between 0 and 1 for this binary prediction problem. We will go through the `sigmoid` activation function in greater detail in the next chapter, Chapter 2, *Predicting Diabetes with Multilayer Perceptrons*.

Putting it all together

Now that we have our complete Python code for doing feedforward and backpropagation, let's apply our neural network on an example and see how well it does.

The following table contains four data points, each with three input variables (x_1, x_2, and x_3) and a target variable (Y):

x_1	x_2	x_3	Y
0	0	1	0
0	1	1	1
1	0	1	1
1	1	1	0

Our neural network should learn the ideal set of weights to represent this function. Note that it isn't exactly trivial for us to work out the weights just by inspection alone.

Let's train the neural network for 1,500 iterations and see what happens. Looking at the following loss-per-iteration graph, we can clearly see the loss monotonically decreasing toward a minimum. This is consistent with the gradient descent algorithm that we discussed earlier:

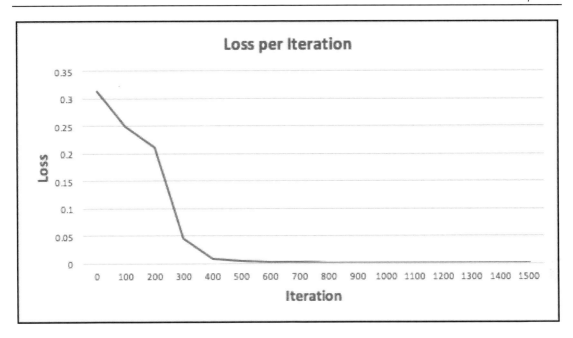

Let's look at the final prediction (output) from the neural network after 1,500 iterations:

Prediction	Y (Actual)
0.023	0
0.979	1
0.975	1
0.025	0

We did it! Our feedforward and backpropagation algorithm trained the neural network successfully and the predictions converged on the true values.

Note that there's a slight difference between the predictions and the actual values. This is desirable, as it prevents overfitting and allows the neural network to generalize better to unseen data.

Now that we understand the inner workings of a neural network, we will introduce the machine learning libraries in Python that we will use for the rest of the book. Don't worry if you find it difficult to create your own neural network from scratch at this point. For the rest of the book, we'll be using libraries that will greatly simplify the process of building and training a neural network.

Deep learning and neural networks

What about deep learning? How is it different from neural networks? To put it simply, deep learning is a machine learning algorithm that uses multiple layers in a neural network for learning (also known as deep nets). While we can think of a single-layer perceptron as the simplest neural network, deep nets are simply neural networks on the opposite end of the complexity spectrum.

In a **deep neural network (DNN)**, each layer learns information of increasing complexity, before passing it to successive layers. For example, when a DNN is trained for the purpose of facial recognition, the first few layers learn to identify edges in faces, followed by contours such as eyes and eventually complete facial features.

Although perceptrons were introduced back in the 1950s, deep learning did not take off until a few years ago. A key reason for the relatively slow progress of deep learning in the past few centuries is largely due to a lack of data and a lack of computation power. In the past few years, however, we have witnessed deep learning driving key innovations in machine learning and AI. Today, deep learning is the algorithm of choice when it comes to image recognition, autonomous vehicles, speech recognition, and game playing. So, what changed over the last few years?

In recent years, computer storage has become affordable enough to collect and store the massive amount of data that deep learning requires. It is becoming increasingly affordable to keep massive amount of data in the cloud, where it can be accessed by a cluster of computers from anywhere on earth. With the affordability of data storage, data is also becoming democratized. For example, websites such as ImageNet provides 14 million different images for deep learning researchers. Data is no longer a commodity that is owned by a privileged few.

The computational power that deep learning requires is also becoming more affordable and powerful. Most of deep learning today is powered by **graphics processing units (GPUs)**, which excel in the computation required by DNNs. Keeping with the theme of democratization, many websites also provides free GPU processing power for deep learning enthusiasts. For example, Google Colab provides a free Tesla K80 GPU in the cloud for deep learning, available for anyone to use.

With these recent advancements, deep learning is becoming available to everyone. In the next few sections, we will introduce the Python libraries that we will use for deep learning.

pandas – a powerful data analysis toolkit in Python

pandas is perhaps the most ubiquitous library in Python for data analysis. Built upon the powerful NumPy library, pandas provides a fast and flexible data structure in Python for handling real-world datasets. Raw data is often presented in tabular form, shared using the .csv file format. pandas provides a simple interface for importing these .csv files into a data structure known as DataFrames that makes it extremely easy to manipulate data in Python.

pandas DataFrames

pandas DataFrames are two-dimensional data structures, which you can think of as spreadsheets in Excel. DataFrames allow us to easily import the .csv files using a simple command. For example, the following sample code allows us to import the raw_data.csv file:

```
import pandas as pd
df = pd.read_csv("raw_data.csv")
```

Once the data is imported as a DataFrame, we can easily perform data preprocessing on it. Let's work through it using the Iris flower dataset. The Iris flower dataset is a commonly used dataset that contains data on the measurements (sepal length and width, petal length and width) of several classes of flowers. First, let's import the dataset as provided for free by **University of California Irvine** (**UCI**). Notice that pandas is able to import a dataset directly from a URL:

```
URL = \
'https://archive.ics.uci.edu/ml/machine-learning-databases/iris/iris.data'
df = pd.read_csv(URL, names = ['sepal_length', 'sepal_width',
                        'petal_length', 'petal_width', 'class'])
```

Now that it's in a DataFrame, we can easily manipulate the data. First, let's get a summary of the data as it is always important to know what kind of data we're working with:

```
print(df.info())
```

The output will be as shown in the following screenshot:

```
<class 'pandas.core.frame.DataFrame'>
RangeIndex: 150 entries, 0 to 149
Data columns (total 5 columns):
sepal_length    150 non-null float64
sepal_width     150 non-null float64
petal_length    150 non-null float64
petal_width     150 non-null float64
class           150 non-null object
dtypes: float64(4), object(1)
memory usage: 5.9+ KB
```

It looks like there are 150 rows in the dataset, with four numeric columns containing information regarding the `sepal_length` and `sepal_width`, along with the `petal_length` and `petal_width`. There is also one non-numeric column containing information regarding the class (that is, species) of the flowers.

We can get a quick statistical summary of the four numeric columns by calling the `describe()` function:

```
print(df.describe())
```

The output is shown in the following screenshot:

	sepal_length	sepal_width	petal_length	petal_width
count	150.000000	150.000000	150.000000	150.000000
mean	5.843333	3.054000	3.758667	1.198667
std	0.828066	0.433594	1.764420	0.763161
min	4.300000	2.000000	1.000000	0.100000
25%	5.100000	2.800000	1.600000	0.300000
50%	5.800000	3.000000	4.350000	1.300000
75%	6.400000	3.300000	5.100000	1.800000
max	7.900000	4.400000	6.900000	2.500000

Next, let's take a look at the first 10 rows of the data:

```
print(df.head(10))
```

The output is shown in the following screenshot:

	sepal_length	sepal_width	petal_length	petal_width	class
0	5.1	3.5	1.4	0.2	Iris-setosa
1	4.9	3.0	1.4	0.2	Iris-setosa
2	4.7	3.2	1.3	0.2	Iris-setosa
3	4.6	3.1	1.5	0.2	Iris-setosa
4	5.0	3.6	1.4	0.2	Iris-setosa
5	5.4	3.9	1.7	0.4	Iris-setosa
6	4.6	3.4	1.4	0.3	Iris-setosa
7	5.0	3.4	1.5	0.2	Iris-setosa
8	4.4	2.9	1.4	0.2	Iris-setosa
9	4.9	3.1	1.5	0.1	Iris-setosa

Simple, isn't it? pandas also allows us to perform data wrangling easily. For example, we can do the following to filter and select rows with sepal_length greater than 5.0:

```
df2 = df.loc[df['sepal_length'] > 5.0, ]
```

The output is shown in the following screenshot:

	sepal_length	sepal_width	petal_length	petal_width	class
0	5.1	3.5	1.4	0.2	Iris-setosa
5	5.4	3.9	1.7	0.4	Iris-setosa
10	5.4	3.7	1.5	0.2	Iris-setosa
14	5.8	4.0	1.2	0.2	Iris-setosa
15	5.7	4.4	1.5	0.4	Iris-setosa
16	5.4	3.9	1.3	0.4	Iris-setosa
17	5.1	3.5	1.4	0.3	Iris-setosa
18	5.7	3.8	1.7	0.3	Iris-setosa
19	5.1	3.8	1.5	0.3	Iris-setosa
20	5.4	3.4	1.7	0.2	Iris-setosa

The loc command allows us to access a group of rows and columns.

Data visualization in pandas

EDA is perhaps one of the most important steps in the machine learning workflow, and pandas makes it extremely easy to visualize data in Python. pandas provides a high-level API for the popular `matplotlib` library, which makes it easy to construct plots directly from DataFrames.

As an example, let's visualize the Iris dataset using pandas to uncover important insights. Let's plot a scatterplot to visualize how `sepal_width` is related to `sepal_length`. We can construct a scatterplot easily using the `DataFrame.plot.scatter()` method, which is built into all DataFrames:

```python
# Define marker shapes by class
import matplotlib.pyplot as plt
marker_shapes = ['.', '^', '*']

# Then, plot the scatterplot
ax = plt.axes()
for i, species in enumerate(df['class'].unique()):
    species_data = df[df['class'] == species]
    species_data.plot.scatter(x='sepal_length',
                              y='sepal_width',
                              marker=marker_shapes[i],
                              s=100,
                              title="Sepal Width vs Length by Species",
                              label=species, figsize=(10,7), ax=ax)
```

We'll get a scatterplot, as shown in the following screenshot:

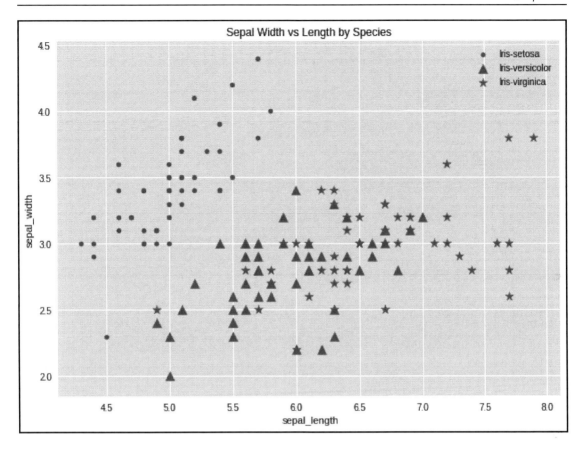

From the scatterplot, we can notice some interesting insights. First, the relationship between `sepal_width` and `sepal_length` is dependent on the species. Setosa (dots) has a fairly linear relationship between `sepal_width` and `sepal_length`, while versicolor (triangle) and virginica (star) tends to have much greater `sepal_length` than Setosa. If we're designing a machine learning algorithm to predict the type of species of flower, we know that the `sepal_width` and `sepal_length` are important features to include in our model.

Next, let's plot a histogram to investigate the distribution. Consistent with scatterplots, pandas DataFrames provides a built in method to plot histograms using the `DataFrame.plot.hist()` function:

```
df['petal_length'].plot.hist(title='Histogram of Petal Length')
```

And we can see the output in the following screenshot:

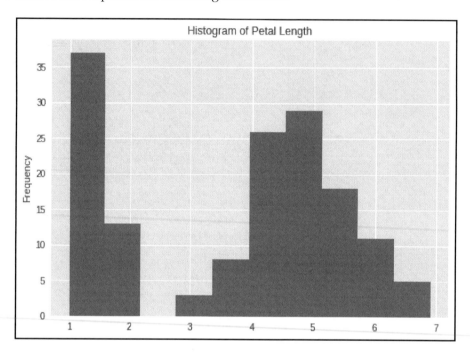

We can see that the distribution of petal lengths is essentially bimodal. It appears that certain species of flowers have shorter petals than the rest. We can also plot a boxplot of the data. The boxplot is an important data visualization tool used by data scientists to understand the distribution of the data based on the first quartile, median, and the third quartile:

```
df.plot.box(title='Boxplot of Sepal Length & Width, and Petal Length & Width')
```

The output is given in the following screenshot:

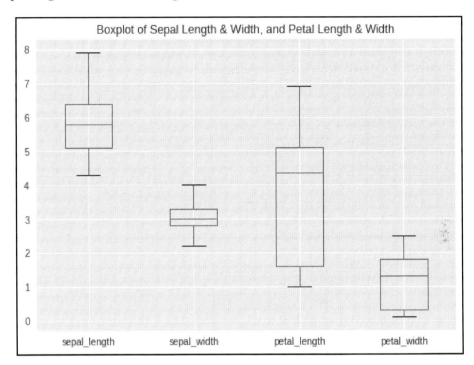

From the boxplot, we can see that the variance of `sepal_width` is much smaller than the other numeric variables, with `petal_length` having the greatest variance.

We have now seen how convenient and easy it is to visualize data using pandas directly. Keep in mind that EDA is a crucial step in the machine learning pipeline, and it is something that we will continue to do in every project for the rest of the book.

Data preprocessing in pandas

Lastly, let's take a look at how we can use pandas for data preprocessing, specifically to encode categorical variables and to impute missing values.

Encoding categorical variables

In machine learning projects, it is common to receive datasets with categorical variables. Here are some examples of categorical variables in datasets:

- **Gender**: Male, female
- **Day**: Monday, Tuesday, Wednesday, Thursday, Friday, Saturday, Sunday
- **Country**: USA, UK, China, Japan

Machine learning algorithms such as neural networks are unable to work with such categorical variables as they expect numerical variables. Therefore, we need to perform preprocessing on these variables before feeding them into a machine learning algorithm.

One common way to convert these categorical variables into numerical variables is a technique known as one-hot encoding, implemented by the `get_dummies()` function in pandas. One-hot encoding is a process that converts a categorical variable with n categories into n distinct binary features. An example is provided in the following table:

	Original Features	One-Hot-Encoding		Day_Monday	Day_Tuesday	Day_Wednesday	Day_Thursday	Day_Friday	Day_Saturday	Day_Sunday
	Day									
1	Monday		1	1	0	0	0	0	0	0
2	Tuesday		2	0	1	0	0	0	0	0
3	Wednesday		3	0	0	1	0	0	0	0
4	Thursday		4	0	0	0	1	0	0	0
5	Friday		5	0	0	0	0	1	0	0
6	Saturday		6	0	0	0	0	0	1	0
7	Sunday		7	0	0	0	0	0	0	1

Essentially, the transformed features are binary features with a **1** value if it represents the original feature, and **0** otherwise. As you can imagine, it would be a hassle to write the code for this manually. Fortunately, pandas has a handy function that does exactly that. First, let's create a DataFrame in pandas using the data in the preceding table:

```
df2 = pd.DataFrame({'Day': ['Monday','Tuesday','Wednesday',
                    'Thursday','Friday','Saturday',
                    'Sunday']})
```

We can see the output in the following screenshot:

	Day
0	Monday
1	Tuesday
2	Wednesday
3	Thursday
4	Friday
5	Saturday
6	Sunday

To one-hot encode the preceding categorical feature using pandas, it is as simple as calling the following function:

```
print(pd.get_dummies(df2))
```

Here's the output:

	Day_Friday	Day_Monday	Day_Saturday	Day_Sunday	Day_Thursday	Day_Tuesday	Day_Wednesday
0	0	1	0	0	0	0	0
1	0	0	0	0	0	1	0
2	0	0	0	0	0	0	1
3	0	0	0	0	1	0	0
4	1	0	0	0	0	0	0
5	0	0	1	0	0	0	0
6	0	0	0	1	0	0	0

Imputing missing values

As discussed earlier, imputing missing values is an essential part of the machine learning workflow. Real-world datasets are messy and usually contain missing values. Most machine learning models such as neural networks are unable to work with missing data, and hence we have to preprocess the data before we feed the data into our models. pandas makes it easy to handle missing values.

Let's use the Iris dataset from earlier. The Iris dataset does not have any missing values by default. Therefore, we have to delete some values on purpose for the sake of this exercise. The following code randomly selects 10 rows in the dataset, and deletes the sepal_length values in these 10 rows:

```
import numpy as np
import pandas as pd

# Import the iris data once again
URL = \
'https://archive.ics.uci.edu/ml/machine-learning-databases/iris/iris.data'
df = pd.read_csv(URL, names = ['sepal_length', 'sepal_width',
                               'petal_length', 'petal_width', 'class'])

# Randomly select 10 rows
random_index = np.random.choice(df.index, replace= False, size=10)

# Set the sepal_length values of these rows to be None
df.loc[random_index,'sepal_length'] = None
```

Let's use this modified dataset to see how we can deal with missing values. First, let's check where our missing values are:

```
print(df.isnull().any())
```

The preceding print function gives the following output:

```
sepal_length      True
sepal_width       False
petal_length      False
petal_width       False
class             False
dtype: bool
```

Unsurprisingly, pandas tells us that there are missing (that is, null) values in the `sepal_length` column. This command is useful to find out which columns in our dataset contains missing values.

One way to deal with missing values is to simply remove any rows with missing values. pandas provides a handy `dropna` function for us to do that:

```
print("Number of rows before deleting: %d" % (df.shape[0]))
df2 = df.dropna()
print("Number of rows after deleting: %d" % (df2.shape[0]))
```

The output is shown in the following screenshot:

```
Number of rows before deleting: 150
Number of rows after  deleting: 140
```

Another way is to replace the missing `sepal_length` values with the mean of the non-missing `sepal_length` values:

```
df.sepal_length = df.sepal_length.fillna(df.sepal_length.mean())
```

pandas will automatically exclude the missing values when calculating the mean using `df.mean()`.

Now let's confirm that there are no missing values:

```
sepal_length    False
sepal_width     False
petal_length    False
petal_width     False
class           False
dtype: bool
```

With the missing values handled, we can then pass the DataFrame to machine learning models.

Using pandas in neural network projects

We have seen how pandas can be used to import tabular data in `.csv` format, and perform data preprocessing and data visualization directly using built-in functions in pandas. For the rest of the book, we will use pandas when the dataset is of a tabular nature. pandas plays a crucial role in data preprocessing and EDA, as we shall see in future chapters.

TensorFlow and Keras – open source deep learning libraries

TensorFlow is an open source library for neural networks and deep learning developed by the Google Brain team. Designed for scalability, TensorFlow runs across a variety of platforms, from desktops to mobile devices and even to clusters of computers. Today, TensorFlow is one of the most popular machine learning libraries and is used extensively in a wide variety of real-world applications. For example, TensorFlow powers the AI behind many online services that we use today, including image search, voice recognition, recommendation engines. TensorFlow has become the silent workhorse powering many AI applications, even though we might not even notice it.

Keras is a high-level API that runs on top of TensorFlow. So, why Keras? Why do we need another library to act as an API for TensorFlow? To put it simply, Keras removes the complexities in building neural networks, and enables rapid experimentation and testing without concerning the user with low-level implementation details. Keras provides a simple and intuitive API for building neural networks using TensorFlow. Its guiding principles are modularity and extensibility. As we shall see later, it is extremely easy to build neural networks by stacking Keras API calls on top of one another, which you can think of like stacking Lego blocks in order to create bigger structures. This beginner-friendly approach has led to the popularity of Keras as one of the top machine learning libraries in Python. In this book, we will use Keras as the primary machine learning library for building our neural network projects.

The fundamental building blocks in Keras

The fundamental building blocks in Keras are layers, and we can stack layers linearly to create a model. The **Loss Function** that we choose will provide the metrics for which we will use to train our model using an **Optimizer.** Recall that while building our neural network from scratch earlier, we had to define and write the code for those terms. We call these the fundamental building blocks in Keras because we can build any neural network using these basic structures.

The following diagram illustrates the relationship between these building blocks in Keras:

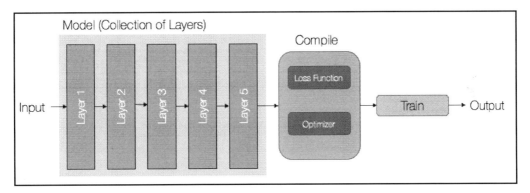

Layers – the atom of neural networks in Keras

You can think of layers in Keras as an atom, because they are the smallest unit of our neural network. Each layer takes in an input performs a mathematical function, then outputs that for the next layer. The core layers in Keras includes dense layers, activation layers, and dropout layers. There are other layers that are more complex, including convolutional layers and pooling layers. In this book, you will be exposed to projects that uses all these layers.

For now, let's take a closer look at dense layers, which are by far the most common type of layer used in Keras. A dense layer is also known as a fully-connected layer. It is fully-connected because it uses all of its input (as opposed to a subset of the input) for the mathematical function that it implements.

A dense layer implements the following function:

$$\hat{y} = \sigma(Wx + b)$$

$\hat{y}$ is the output, σ is the activation function, x is the input, and W and b are the weights and biases respectively.

This equation should look familiar to you. We used the fully-connected layer when we were building our neural network from scratch earlier.

Models – a collection of layers

If layers can be thought of as atoms, then models can be thought of as molecules in Keras. A model is simply a collection of layers, and the most commonly used model in Keras is the `Sequential` model. A `Sequential` model allows us to linearly stack layers on one another, where a single layer is connected to one other layer only. This allows us to easily design model architectures without worrying about the underlying math. As we will see in later chapters, there is a significant amount of thought needed to ensure that consecutive layer dimensions are compatible with one another, something that Keras takes care for us under the hood!

Once we have defined our model architecture, we need to define our training process, which is done using the `compile` method in Keras. The `compile` method takes in several arguments, but the most important arguments we need to define is the optimizer and the loss function.

Loss function – error metric for neural network training

In an earlier section, we defined the loss function as a way to evaluate the goodness of our predictions (that is, how far off our predictions are). The nature of our problem should dictate the loss function used. There are several loss functions implemented in Keras, but the most commonly used loss functions are `mean_squared_error`, `categorical_crossentropy`, and `binary_crossentropy`.

As a general rule of thumb, this is how you should choose which loss function to use:

- `mean_squared_error` if the problem is a regression problem
- `categorical_crossentropy` if the problem is a multiclass classification problem
- `binary_crossentropy` if the problem is a binary classification problem

In certain cases, you might find that the default loss functions in Keras are unsuitable for your problem. In that case, you can define your own loss function by defining a custom function in Python, then passing that custom function to the `compile` method in Keras.

Optimizers – training algorithm for neural networks

An optimizer is an algorithm for updating the weights of the neural network in the training process. Optimizers in Keras are based on the gradient descent algorithm, which we have covered in an earlier section.

While we won't cover in detail the differences between each optimizer, it is important to note that our choice of optimizer should depend on the nature of the problem. In general, researchers have found that the `Adam` optimizer works best for DNNs, while the `sgd` optimizer works best for shallow neural networks. The `Adagrad` optimizer is also a popular choice, and it adapts the learning rate of the algorithm based on how frequent a particular set of weights are updated. The main advantage of this approach is that it eliminates the need to manually tune the learning rate hyperparameter, which is a time-consuming process in the machine learning workflow.

Creating neural networks in Keras

Let's take a look at how we can use Keras to build the two-layer neural network that we introduced earlier. To build a linear collection of layers, first declare a `Sequential` model in Keras:

```
from keras.models import Sequential
model = Sequential()
```

This creates an empty `Sequential` model that we can now add layers to. Adding layers in Keras is simple and similar to stacking Lego blocks on top of one another. We start by adding layers from the left (the layer closest to the input):

```
from keras.layers import Dense
# Layer 1
model.add(Dense(units=4, activation='sigmoid', input_dim=3))
# Output Layer
model.add(Dense(units=1, activation='sigmoid'))
```

Stacking layers in Keras is as simple as calling the `model.add()` command. Notice that we had to define the number of units in each layer. Generally, increasing the number of units increases the complexity of the model, as it means that there are more weights to be trained. For the first layer, we had to define `input_dim`. This informs Keras the number of features (that is, columns) in the dataset. Also, note that we have used a `Dense` layer. A `Dense` layer is simply a fully connected layer. In later chapters, we will introduce other kinds of layers, specific to different types of problems.

We can verify the structure of our model by calling the `model.summary()` function:

```
print(model.summary())
```

The output is shown in the following screenshot:

```
Layer (type)                    Output Shape                Param #
=================================================================
dense_1 (Dense)                 (None, 4)                   16
_____
dense_2 (Dense)                 (None, 1)                   5
=================================================================
Total params: 21
Trainable params: 21
Non-trainable params: 0
```

The number of params is the number of weights and biases we need to train for the model that we have just defined.

Once we are satisfied with our model's architecture, let's compile it and start the training process:

```
from keras import optimizers
sgd = optimizers.SGD(lr=1)
model.compile(loss='mean_squared_error', optimizer=sgd)
```

 Note that we have defined the learning rate of the `sgd` optimizer to be 1.0 (`lr=1`). In general, the learning rate is a hyperparameter of the neural network that needs to be tuned carefully depending on the problem. We will take a closer look at tuning hyperparameters in later chapters.

The `mean_squared_error` loss function in Keras is similar to the sum-of-squares error that we have defined earlier. We are using the SGD optimizer to train our model. Recall that gradient descent is the method of updating the weights and biases by moving it toward the derivative of the loss function with respect to the weights and biases.

Let's use the same data that we used earlier to train our neural network. This will allow us to compare the predictions obtained using Keras versus the predictions obtained when we created our neural network from scratch earlier.

Let's define an X and Y NumPy array, corresponding to the features and the target variables respectively:

```
import numpy as np
# Fixing a random seed ensures reproducible results
np.random.seed(9)

X = np.array([[0,0,1],
              [0,1,1],
              [1,0,1],
              [1,1,1]])
y = np.array([[0],[1],[1],[0]])
```

Finally, let's train the model for 1500 iterations:

```
model.fit(X, y, epochs=1500, verbose=False)
```

To get the predictions, run the model.predict() command on our data:

```
print(model.predict(X))
```

The preceding code gives the following output:

```
[[0.04623432]
 [0.94387746]
 [0.94575524]
 [0.06039287]]
```

Comparing this to the predictions that we obtained earlier, we can see that the results are extremely similar. The major advantage of using Keras is that we did not have to worry about the low-level implementation details and mathematics while building our neural network, unlike what we did earlier. In fact, we did no math at all. All we did in Keras was to call a series of APIs to build our neural network. This allows us to focus on high-level details, enabling rapid experimentation.

Other Python libraries

Besides pandas and Keras, we will also be using other Python libraries, such as scikit-learn and seaborn. scikit-learn is an open source machine learning library that is widely used in machine learning projects. The main functionality that we use in scikit-learn is to separate our data into a training and testing set during data preprocessing. seaborn is an alternative data visualization in Python that has been gaining traction recently. In the later chapters, we'll see how we can use seaborn to make data visualizations.

Summary

In this chapter, we have seen what machine learning is, and looked at the complete end-to-end workflow for every machine learning project. We have also seen what neural networks and deep learning is, and coded up our own neural network from scratch and in Keras.

For the rest of the book, we will create our own real-world neural network projects. Each chapter will cover one project, and the projects are listed in order of increasing complexity. By the end of the book, you will have created your own neural network projects in medical diagnosis, taxi fare predictions, image classification, sentiment analysis, and much more. In the next chapter, Chapter 2, *Predicting Diabetes with Multilayer Perceptrons* we will cover diabetes prediction with **multilayer perceptrons (MLPs)**. Let's get started!

2
Predicting Diabetes with Multilayer Perceptrons

In the first chapter, we went through the inner workings of a neural network, how to build our own neural network using Python libraries such as Keras, as well as the end-to-end machine learning workflow. In this chapter, we will apply what we have learned to build a **multilayer perceptron** (**MLP**) that can predict whether a patient is at risk of diabetes. This marks the first neural network project that we will build from scratch.

In this chapter, we will cover the following topics:

- Understanding the problem that we're trying to tackle—diabetes mellitus
- How AI is being used in healthcare today, and how AI will continue to transform healthcare
- An in-depth analysis of the diabetes mellitus dataset, including data visualization using Python
- Understanding MLPs, and the model architecture that we will use
- A step-by-step guide to implement and train an MLP with Keras
- Analysis of our results

Technical requirements

The key Python libraries required for this chapter are as follows:

- matplotlib 3.0.2
- pandas 0.23.4
- Keras 2.2.4
- NumPy 1.15.2
- seaborn 0.9.0
- scikit-learn 0.20.2

 To download the dataset required for this project, please refer to the instructions at https://raw.githubusercontent.com/PacktPublishing/ Neural-Network-Projects-with-Python/master/Chapter02/how_to_ download_the_dataset.txt.

The code for this chapter can be found in the GitHub repository for the book at https:// github.com/PacktPublishing/Neural-Network-Projects-with-Python.

To download the code into your computer, you may run the following git clone command:

```
$ git clone
https://github.com/PacktPublishing/Neural-Network-Projects-with-Python.git
```

After the process is complete, there will be a folder titled Neural-Network-Projects- with-Python . Enter the folder by running this command:

```
$ cd Neural-Network-Projects-with-Python
```

To install the required Python libraries in a virtual environment, run the following command:

```
$ conda env create -f environment.yml
```

Note that you should have installed Anaconda on your computer first before running this command. To enter the virtual environment, run the following command:

```
$ conda activate neural-network-projects-python
```

Navigate to the Chapter02 folder by running the following command:

```
$ cd Chapter02
```

The following files are located in the folder:

- `main.py`: This is the main code for the neural network.
- `utils.py`: This file contains auxiliary utility code that will help us in the implementation of our neural network.
- `visualize.py`: This file contains code for exploratory data analysis and data visualization.

To run the code for the neural network, simply execute the `main.py` file:

```
$ python main.py
```

To recreate the data visualizations covered in this chapter, execute the `visualize.py` file:

```
$ python visualize.py
```

Diabetes – understanding the problem

Diabetes is a chronic medical condition that is associated with elevated blood sugar levels in the body. Diabetes often leads to cardiovascular disease, stroke, kidney damage, and long-term damage to the extremities (that is, limbs and eyes).

It is estimated that there are 415 million people in the world suffering from diabetes, with up to 5 million deaths every year attributed to diabetes-related complications. In the United States, diabetes is estimated to be the seventh highest cause of death. Clearly, diabetes is a cause of concern to the wellbeing of modern society.

Diabetes can be divided into two subtypes: type 1 and type 2. Type 1 diabetes results from the body's inability to produce sufficient insulin. Type 1 diabetes is relatively rare compared to type 2 diabetes, and it only accounts for approximately 5% of diabetes. Unfortunately, the exact cause of type 1 diabetes is unknown and therefore, it is difficult to prevent the onset of type 1 diabetes.

Type 2 diabetes results from the body's gradual resistance to insulin. Type 2 diabetes is the prevalent form of diabetes in the world, and it is caused by excessive body weight, irregular exercise, and a poor diet. Fortunately, the onset of type 2 diabetes can be prevented and reversed if diagnosed early.

One of the barriers for early detection and diagnosis of diabetes is that the early stages of diabetes are often non-symptomatic. People who are on the path to diabetes (also known as prediabetes) often do not know that they have diabetes until it is too late.

How can we use machine learning to address this problem? If we have a labeled dataset that contains some vital measurements of patients (for example, age and blood insulin level), as well as a true label indicating the onset of diabetes in the patient sometime after the measurements were taken, then we can train a neural network (machine learning classifier) on this data and use it to make predictions on new patients:

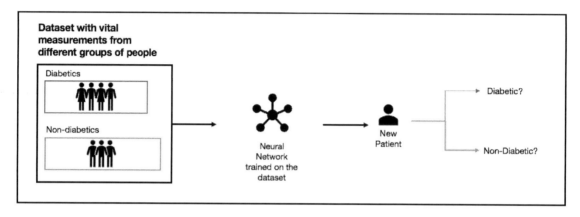

In the next section, we'll briefly explore how AI is transforming healthcare.

AI in healthcare

Beyond predicting diabetes using machine learning, the field of healthcare, in general, is ripe for disruption by AI. According to a study by Accenture, the market for AI in healthcare is set for explosive growth, with an estimated compound annual growth rate of 40% by 2021. This significant growth is driven by a proliferation of AI and tech companies in healthcare.

Apple's chief executive officer, Tim Cook, believes that Apple can make significant contributions in healthcare. Apple's vision for disrupting healthcare can be exemplified by its developments in wearable technology. In 2018, Apple announced a new generation of smartwatches with active monitoring of cardiovascular health. Apple's smartwatches can now conduct electrocardiography in real time, and even warn you when your heart rate becomes abnormal, which is an early sign of cardiovascular failure. Apple's smartwatches also collect accelerometer and gyroscope measurements to predict in real time if a significant fall has occurred. Clearly, the impact of AI on healthcare will be far-reaching.

The value of AI in healthcare is not in replacing physicians and other healthcare workers, but rather to augment their activities. AI has the potential to support healthcare workers throughout a patient's journey and to assist healthcare workers in discovering insights into a patient's wellbeing using data. According to experts, AI in healthcare will see the most growth in the following areas:

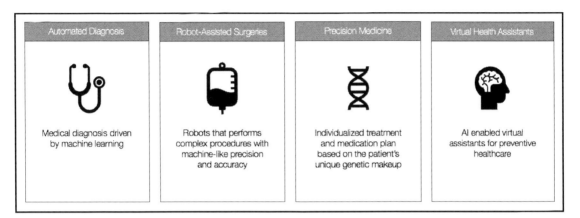

Automated diagnosis

Let's zoom in on automated diagnosis as that is the area of concern for this project. Experts believe that AI will greatly augment the way medical diagnosis is conducted. At the moment, most medical diagnosis is performed by skilled medical experts. In the case of medical diagnosis through images (such as X-rays and MRI scans), skilled radiologists are required to provide their expertise in the diagnostic process. These skilled medical professionals go through years of rigorous training before being certified, and there is a shortage of these medical experts in certain countries, which contributes to poor outcomes. The role of AI is to augment these experts and to offload low-level routine diagnosis, which can be done by an AI agent with a high degree of accuracy.

This ties back to our original problem statement; using AI to predict which patients are at risk of diabetes. As we shall see, we can use machine learning and neural networks to make this prediction. In this chapter, we will design and implement an MLP that can predict the onset of diabetes using machine learning.

The diabetes mellitus dataset

The dataset that we will be using for this project comes from the Pima Indians Diabetes dataset, as provided by the National Institute of Diabetes and Digestive and Kidney Diseases (and hosted by Kaggle).

The Pima Indians are a group of native Americans living in Arizona, and they are a highly studied group of people due to their genetic predisposition to diabetes. It is believed that the Pima Indians carry a gene that allows them to survive long periods of starvation. This thrifty gene allowed the Pima Indians to store in their bodies whatever glucose and carbohydrates they may eat, which is genetically advantageous in an environment where famines were common.

However, as society modernized and the Pima Indians began to change their diet to one of processed food, the rate of type 2 diabetes among them began to increase as well. Today, the incidence of type 2 diabetes among the Pima Indians is the highest in the world. This makes them a highly studied group of people, as researchers attempt to find the genetic link of diabetes among the Pima Indians.

The Pima Indians diabetes dataset consists of diagnostic measurements collected from a sample of female Pima Indians, along with a label indicating whether the patient developed diabetes within five years of the initial measurement. In the next section, we'll perform exploratory data analysis on the Pima Indians diabetes dataset to uncover important insights about the data.

Exploratory data analysis

Let's dive into the dataset to understand the kind of data we are working with. We import the dataset into pandas:

```
import pandas as pd

df = pd.read_csv('diabetes.csv')
```

Let's take a quick look at the first five rows of the dataset by calling the df.head() command:

```
print(df.head())
```

We get the following output:

	Pregnancies	Glucose	BloodPressure	SkinThickness	Insulin	BMI	DiabetesPedigreeFunction	Age	Outcome
0	6	148	72	35	0	33.6	0.627	50	1
1	1	85	66	29	0	26.6	0.351	31	0
2	8	183	64	0	0	23.3	0.672	32	1
3	1	89	66	23	94	28.1	0.167	21	0
4	0	137	40	35	168	43.1	2.288	33	1

It looks like there are nine columns in the dataset, which are as follows:

- Pregnancies: Number of previous pregnancies
- Glucose: Plasma glucose concentration
- BloodPressure: Diastolic blood pressure
- SkinThickness: Skin fold thickness measured from the triceps
- Insulin : Blood serum insulin concentration
- BMI: Body mass index
- DiabetesPedigreeFunction: A summarized score that indicates the genetic predisposition of the patient for diabetes, as extrapolated from the patient's family record for diabetes
- Age: Age in years
- Outcome: The target variable we are trying to predict, 1 for patients that developed diabetes within five years of the initial measurement, and 0 otherwise

Let's start by visualizing the distribution of the nine variables in the dataset. We can do this by plotting a histogram:

```
from matplotlib import pyplot as plt

df.hist()
plt.show()
```

We get the following output:

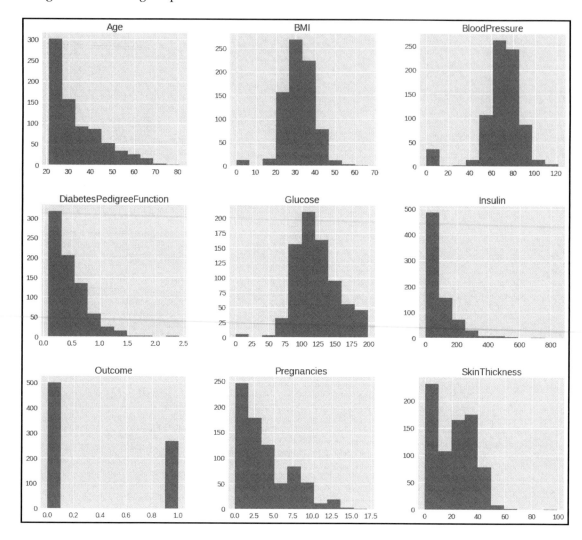

The histogram provides some interesting insights into the data. From the histogram for Age, we can see that most of the data was collected from young people, with the most common age group between **20-30** years old. We can also see that the distribution for BMI, BloodPressure, and Glucose concentration is normally distributed (that is, a bell curve shape), which is what we we expect when we collect such statistics from a population. However, note that the tail of the Glucose concentration distribution shows some rather extreme values. It appears that there are people with plasma Glucose concentration that is almost **200**. On the opposite end of the distribution, we can see that there are people with **0** values for BMI, BloodPressure, and Glucose. Logically, we know that it is not possible to have a **0** value for these measurements. Are these missing values? We shall explore more in the next section on data preprocessing.

If we look at the distribution for the number of previous Pregnancies, we can see some outliers as well. We can see that some patients had more than 15 previous pregnancies. While that may not be entirely surprising, we should keep such outliers in mind when we do our analysis, as it can skew our results.

The distribution of outcome shows that approximately 65% of the population belongs to class 0 (no diabetes), while the remaining 35% belongs to class 1 (diabetes). When building a machine learning classifier, we should always keep in mind the distribution of classes in our training data. In order to ensure that our machine learning classifier works well in the real world, we should ensure that the distribution of classes in our training data mirrors that of the real world. In this case, the distribution of the classes does not match those in the real world, as it is estimated by the **World Health Organization (WHO)** that only 8.5% of the world population suffers from diabetes.

We do not need to worry about the distribution of classes in our training data for this project, as we are not going to deploy our classifier in the real world. Nevertheless, it is a good practice for data scientists and machine learning engineers to check the distribution of classes in the training data, in order to ensure strong model performance in the real world.

Lastly, it is important to note that the variables are on different scales. For example, the DiabetesPedigreeFunction variable ranges from **0** to ~**2.5**, while the Insulin variable ranges from **0** to ~**800**. This difference in scale can cause problems in training our neural network, as variables with larger scales tend to dominate variables with smaller scales. In the next section on data preprocessing, we will look at how we can standardize the variables.

We can also plot a density plot to investigate the relationship between each variable and the target variable. To do so, we will use seaborn. seaborn is a Python data visualization library based on matplotlib.

The following code snippet shows how to plot a density plot for each variable. To visualize the difference in distribution between diabetics and non-diabetics, we will also plot them separately on each plot:

```python
import seaborn as sns

# create a subplot of 3 x 3
plt.subplots(3,3,figsize=(15,15))

# Plot a density plot for each variable
for idx, col in enumerate(df.columns):
    ax = plt.subplot(3,3,idx+1)
    ax.yaxis.set_ticklabels([])
    sns.distplot(df.loc[df.Outcome == 0][col], hist=False, axlabel= False,
    kde_kws={'linestyle':'-',
    'color':'black', 'label':"No Diabetes"})
    sns.distplot(df.loc[df.Outcome == 1][col], hist=False, axlabel= False,
    kde_kws={'linestyle':'--',
    'color':'black', 'label':"Diabetes"})
    ax.set_title(col)

# Hide the 9th subplot (bottom right) since there are only 8 plots
plt.subplot(3,3,9).set_visible(False)

plt.show()
```

We'll get the output shown in the following screenshot:

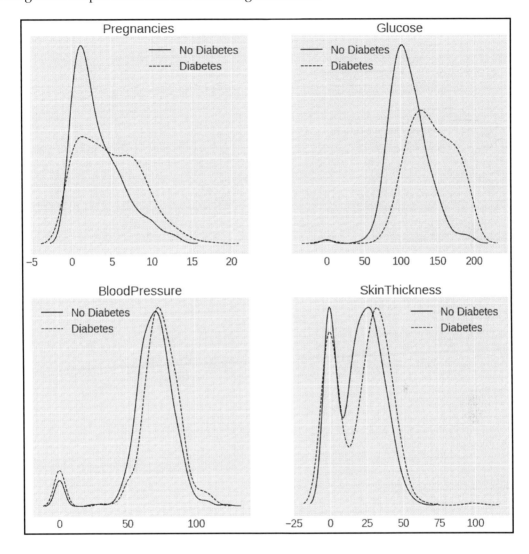

The following screenshot shows the output in continuation to the preceding one:

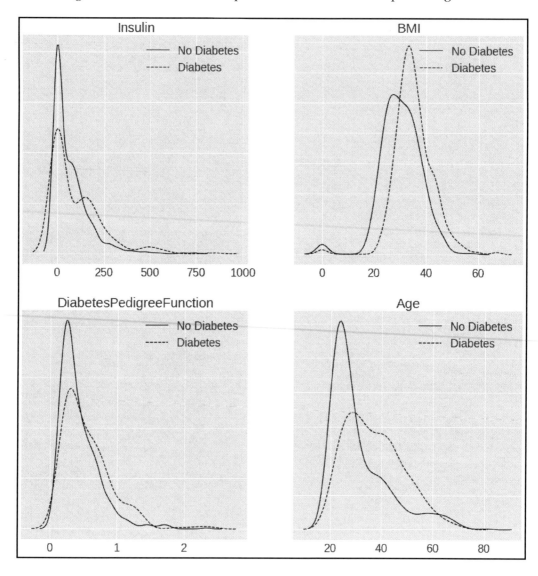

The preceding density plots look complicated, but let's focus on each individual plot and see what insights can we gain. If we look at the plot for the Glucose variable, we can see that among the non-diabetics (solid line), the curve has a normal distribution centered around the value 100. This tells us that among non-diabetics, most people have a blood glucose value of 100 mg/dL. On the other hand, if we look at the Diabetics (dashed line), the curve is wider and is centered around a value of 150. This tells us that diabetics tends to have a wider range of blood glucose value, and the average blood glucose value is around 150 mg/dL. Therefore, there is a significant difference in blood glucose values for diabetes vs non-diabetics. A similar analysis can also be made for the variable BMI and Age. In other words, the Glucose, BMI, and Age variables are strong predictors for diabetes. People with diabetes tend to have higher blood glucose level, higher BMI, and are older.

On the other hand, we can see that for variables such as BloodPressure and SkinThickness, there is no significant difference in the distribution between diabetics and non-diabetics. The two groups of people tend to have similar blood pressure and skin thickness values. Therefore, BloodPressure and SkinThickness are poorer predictors for diabetes.

Data preprocessing

In the previous section, *Exploratory data analysis*, we have discovered that there are 0 values in certain columns, which indicates missing values. We have also seen that the variables have different scales, which can negatively impact model performance. In this section, we will perform data preprocessing to handle these issues.

Handling missing values

First, let's call the isnull() function to check whether there are any missing values in the dataset:

```
print(df.isnull().any())
```

We'll see the following output:

```
Pregnancies                 False
Glucose                     False
BloodPressure               False
SkinThickness               False
Insulin                     False
BMI                         False
DiabetesPedigreeFunction    False
Age                         False
Outcome                     False
dtype: bool
```

It seems like there are no missing values in the dataset, but are we sure? Let's get a statistical summary of the dataset to investigate further:

```
print(df.describe())
```

The output is as follows:

	Pregnancies	Glucose	BloodPressure	SkinThickness	Insulin	BMI	DiabetesPedigreeFunction	Age	Outcome
count	768.000000	768.000000	768.000000	768.000000	768.000000	768.000000	768.000000	768.000000	768.000000
mean	3.845052	120.894531	69.105469	20.536458	79.799479	31.992578	0.471876	33.240885	0.348958
std	3.369578	31.972618	19.355807	15.952218	115.244002	7.884160	0.331329	11.760232	0.476951
min	0.000000	0.000000	0.000000	0.000000	0.000000	0.000000	0.078000	21.000000	0.000000
25%	1.000000	99.000000	62.000000	0.000000	0.000000	27.300000	0.243750	24.000000	0.000000
50%	3.000000	117.000000	72.000000	23.000000	30.500000	32.000000	0.372500	29.000000	0.000000
75%	6.000000	140.250000	80.000000	32.000000	127.250000	36.600000	0.626250	41.000000	1.000000
max	17.000000	199.000000	122.000000	99.000000	846.000000	67.100000	2.420000	81.000000	1.000000

We can see that there are `768` rows of data, and the `Pregnancies`, `Glucose`, `BloodPressure`, `SkinThickness`, `Insulin`, and `BMI` columns have a minimum value of `0`. This doesn't quite make sense. The measurements for `Glucose`, `BloodPressure`, `SkinThickness`, `Insulin`, and `BMI` should never be `0`. This is an indication that there are missing values in our dataset. The values were probably recorded as `0` due to certain issues during data collection. Perhaps the equipment was faulty, or the patient was unwilling to have their measurements taken.

In any case, we need to handle these 0 values. Let's take a look at how many 0 values are there in each column to understand the extent of the problem:

```
print("Number of rows with 0 values for each variable")
for col in df.columns:
    missing_rows = df.loc[df[col]==0].shape[0]
    print(col + ": " + str(missing_rows))
```

We get the following result:

```
Number of rows with 0 values for each variable
Pregnancies: 111
Glucose: 5
BloodPressure: 35
SkinThickness: 227
Insulin: 374
BMI: 11
DiabetesPedigreeFunction: 0
Age: 0
```

In the `Insulin` column, there are `374` rows with 0 values. That is almost half of the data that we have! Clearly, we cannot discard these rows with 0 values as that will cause a significant drop in model performance.

There are several techniques to handle these missing values:

- Remove (discard) any rows with missing values.
- Replace the missing values with the mean/median/mode of the non-missing values.
- Predict the actual values using a separate machine learning model.

Since the missing values comes from continuous variables such as `Glucose`, `BloodPressure`, `SkinThickness`, `Insulin`, and `BMI`, we will replace the missing values with the mean of the non-missing values.

First, let's replace the 0 values in the Glucose, BloodPressure, SkinThickness, Insulin, and BMI columns with NaN. This way, pandas will understand that these values are invalid:

```
import numpy as np

df['Glucose'] = df['Glucose'].replace(0, np.nan)
df['BloodPressure'] = df['BloodPressure'].replace(0, np.nan)
df['SkinThickness'] = df['SkinThickness'].replace(0, np.nan)
df['Insulin'] = df['Insulin'].replace(0, np.nan)
df['BMI'] = df['BMI'].replace(0, np.nan)
```

Now let's confirm that the Glucose, BloodPressure, SkinThickness, Insulin, and BMI columns no longer contain 0 values:

```
print("Number of rows with 0 values for each variable")
for col in df.columns:
    missing_rows = df.loc[df[col]==0].shape[0]
    print(col + ": " + str(missing_rows))
```

We get the following result:

```
Number of rows with 0 values for each variable
Pregnancies: 111
Glucose: 0
BloodPressure: 0
SkinThickness: 0
Insulin: 0
BMI: 0
DiabetesPedigreeFunction: 0
Age: 0
```

Note that we did not modify the Pregnancies column as 0 values in that column (that is, 0 previous pregnancies) are perfectly valid.

Now, let's replace the NaN values with the mean of the non-missing values. We can do this using the handy fillna() function in pandas:

```
df['Glucose'] = df['Glucose'].fillna(df['Glucose'].mean())
df['BloodPressure'] =
df['BloodPressure'].fillna(df['BloodPressure'].mean())
df['SkinThickness'] =
df['SkinThickness'].fillna(df['SkinThickness'].mean())
df['Insulin'] = df['Insulin'].fillna(df['Insulin'].mean())
df['BMI'] = df['BMI'].fillna(df['BMI'].mean())
```

Data standardization

Data standardization is another important technique in data preprocessing. The goal of data standardization is to transform the numeric variables so that each variable has zero mean and unit variance.

Standardization of variables as a preprocessing step is a requirement for many machine learning algorithms. In neural networks, it is important to standardize the data in order to ensure that the backpropagation algorithm works as intended. Another positive effect of data standardization is that it shrinks the magnitude of the variables, transforming them to a scale that is more proportional.

As we have seen earlier, variables such as Insulin and DiabetesPedigreeeFunction have vastly different scales; the maximum value for Insulin is 846 while the maximum value for DiabetesPedigreeeFunction is only 2.42. With such different scales, the variable with the greater scale tends to dominate when training the neural network, causing the neural network to inadvertently place more emphasis on the variable with a greater scale.

To standardize our data, we can use the preprocessing class from scikit-learn. Let's import the preprocessing class from scikit-learn and use it to scale our data:

```
from sklearn import preprocessing

df_scaled = preprocessing.scale(df)
```

Since the object returned by the preprocessing.scale() function is no longer a pandas DataFrame, let's convert it back:

```
df_scaled = pd.DataFrame(df_scaled, columns=df.columns)
```

Lastly, since we do not want to scale the Outcome column (which is the target variable that we are trying to predict) let's use the original Outcome column:

```
df_scaled['Outcome'] = df['Outcome']
df = df_scaled
```

Let's take a look at the mean, standard deviation and the max of each of the transformed variables:

```
print(df.describe().loc[['mean', 'std','max'],].round(2).abs())
```

We get the following result:

	Pregnancies	Glucose	BloodPressure	SkinThickness	Insulin	BMI	DiabetesPedigreeFunction	Age
mean	0.00	0.00	0.0	0.00	0.00	0.00	0.00	0.00
std	1.00	1.00	1.0	1.00	1.00	1.00	1.00	1.00
max	3.91	2.54	4.1	7.95	8.13	5.04	5.88	4.06

We can see that the scale of each variable is now a lot closer to one another.

Splitting the data into training, testing, and validation sets

The last step in data preprocessing is to split the data into training, testing, and validation sets:

- **Training set**: The neural network will be trained on this subset of the data.
- **Validation set**: This set of data allows us to perform hyperparameter tuning (that is, tuning the number of hidden layers) using an unbiased source of data.
- **Testing set**: The final evaluation of the neural network will be based on this subset of the data.

The purpose of splitting the data into training, testing, and validation sets is to avoid overfitting and to provide an unbiased source of data for evaluating model performance. Typically, we will use the training and validation set to tune and improve our model. The validation set can be used for early stopping of training, that is, we continue to train our neural network only to the point where model performance on the validation set stops improving. This allows us to avoid overfitting the neural network.

The testing set is also known as the holdout dataset, as the neural network will never be trained using it. Instead, we will use the testing set to evaluate the model at the end. This provides us with an accurate reflection of the real-world performance of our model.

How do we decide the proportion of each split? The competing concerns, in this case, is that if we allocate most of the data for training purposes, model performance will increase at the detriment of our ability to avoid overfitting. Similarly, if we allocate most of the data for validation and testing purposes, model performance will decrease as there might be insufficient data for training.

As a general rule of thumb, we should split the original data into 80% training and 20% testing, and then to split the training data into 80% training and 20% validation again. The following diagram illustrates this process:

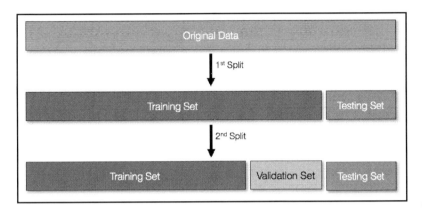

One important point to note is that the splitting of data must be done at random. If we were to use a non-random method of splitting the data (for example, the first 80% of rows go to the **Training Set** and the last 20% of rows go to the **Testing Set**), we could potentially be introducing bias into our training and testing set. For example, the original data could be sorted in chronological order, so a non-random method of splitting the data could mean that our model is only trained on data from a certain date, which is highly biased and would not work as well in the real world.

The `train_test_split` function from scikit-learn allows us to randomly split a dataset easily.

First, let's separate the dataset into X (input features) and y (target variable):

```
from sklearn.model_selection import train_test_split

X = df.loc[:, df.columns != 'Outcome']
y = df.loc[:, 'Outcome']
```

Then, make the first split to split the data into the training set (80%) and the testing set (20%) according to the preceding diagram:

```
X_train, X_test, y_train, y_test = train_test_split(X, y, test_size=0.2)
```

Finally, make the second split to create the final training set and the validation set:

```
X_train, X_val, y_train, y_val = train_test_split(X_train, y_train,
test_size=0.2)
```

MLPs

Now that we have completed exploratory data analysis and data preprocessing, let's turn our attention towards designing the neural network architecture. In this project, we will be using MLPs.

An MLP is a class of feedforward neural network, and it distinguishes itself from the single-layer perceptron that we've discussed in Chapter 1, *Machine Learning and Neural Networks 101*, by having at least one hidden layer, with each layer activated by a non-linear activation function. This multilayer neural network architecture and non-linear activation allows MLPs to produce non-linear decision boundaries, which is crucial in multi-dimensional real-world datasets such as the Pima Indians Diabetes dataset.

Model architecture

The model architecture of the MLP can be represented graphically as follows:

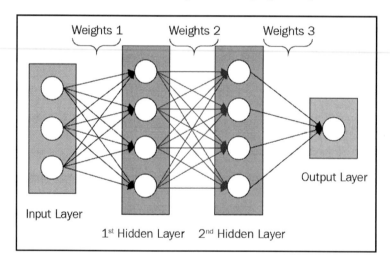

As discussed in Chapter 1, *Machine Learning and Neural Networks 101*, we can use an arbitrary number of hidden layers in our MLP. For this project, we will use two hidden layers in our MLP.

Input layer

Each node in the **input layer** (illustrated by the circles in the pink rectangle) refers to each feature (that is, column) in the dataset. Since there are eight features in the Pima Indians dataset, there should be eight nodes in the input layer of our MLP.

Hidden layers

The next layer after the input layer is known as a **hidden layer.** As we have seen in `Chapter 1`, *Machine Learning and Neural Networks 101*, the hidden layer takes the input layer and applies a **non-linear activation function** to it. Mathematically, we can represent the function of the hidden layer as follows:

$$Output\ from\ Hidden\ Layer = \sigma(Wx + b)$$

x refers to the input passed from the previous layer, σ refers to the non-linear activation function, W are the weights, and b refers to the biases.

To keep things simple, we will only use two hidden layers in our model for this project. Increasing the number of hidden layers tends to increase the model complexity and training time. For this project, two hidden layers will suffice, as we shall see later when we look at the model performance.

Activation functions

When designing the neural network model architecture, we also need to decide what activation functions to use for each layer. Activation functions have an important role to play in neural networks. You can think of activation functions as *transformers* in neural networks; they take an input value, transform the input value, and pass the transformed value to the next layer.

In this project, we will use the **rectified linear unit (ReLU)** and the **sigmoid** as our activation functions.

ReLU

As a general rule of thumb, ReLU is always used as the activation function for our intermediate hidden layers (that is, non-output layer). In 2011, it was proved by researchers that ReLU is superior to all previously used activation functions for training **deep neural networks (DNNs)**. Today, ReLU is the most popular choice of activation function for DNNs, and it has become a default choice for activation functions.

Mathematically, we can represent ReLU as follows:

$$f(x) = max(0, x)$$

What the ReLU function does is to simply consider only the non-negative portion of the original x, and to treat the negative portion as 0. The following graph illustrates this:

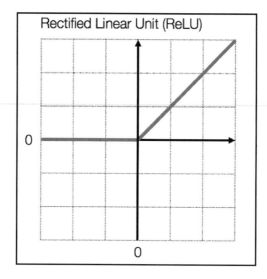

Sigmoid activation function

For the final output layer, we need an activation function that makes a prediction on the class of the label. For this project, we are making a simple binary prediction on the class: 1 for patients with onset of diabetes and 0 for patients without the onset of diabetes. The sigmoid activation function is ideal for binary classification problems.

Mathematically, we can represent the sigmoid activation function as follows:

$$f(x) = \frac{1}{1 + e^{-x}}$$

Although this looks complicated, the underlying function is actually pretty simple. The **Sigmoid Activation Function** simply takes a value and squashes it between **0** and **1**:

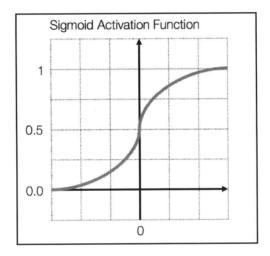

If the transformed value $f(x)$ is greater than **0.5**, then we classify it as class **1**. Similarly, if the transformed value is less than **0.5**, we classify it as class **0**. The **Sigmoid Activation Function** allows us to take an input value and outputs a binary class (**1** or **0**), which is exactly what we require for this project (that is, to predict whether a person has diabetes or not).

Model building in Python using Keras

We're finally ready to build and train our MLP in Keras.

Model building

As we mentioned in Chapter 1, *Machine Learning and Neural Networks 101*, the Sequential() class in Keras allows us to construct a neural network like Lego, stacking layers on top of one another.

Let's create a new Sequential() class:

```
from keras.models import Sequential

model = Sequential()
```

Next, let's stack our first hidden layer. The first hidden will have 32 nodes, and the input dimensions will be 8 (because there are 8 columns in X_train). Notice that for the very first hidden layer, we need to indicate the input dimensions. Subsequently, Keras will take care of the size compatibility of other hidden layers automatically.

Another point to note is that we have arbitrarily decided on the number of nodes for the first hidden layer. This variable is a hyperparameter that should be carefully selected through trial and error. In this project, we will skip hyperparameter tuning and just use 32 as the number of nodes since it does not necessarily make much of a difference for this simple dataset.

Let's add the first hidden layer:

```
from keras.layers import Dense
# Add the first hidden layer
model.add(Dense(32, activation='relu', input_dim=8))
```

The activation function used is relu, as discussed in the previous section.

Next, let's stack on the second hidden layer. Adding more hidden layers increases the complexity of our model, but can sometimes cause the model to overfit. For this project, we will use two hidden layers only, as that is sufficient to produce a satisfactory model.

Let's add our second hidden layer:

```
# Add the second hidden layer
model.add(Dense(16, activation='relu'))
```

Finally, finish off the MLP by adding the output layer. This layer has only one single node, as we're dealing with binary classification here. The `activation` function used is the `sigmoid` function, and it *squashes* the output between 0 and 1 (binary output).

Now we add the output layer as follows:

```
# Add the output layer
model.add(Dense(1, activation='sigmoid'))
```

Model compilation

Before we start training our model, we need to define the parameters of the training process, which is done via the `compile` method.

There are three different parameters we need to define for the training process:

- **Optimizer**: Let's use the `adam` optimizer, which is a popular optimizer in Keras. For most datasets, the `adam` optimizer will work well without much tuning.
- **Loss function**: We'll use `binary_crossentropy` as our `loss` function since the problem at hand is a binary classification problem.
- **Metrics**: We'll use `accuracy` (that is, the percentage of correctly classified samples) as our evaluation metric.

Then, we can run the `compile()` function as follows:

```
# Compile the model
model.compile(optimizer='adam',
              loss='binary_crossentropy',
              metrics=['accuracy'])
```

Model training

To train our MLP model defined in earlier steps, let's call the `fit` function. Let's train our model for 200 iterations:

```
# Train the model for 200 epochs
model.fit(X_train, y_train, epochs=200)
```

We get the following result:

```
Epoch 1/200
491/491 [==============================] - 1s 1ms/step - loss: 0.6387 - acc: 0.6640
Epoch 2/200
491/491 [==============================] - 0s 30us/step - loss: 0.5772 - acc: 0.7189
Epoch 3/200
491/491 [==============================] - 0s 32us/step - loss: 0.5410 - acc: 0.7332
Epoch 4/200
491/491 [==============================] - 0s 35us/step - loss: 0.5159 - acc: 0.7434
Epoch 5/200
491/491 [==============================] - 0s 32us/step - loss: 0.4976 - acc: 0.7617
Epoch 6/200
491/491 [==============================] - 0s 29us/step - loss: 0.4869 - acc: 0.7597
Epoch 7/200
491/491 [==============================] - 0s 32us/step - loss: 0.4770 - acc: 0.7617
Epoch 8/200
491/491 [==============================] - 0s 32us/step - loss: 0.4697 - acc: 0.7637
Epoch 9/200
491/491 [==============================] - 0s 32us/step - loss: 0.4642 - acc: 0.7678
Epoch 10/200
491/491 [==============================] - 0s 31us/step - loss: 0.4600 - acc: 0.7658



                                   .


                                   .


                                   .


Epoch 190/200
491/491 [==============================] - 0s 31us/step - loss: 0.2488 - acc: 0.8941
Epoch 191/200
491/491 [==============================] - 0s 30us/step - loss: 0.2476 - acc: 0.9002
Epoch 192/200
491/491 [==============================] - 0s 30us/step - loss: 0.2492 - acc: 0.8982
Epoch 193/200
491/491 [==============================] - 0s 30us/step - loss: 0.2466 - acc: 0.9022
Epoch 194/200
491/491 [==============================] - 0s 33us/step - loss: 0.2476 - acc: 0.8961
Epoch 195/200
491/491 [==============================] - 0s 32us/step - loss: 0.2490 - acc: 0.8921
Epoch 196/200
491/491 [==============================] - 0s 36us/step - loss: 0.2473 - acc: 0.8961
Epoch 197/200
491/491 [==============================] - 0s 32us/step - loss: 0.2455 - acc: 0.8961
Epoch 198/200
491/491 [==============================] - 0s 35us/step - loss: 0.2422 - acc: 0.9022
Epoch 199/200
491/491 [==============================] - 0s 31us/step - loss: 0.2428 - acc: 0.8961
Epoch 200/200
491/491 [==============================] - 0s 32us/step - loss: 0.2412 - acc: 0.9022
```

As we can see, the loss decreases and the accuracy increases over each epoch, as the learning algorithm continuously updates the weights and biases in the MLP according to the training data. Note that the accuracy shown in the preceding screenshot refers to the accuracy based on the training data. In the next section, we will take a look at the performance of the MLP based on the held out testing data, as well as some other important metrics.

Results analysis

Having successfully trained our MLP, let's evaluate our model based on the testing accuracy, confusion matrix, and **receiver operating characteristic** (**ROC**) curve.

Testing accuracy

We can evaluate our model on the training set and testing set using the `evaluate()` function:

```
scores = model.evaluate(X_train, y_train)
print("Training Accuracy: %.2f%%\n" % (scores[1]*100))

scores = model.evaluate(X_test, y_test)
print("Testing Accuracy: %.2f%%\n" % (scores[1]*100))
```

We get the following result:

```
491/491 [==============================] - 0s 45us/step
Training Accuracy: 91.85%

154/154 [==============================] - 0s 48us/step
Testing Accuracy: 78.57%
```

The accuracy is **91.85%** and **78.57%** on the training set and testing set respectively. The difference in accuracy between the training and testing set isn't surprising since the model was trained on the training set. In fact, by training the model over more iterations, we can achieve 100% accuracy on the training set, but that would not be desirable as it just means that we are overfitting our model. The testing accuracy should always be used to evaluate the real-world performance of our model, as the testing set represents real-world data that the model has never seen before.

The testing accuracy of **78.57%** is pretty impressive for our simple MLP with just two hidden layers. What this means is that given the eight measurements from a new patient (glucose, blood pressure, insulin, and so on), our MLP is able to predict with ~80% accuracy whether that patient will develop diabetes within the next five years. In essence, we have developed our first AI agent!

Confusion matrix

The confusion matrix is a useful visualization tool that provides analysis on the true negative, false positive, false negative, and true positives made by our model. Beyond a simple accuracy metric, we should also look at the confusion matrix to understand the performance of the model.

The definition of true negative, false positive, false negative, and true positives are as follows:

- **True negative**: Actual class is negative (no diabetes), and the model predicted negative (no diabetes)
- **False positive**: Actual class is negative (no diabetes), but the model predicted positive (diabetes)
- **False negative**: Actual class is positive (diabetes), but the model predicted negative (no diabetes)
- **True positive**: Actual class is positive (diabetes), and the model predicted positive (diabetes)

Clearly, we want our false positive and false negative numbers to be as low as possible, and for the true negative and true positive numbers to be as high as possible.

We can construct a confusion matrix using the `confusion_matrix` class from `sklearn`, using `seaborn` for the visualization:

```
from sklearn.metrics import confusion_matrix
import seaborn as sns

y_test_pred = model.predict_classes(X_test)
c_matrix = confusion_matrix(y_test, y_test_pred)
ax = sns.heatmap(c_matrix, annot=True,
                 xticklabels=['No Diabetes','Diabetes'],
                 yticklabels=['No Diabetes','Diabetes'],
                 cbar=False, cmap='Blues')
ax.set_xlabel("Prediction")
ax.set_ylabel("Actual")
```

And the result is as follows:

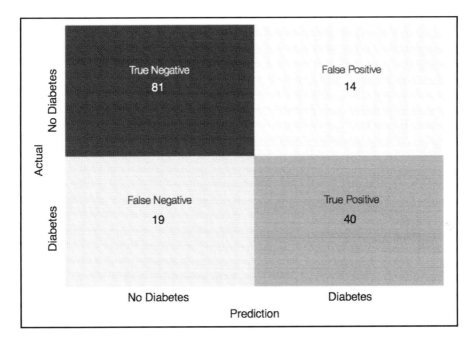

From the preceding confusion matrix, we can see that most predictions are true negatives and true positives (as indicated by the 78.57% test accuracy in the previous section). The remaining **19** predictions are false negatives and **14** other predictions are false positives, which are undesirable.

For diabetes prediction, a false negative is perhaps more damaging than a false positive. A false negative means telling the patient that they will not develop diabetes within the next five years, when in fact they would. Therefore, when we evaluate the performance of different models for predicting the onset of diabetes, a model with a lower false negative is more desirable.

ROC curve

For classification tasks, we should also look at the ROC curve to evaluate our model. The ROC curve is a plot with the **True Positive Rate** (**TPR**) on the y axis and the **False Positive Rate** (**FPR**) on the x axis. TPR and FPR are defined as follows:

$$True\ Positive\ Rate\ (TPR) = \frac{True\ Positive}{True\ Positive\ +\ False\ Negative}$$

$$False\ Positive\ Rate\ (FPR) = \frac{False\ Positive}{True\ Negative\ +\ False\ Positive}$$

When we analyze the ROC curve, we look at the **area under the curve** (**AUC**) to evaluate the performance of the model that produced the curve. A large AUC indicates that the model is able to differentiate the respective classes with high accuracy, while a low AUC indicates that the model makes poor, often wrong predictions. A ROC curve that lies on the diagonal indicates that the model does no better than random. The following diagram illustrates this:

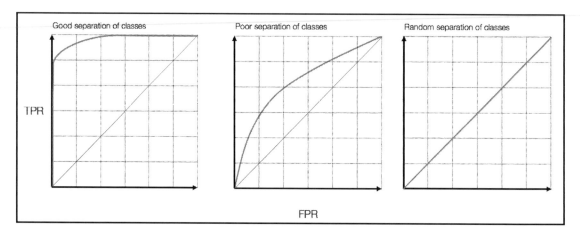

Let's plot the ROC curve for our model and analyze its performance. As always, scikit-learn provides a useful `roc_curve` class to help us do this. But first, let's get the predicted probabilities of each class using the `predict()` function:

```
from sklearn.metrics import roc_curve
import matplotlib.pyplot as plt

y_test_pred_probs = model.predict(X_test)
```

Then, run the `roc_curve` function in order to get the corresponding false positive rate and true positive rate for the ROC curve:

```
FPR, TPR, _ = roc_curve(y_test, y_test_pred_probs)
```

Now plot the values on a plot using matplotlib:

```
plt.plot(FPR, TPR)
plt.plot([0,1],[0,1],'--', color='black') #diagonal line
plt.title('ROC Curve')
plt.xlabel('False Positive Rate')
plt.ylabel('True Positive Rate')
```

We get the following result:

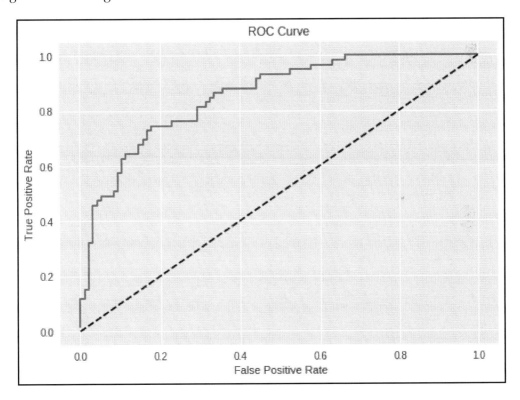

From the preceding **ROC Curve**, we can see that the model performs rather well, close to the model **ROC Curve** shown in the preceding diagram. This shows that our model is able to differentiate samples of different classes, making good predictions.

Further improvements

At this point, it is worth wondering if it is possible to further improve the performance of our model. How can we further improve the accuracy of our model and/or improve the false negative and false positive rate?

In general, any limitation in performance is usually due to the lack of strong features in the dataset, rather than the complexity of the neural network used. The Pima Indians Diabetes dataset only consists of eight features, and it can be argued that these features alone are insufficient to really predict the onset of diabetes.

One way to increase the number of features we provide to the model is via **feature engineering**. Feature engineering is the process of using one's domain knowledge of the problem to create new features for the machine learning algorithm. Feature engineering is one of the most important aspects of data science. In fact, many past winners of Kaggle competitions have credited their success to feature engineering, and not just tuning of the machine learning model. However, feature engineering is a double-edged sword and must be done carefully. Adding inappropriate features may create noise for our machine learning model, affecting the performance of our model.

On the opposite spectrum, we may also consider removing features in order to improve model performance. This is known as **feature selection**. Feature selection is used when we believe that the original dataset contains too much noise, and removing the noisy features (features that are not strong predictors) may improve model performance. One popular way to do feature selection is to use decision trees.

Decision trees are a separate class of machine learning models with a tree-like data structure. Decision trees are useful as they calculate and rank the most important features according to certain statistical criteria. We can first fit the data using the decision tree, and then use the output from the decision tree to remove features that are deemed unimportant, before providing the reduced dataset to our neural network. Again, feature selection is a double-edged sword that can potentially affect model performance.

Although feature engineering and feature selection were not done in this project, we will see it being used in other projects in later chapters, as we gradually take on more challenging problems.

Summary

In this chapter, we have designed and implemented an MLP that is capable of predicting the onset of diabetes with ~80% accuracy.

We first performed exploratory data analysis where we looked at the distribution of each variable, as well as the relationship between each variable and the target variable. We then performed data preprocessing to remove missing data and we also standardized our data such that each variable has a mean of 0 with unit standard deviation. Finally, we split our original data randomly into a training set, a validation set, and a testing set.

We then looked at the architecture of the MLP that we used, which consists of 2 hidden layers, with 32 nodes in the first hidden layer and 16 nodes in the second hidden layer. We then implemented this MLP in Keras using the sequential model, which allows us to stack layers on one another. We then trained our MLP using the training set, where Keras used the Adam optimizer algorithm to modify the weights and biases in the neural network over 200 iterations, gradually improving model's accuracy.

Finally, we evaluated our model using metrics such as the testing accuracy, confusion matrix, and ROC curve. We saw the importance of looking at metrics such as false negatives and false positives when evaluating our model, and how false negatives and false positives are important metrics, especially for a classifier that predicts the onset of diabetes.

This concludes the chapter on using a simple MLP to predict the onset of diabetes. In the next chapter, Chapter 3, *Predicting Taxi Fares with Deep Feedforward Networks*, we will use a more complicated dataset that utilizes temporal and geolocation information to make predictions of taxi fares.

Questions

1. How do we plot a histogram of each variable in a pandas DataFrame, and why are histograms useful?

   We can plot a histogram by calling the df.hist() function built into a pandas DataFrame class. A histogram provides an accurate representation of the distribution of our numerical data.

2. How do we check for missing values (NaN values) in a pandas DataFrame?

   We can call the df.isnull().any() function to easily check whether there are any null values in each column of the dataset.

3. Besides NaN values, what other kinds of missing values could appear in a dataset?

    Missing values can also appear in the form of 0 values. Missing values are often recorded as 0 in a dataset due to certain issues during data collection—perhaps the equipment was faulty, or there are other issues hindering data collection.

4. Why is it crucial to remove missing values in a dataset before training a neural network with it?

    Neural networks are unable to handle NaN values. Neural networks require all of their inputs to be numerical due to the kind of mathematical operations they perform during forward and back propagation.

5. What does data standardization do, and why is it important to perform data standardization before training a neural network with the data?

    The goal of data standardization is to transform the numeric variables so that each variable has zero mean and unit variance. When training neural networks, it is important to ensure that the data has been standardized. This ensures that features with a larger scale does not dominate features with a smaller scale when training a neural network.

6. How do we split our dataset to ensure unbiased evaluation of model performance?

    Before training a neural network, we should split our dataset into a training set, validation set, and testing set. The neural network will be trained on the training set, while the validation set allows us to perform hyperparameter tuning using an unbiased source of data. Finally, the testing set provides an unbiased source of data to evaluate the performance of the neural network.

7. What are the characteristic features of the model architecture of a MLP?

    MLPs are feedforward neural networks, and they have at least one hidden layer, with each layer activated by a non-linear activation function. This multilayer neural network architecture and non-linear activation allows MLPs to produce non-linear decision boundaries.

8. What is the purpose of activation functions in neural networks?

Activation functions performs a non-linear transformation on the weights and biases before passing it to the next layer. The most popular and effective activation function between hidden layers is the ReLU activation function.

9. What is a suitable loss function to use when training our neural network for a binary classification problem?

The binary cross entropy is the most appropriate loss function to use when training our neural network for a binary classification problem.

10. What does a confusion matrix represent, and how can we use it to evaluate the performance of our neural network?

A confusion matrix provides values on the true negative, false positive, false negative, and true positives made by our neural network. Beyond a simple accuracy metric, the confusion matrix allows us to drill down into the kind of mistakes made by our neural network (false positives and false negatives).

Predicting Taxi Fares with Deep Feedforward Networks

3

In this chapter, we will use a deep feedforward neural network to predict taxi fares in **New York City** (**NYC**), given inputs such as the pickup and drop off locations.

In the previous chapter, Chapter 2, *Predicting Diabetes with Multilayer Perceptrons*, we saw how we can use a MLP with two hidden layers to perform a classification task (whether the patient is at risk of diabetes or not). In this chapter, we will build a deep neural network to perform a regression task of estimating taxi fares. As we shall see, we will need a deeper (that is, more complex) neural network to achieve this goal.

In this chapter, we will cover the following topics:

- The motivation for the problem that we're trying to tackle—making accurate predictions of taxi fares
- Classification versus regression problems in machine learning
- In-depth analysis of the NYC taxi fares dataset, including geolocation data visualization
- Architecture of a deep feedforward neural network
- Training a deep feedforward neural network in Keras for regression problems
- Analysis of our results

Technical requirements

The key Python libraries required for this chapter are as follows:

- matplotlib 3.0.2
- pandas 0.23.4
- Keras 2.2.4
- NumPy 1.15.2
- scikit-learn 0.20.2

 To download the dataset required for this project, please refer to the instructions at `https://raw.githubusercontent.com/PacktPublishing/ Neural-Network-Projects-with-Python/master/Chapter03/how_to_ download_the_dataset.txt`.

The code for this chapter can be found in the GitHub repository for the book at `https:// github.com/PacktPublishing/Neural-Network-Projects-with-Python`.

To download the code into your computer, run the following `git clone` command:

```
$ git clone
https://github.com/PacktPublishing/Neural-Network-Projects-with-Python.git
```

After the process is complete, there will be a folder titled `Neural-Network-Projects- with-Python`. Enter the folder by running the following command:

```
$ cd Neural-Network-Projects-with-Python
```

To install the required Python libraries in a virtual environment, run the following command:

```
$ conda env create -f environment.yml
```

Note that you should have installed Anaconda on your computer first before running this command. To enter the virtual environment, run the following command:

```
$ conda activate neural-network-projects-python
```

Navigate to the `Chapter03` folder by running the following command:

```
$ cd Chapter03
```

The following files are located in this folder:

- `main.py`: This is the main code for the neural network.
- `utils.py`: This file contains auxiliary utility code that will help us in the implementation of our neural network.
- `visualize.py`: This file contains all the necessary code for exploratory data analysis and data visualization. Every plot in this chapter can be recreated by running this file.

To run the code for the neural network, simply execute the `main.py` file:

```
$ python main.py
```

To recreate the data visualizations covered in this chapter, execute the `visualize.py` file:

```
$ python visualize.py
```

Predicting taxi fares in New York City

Yellow cabs in NYC are perhaps one of the most recognizable icons in the city. Tens of thousands of commuters in NYC rely on taxis as a mode of transportation around the bustling metropolis. In recent years, the taxi industry in NYC has been put under increasing pressure from ride-hailing apps such as Uber.

In order to rise to the challenge from ride-hailing apps, yellow cabs in NYC are looking to modernize their operations, and to provide a user experience on par with Uber. In August 2018, the Taxi and Limousine Commission of NYC launched a new app that allows commuters to book a yellow cab from their phones. The app provides fare pricing upfront before they hail a cab. Creating an algorithm to provide fare pricing upfront is no simple feat. The algorithm needs to consider various environmental variables such as traffic conditions, time of day, and pick up and drop off locations in order to make an accurate fare prediction. The best way to do that is to leverage machine learning. By the end of this chapter, you will have created and trained a neural network to do exactly that.

The NYC taxi fares dataset

The dataset that we will be using for this project is the NYC taxi fares dataset, as provided by Kaggle. The original dataset contains a massive 55 million trip records from 2009 to 2015, including data such as the pick up and drop off locations, number of passengers, and pickup datetime. This dataset provides an interesting opportunity to use big datasets in machine learning projects, as well to visualize geolocation data.

Exploratory data analysis

Let's dive right into the dataset. The instructions to download the NYC taxi fares dataset can be found in the accompanying GitHub repository for the book (refer to the *Technical requirements* section). Unlike in the previous chapter, `Chapter 2`, *Predicting Diabetes with Multilayer Perceptrons*, we're not going to import the original dataset of 55 million rows. In fact, most computers would not be able to store the entire dataset in memory! Instead, let's just import the first 0.5 million rows. Doing this does have its drawbacks, but it is a necessary tradeoff in order to use the dataset in an efficient manner.

To do this, run the `read_csv()` function with `pandas`:

```
import pandas as pd

df = pd.read_csv('NYC_taxi.csv', parse_dates=['pickup_datetime'],
nrows=500000)
```

 The `parse_dates` parameter in `read_csv` allows `pandas` to easily recognize certain columns as dates, giving us the flexibility to work with such `datetime` values, as we shall see later in the chapter.

Let's take a look at the first five rows of the dataset by calling the `df.head()` command:

```
print(df.head())
```

We get the following output:

	key	fare_amount	pickup_datetime	pickup_longitude	pickup_latitude	dropoff_longitude	dropoff_latitude	passenger_count
0	2009-06-15 17:26:21.0000001	4.5	2009-06-15 17:26:21	-73.844311	40.721319	-73.841610	40.712278	1
1	2010-01-05 16:52:16.0000002	16.9	2010-01-05 16:52:16	-74.016048	40.711303	-73.979268	40.782004	1
2	2011-08-18 00:35:00.00000049	5.7	2011-08-18 00:35:00	-73.982738	40.761270	-73.991242	40.750562	2
3	2012-04-21 04:30:42.0000001	7.7	2012-04-21 04:30:42	-73.987130	40.733143	-73.991567	40.758092	1
4	2010-03-09 07:51:00.000000135	5.3	2010-03-09 07:51:00	-73.968095	40.768008	-73.956655	40.783762	1

We can see that there are eight columns in the dataset:

- `key`: This column seems identical to the `pickup_datetime` column. It was probably used as an unique identifier in the database it was stored in. We can safely remove this column without any loss of information.
- `fare_amount`: This is the target variable we are trying to predict, the fare amount paid at the end of the trip.
- `pickup_datetime`: This column contains information on the pickup date (year, month, day of month), as well as the time (hour, minute, seconds).
- `pickup_longitude` and `pickup_latitude`: The longitude and latitude of the pickup location.
- `dropoff_longitude` and `dropoff_latitude`: The longitude and latitude of the drop off location.
- `passenger_count`: The number of passengers.

Visualizing geolocation data

The pick-up and drop-off longitude and latitude data are crucial to predicting the fare amount. After all, fares in NYC taxis are largely determined by the distance traveled.

First, let's understand what latitude and longitude represents. Latitude and longitude are coordinates in a geographic coordinate system. Basically, the latitude and longitude allows us to specify any location on Earth using a set of coordinates.

The following diagram shows the **Latitude** and **Longitude** coordinate system:

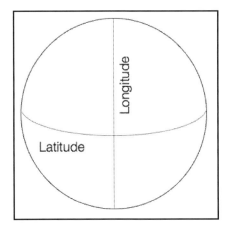

We can think of the Earth as a scatterplot, with the **Longitude** and the **Latitude** being the axes. Then, every location on Earth is simply a point on the scatterplot. In fact, let's do exactly that; let's plot the pickup and drop off latitudes and longitudes on a scatterplot.

First, let's restrict our data points to only pickups and drop offs within NYC. NYC has an approximate longitude range of -74.05 to -73.75 and a latitude range of 40.63 to 40.85:

```
# range of longitude for NYC
nyc_min_longitude = -74.05
nyc_max_longitude = -73.75

# range of latitude for NYC
nyc_min_latitude = 40.63
nyc_max_latitude = 40.85

df2 = df.copy(deep=True)
for long in ['pickup_longitude', 'dropoff_longitude']:
    df2 = df2[(df2[long] > nyc_min_longitude) & (df2[long] <
                                        nyc_max_longitude)]

for lat in ['pickup_latitude', 'dropoff_latitude']:
    df2 = df2[(df2[lat] > nyc_min_latitude) & (df2[lat] <
                                        nyc_max_latitude)]
```

Note that we copied the original DataFrame, df, into a new DataFrame, df2, to avoid overwriting the original DataFrame.

Now, let's define a new function that will take our DataFrame as an input, and plot the pickup locations on a scatterplot. We are also interested in overlaying the scatterplot with a few key landmarks in NYC. A quick Google search tells us that there are two main airports in NYC (JFK and LaGuardia), and their coordinates, along with the main districts in NYC, are as follows:

```
landmarks = {'JFK Airport': (-73.78, 40.643),
            'Laguardia Airport': (-73.87, 40.77),
            'Midtown': (-73.98, 40.76),
            'Lower Manhattan': (-74.00, 40.72),
            'Upper Manhattan': (-73.94, 40.82),
            'Brooklyn': (-73.95, 40.66)}
```

And here's our function using `matplotlib` to plot the pickup locations on a scatterplot:

```
import matplotlib.pyplot as plt

def plot_lat_long(df, landmarks, points='Pickup'):
    plt.figure(figsize = (12,12)) # set figure size
    if points == 'pickup':
        plt.plot(list(df.pickup_longitude), list(df.pickup_latitude),
                 '.', markersize=1)
    else:
        plt.plot(list(df.dropoff_longitude), list(df.dropoff_latitude),
                 '.', markersize=1)

    for landmark in landmarks:
        plt.plot(landmarks[landmark][0], landmarks[landmark][1],
                 '*', markersize=15, alpha=1, color='r')
        plt.annotate(landmark, (landmarks[landmark][0]+0.005,
                     landmarks[landmark][1]+0.005), color='r',
                     backgroundcolor='w')

    plt.title("{} Locations in NYC Illustrated".format(points))
    plt.grid(None)
    plt.xlabel("Latitude")
    plt.ylabel("Longitude")
    plt.show()
```

Let's run the function we just defined:

```
plot_lat_long(df2, landmarks, points='Pickup')
```

We'll see the following scatterplot showing the pickup locations:

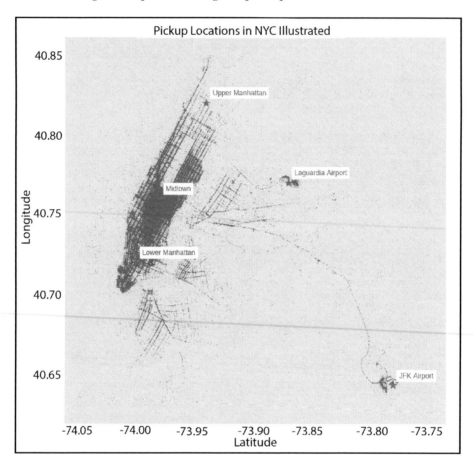

Isn't it beautiful? Just by plotting the pickup locations on a scatterplot, we can clearly see a map of NYC, along with the grids that streets in NYC are known for. From the preceding scatterplot, we can make a few observations:

- In Manhattan, most pickups were around the `Midtown` area, followed by `Lower Manhattan`. In comparison, there are much fewer pickups in `Upper Manhattan`. This makes sense, since `Upper Manhattan` is a residential area, whereas more offices and tourist attractions are located at `Midtown` and `Lower Manhattan`.
- Pickups are sparse outside Manhattan. The only two outliers were at `LaGuardia Airport` and `JFK Airport`.

Let's also plot the scatterplot for drop off locations and see how it differs:

```
plot_lat_long(df2, landmarks, points='Drop Off')
```

We'll see the following scatterplot:

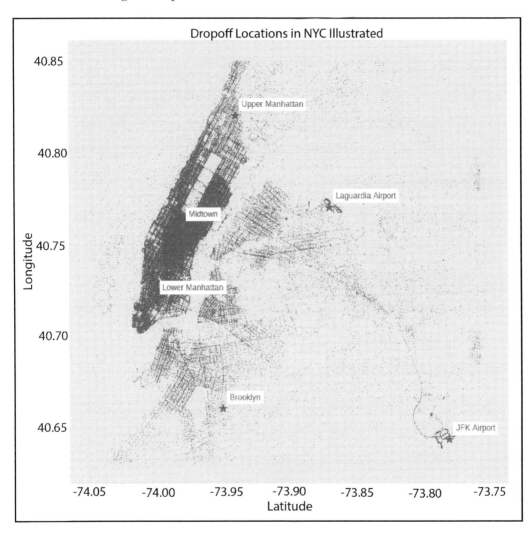

Comparing the pickup and drop off scatterplots, we can clearly see that there are more drop offs than pickups in residential areas such as Upper Manhattan and Brooklyn. Neat!

Ridership by day and hour

Next, let's investigate how the number of rides varies by day and hour.

Recall that the raw data contains a single `pickup_datetime` column that contains the pickup date and time in `datetime` format. First, let's separate the pickup year, month, day, day of week, and hour from the original `pickup_datetime` column into different columns:

```
df['year'] = df['pickup_datetime'].dt.year
df['month'] = df['pickup_datetime'].dt.month
df['day'] = df['pickup_datetime'].dt.day
df['day_of_week'] = df['pickup_datetime'].dt.dayofweek
df['hour'] = df['pickup_datetime'].dt.hour
```

Since we have previously used the `parse_dates` parameter when we imported the data into pandas, we can easily identify and separate the year, month, day and hour components using the `dt` function in pandas.

Now, let's plot a histogram to analyze the distribution of rides throughout the week:

```
import numpy as np
df['day_of_week'].plot.hist(bins=np.arange(8)-0.5, ec='black',
                    ylim=(60000,75000))
plt.xlabel('Day of Week (0=Monday, 6=Sunday)')
plt.title('Day of Week Histogram')
plt.show()
```

We'll see the following histogram:

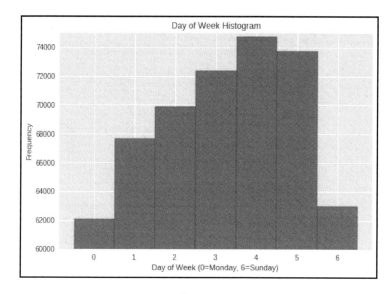

Interestingly, we can see that the number of rides is not evenly distributed across each weekday. Instead, the number of rides increases linearly from Monday through Friday, and peaking on Friday. The weekends see a slight drop in the number of rides on Saturday, before falling sharply on Sunday.

We can also visualize ridership by hour:

```
df['hour'].plot.hist(bins=24, ec='black')
plt.title('Pickup Hour Histogram')
plt.xlabel('Hour')
plt.show()
```

We'll see the following histogram for pickup hour:

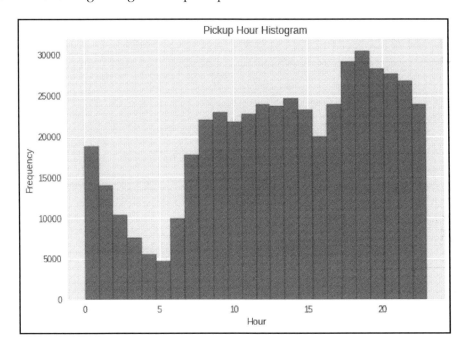

We can see that there are more rides during the evening rush hour, as compared to the morning rush hour. In fact, the number of rides is pretty constant throughout the day. Starting at 6 P.M., the number of rides increases and peaks at 7 P.M., before falling from 11 P.M. onwards.

Data preprocessing

Recall from the previous project that we had to preprocess the data by removing missing values and other data anomalies. In this project, we'll perform the same process. We'll also perform feature engineering to improve both the quality and quantity of the features before training our neural network on it.

Handling missing values and data anomalies

Let's do a check to see whether there are any missing values in our dataset:

```
print(df.isnull().sum())
```

We'll see the following output showing the number of missing values in each column:

```
key                  0
fare_amount          0
pickup_datetime      0
pickup_longitude     0
pickup_latitude      0
dropoff_longitude    5
dropoff_latitude     5
passenger_count      0
dtype: int64
```

We can see that there are only five rows (out of 500,000 rows) with missing data. With a missing data percentage of just 0.001%, it seems that we don't have a problem with missing data. Let's go ahead and remove those five rows with missing data:

```
df = df.dropna()
```

At this point, we should also check the data for outliers. In a dataset as massive as this, there are bound to be outliers, which can skew our model. Let's run a quick statistical summary on our data to look at the distribution:

```
print(df.describe())
```

The `describe` method produces the following table:

	fare_amount	pickup_longitude	pickup_latitude	dropoff_longitude	dropoff_latitude	passenger_count
count	499995.000000	499995.000000	499995.000000	499995.000000	499995.000000	499995.000000
mean	11.358182	-72.520091	39.920350	-72.522435	39.916526	1.683445
std	9.916069	11.856446	8.073318	11.797362	7.391002	1.307391
min	-44.900000	-2986.242495	-3116.285383	-3383.296608	-2559.748913	0.000000
25%	6.000000	-73.992047	40.734916	-73.991382	40.734057	1.000000
50%	8.500000	-73.981785	40.752670	-73.980126	40.753152	1.000000
75%	12.500000	-73.967117	40.767076	-73.963572	40.768135	2.000000
max	500.000000	2140.601160	1703.092772	40.851027	404.616667	6.000000

The lowest fare in the dataset is $-44.90. That doesn't make sense; fares can't be negative! Also, the highest fare is $500. Did the passenger get ripped off? Or was it just an error? Let's plot a histogram to better understand the distribution of fares:

```
df['fare_amount'].hist(bins=500)
plt.xlabel("Fare")
plt.title("Histogram of Fares")
plt.show()
```

We'll get the following histogram:

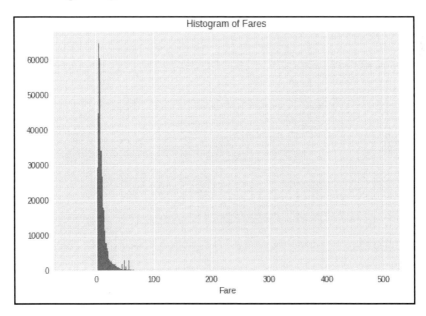

It doesn't seem like that there are too many outliers, so we can safely remove them. Another interesting trend that we can observe from the histogram is that there is a small spike in fares around $50. Could this be a fixed fare from a specific location? Cities usually implement fixed fares for trips to and from airports. A quick Google search tells us that trips to and from JFK airport incurs a flat fare of $52 plus tolls. This could be the reason for the spike in the histogram around $50! We'll keep this important fact in mind when we do feature engineering later on.

For now, let's remove rows with fares less than $0 and more than $100:

```
df = df[(df['fare_amount'] >=0) & (df['fare_amount'] <= 100)]
```

From the previous table, we can see that there are also outliers in the passenger_count column. Let's plot a histogram of Passenger Count to look at its distribution:

```
df['passenger_count'].hist(bins=6, ec='black')
plt.xlabel("Passenger Count")
plt.title("Histogram of Passenger Count")
plt.show()
```

This gives us the following histogram:

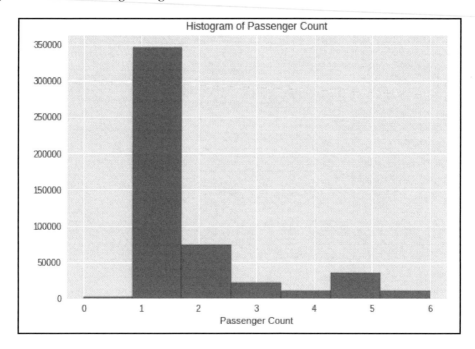

We can see that there's a small percentage of rows with 0 passenger counts. Instead of discarding those rows, let's replace the outliers with the mode (that is, 1 passenger count):

```
df.loc[df['passenger_count']==0, 'passenger_count'] = 1
```

 We can also remove these outliers entirely, since only a few rows are affected. Instead, we chose to replace the outlier passenger count with the mode. Both methods are perfectly valid, but we chose the latter to illustrate the importance of visualizing your data with a histogram to identify outlier values, as well as the mode.

Next, let's inspect the pickup and drop off latitude and longitude data to check for outliers. In the previous section on data visualization, we plotted a scatterplot with the restriction that the points should be located within the boundaries of NYC. Let's plot a scatterplot now without that restriction:

```
df.plot.scatter('pickup_longitude', 'pickup_latitude')
plt.show()
```

We'll see the following scatterplot:

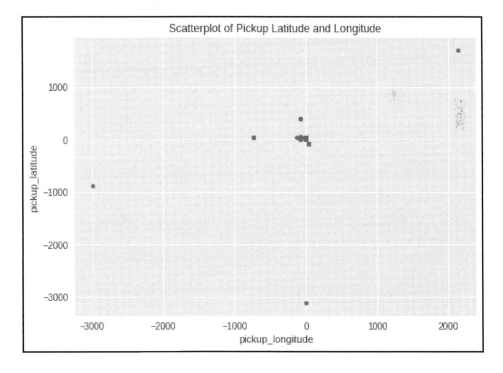

Do you see where the outliers are? The dots at the periphery of the scatterplot are outliers. They have latitude values as high as **1000** and as low as **-3000**. Earth's geographic coordinate system does not have such extreme latitudes and longitudes! Let's remove these outliers:

```
# range of longitude for NYC
nyc_min_longitude = -74.05
nyc_max_longitude = -73.75

# range of latitude for NYC
nyc_min_latitude = 40.63
nyc_max_latitude = 40.85

# only consider locations within NYC
for long in ['pickup_longitude', 'dropoff_longitude']:
    df = df[(df[long] > nyc_min_longitude) & (df[long] <
                                          nyc_max_longitude)]

for lat in ['pickup_latitude', 'dropoff_latitude']:
    df = df[(df[lat] > nyc_min_latitude) & (df[lat] <
                                          nyc_max_latitude)]
```

Let's summarize what we have done for data preprocessing. We first saw that missing values only constitute 0.001% of the dataset, so we can remove them safely without affecting the quantity of our training data. Next, we saw that there are outliers in `fare_amount`, and `passenger_count`, as well as the pickup and drop off latitude and longitude. We removed the outliers for the `fare_amount`, latitude and longitude. For the `passenger_count`, we replaced those rows that had a 0 passenger count with the `passenger count` = 1 mode.

Let's create a helper function to help us do all that data preprocessing. In machine learning projects, the number of steps can often get out of hand. It is important to adhere to strong software engineering practices, such as code modularization, to keep our project on track.

The following code takes a pandas DataFrame as input, and returns the DataFrame after performing data preprocessing:

```
def preprocess(df):
    # remove missing values in the dataframe
    def remove_missing_values(df):
        df = df.dropna()
        return df

    # remove outliers in fare amount
    def remove_fare_amount_outliers(df, lower_bound, upper_bound):
        df = df[(df['fare_amount'] >= lower_bound) &
```

```
                    (df['fare_amount'] <= upper_bound)]
        return df

# replace outliers in passenger count with the mode
def replace_passenger_count_outliers(df):
    mode = df['passenger_count'].mode()
    df.loc[df['passenger_count'] == 0, 'passenger_count'] = mode
    return df

# remove outliers in latitude and longitude
def remove_lat_long_outliers(df):
    # range of longitude for NYC
    nyc_min_longitude = -74.05
    nyc_max_longitude = -73.75
    # range of latitude for NYC
    nyc_min_latitude = 40.63
    nyc_max_latitude = 40.85
    # only consider locations within New York City
    for long in ['pickup_longitude', 'dropoff_longitude']:
        df = df[(df[long] > nyc_min_longitude) &
                (df[long] < nyc_max_longitude)]
    for lat in ['pickup_latitude', 'dropoff_latitude']:
        df = df[(df[lat] > nyc_min_latitude) &
                (df[lat] < nyc_max_latitude)]
    return df

df = remove_missing_values(df)
df = remove_fare_amount_outliers(df, lower_bound = 0,
                                 upper_bound = 100)
df = replace_passenger_count_outliers(df)
df = remove_lat_long_outliers(df)
return df
```

We'll save this helper function under `utils.py` in our project folder. Then, to call our helper function for data preprocessing, we just have to call `from utils import preprocess` and we'll have access to this helper function. This keeps our code neat and manageable!

Feature engineering

As briefly discussed in the previous chapter, `Chapter 2`, *Predicting Diabetes with Multilayer Perceptrons* feature engineering is the process of using one's domain knowledge of the problem to create new features for the machine learning algorithm. In this section, we shall create features based on the date and time of pickup, and location-related features.

Temporal features

As we've seen earlier in the section on data visualization, ridership volume depends heavily on the day of the week, as well as the time of day.

Let's look at the format of the `pickup_datetime` column by running the following code:

```
print(df.head()['pickup_datetime'])
```

We get the following output:

```
0    2009-06-15 17:26:21
1    2010-01-05 16:52:16
2    2011-08-18 00:35:00
3    2012-04-21 04:30:42
4    2010-03-09 07:51:00
Name: pickup_datetime, dtype: datetime64[ns]
```

Recall that neural networks require numerical features. Therefore, we can't train our neural network using such a datetime string. Let's separate the `pickup_datetime` column into different columns for `year`, `month`, `day`, `day_of_week`, and `hour`:

```
df['year'] = df['pickup_datetime'].dt.year
df['month'] = df['pickup_datetime'].dt.month
df['day'] = df['pickup_datetime'].dt.day
df['day_of_week'] = df['pickup_datetime'].dt.dayofweek
df['hour'] = df['pickup_datetime'].dt.hour
```

Let's take a look at the new columns:

```
print(df.loc[:5,['pickup_datetime', 'year', 'month',
                 'day', 'day_of_week', 'hour']])
```

We get the following output:

	pickup_datetime	year	month	day	day_of_week	hour
0	2009-06-15 17:26:21	2009	6	15	0	17
1	2010-01-05 16:52:16	2010	1	5	1	16
2	2011-08-18 00:35:00	2011	8	18	3	0
3	2012-04-21 04:30:42	2012	4	21	5	4
4	2010-03-09 07:51:00	2010	3	9	1	7
5	2011-01-06 09:50:45	2011	1	6	3	9

We can see that the new columns capture the original information from the `pickup_datetime` column in a format that's suitable for our neural network. Let's drop the `pickup_datetime` column from our DataFrame:

```
df = df.drop(['pickup_datetime'], axis=1)
```

Geolocation features

As we have seen earlier, the dataset contains information regarding the pickup and drop off coordinates. However, there is no information regarding the distance between the pickup and drop off points, which is arguably the most important factor in deciding taxi fares. Therefore, let's create a new feature that calculates the distance between each pair of pickup and drop off points.

Recall from geometry that the *Euclidean Distance* is the straight-line distance between any two points:

$$Euclidean\ Distance = \sqrt{(x_2 - x_1)^2 + (y_2 - y_1)^2}$$

Let's define a function to calculate the Euclidean distance between any two points, given the latitude and longitudes of the two points:

```
def euc_distance(lat1, long1, lat2, long2):
    return(((lat1-lat2)**2 + (long1-long2)**2)**0.5)
```

And let's apply the function to the DataFrame to create the new `distance` column:

```
df['distance'] = euc_distance(df['pickup_latitude'],
                              df['pickup_longitude'],
                              df['dropoff_latitude'],
                              df['dropoff_longitude'])
```

Our hypothesis was that the trip fare is closely correlated to the distance traveled. We can now plot the two variables on a scatterplot to analyze the correlation and see if our intuition was right:

```
df.plot.scatter('fare_amount', 'distance')
plt.show()
```

We get the following scatterplot:

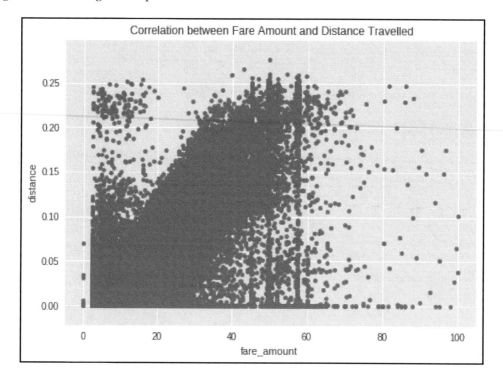

Nice! We can clearly see that our hypothesis is right. However, the distance traveled alone does not tell the whole story. If we look at the center of the graph, we can see three vertical lines of dots. These outlier data seems to suggest that there are certain trips where the distance traveled did not have an impact on the fare amount (which is between **$40** and **$60** for these outliers). Recall in the previous section on data visualization where we saw that there are certain pickups near airports, and these airport pickups have a flat fare of $52 plus tolls. This could explain the three vertical lines of dots between **$40** and **$60**!

Clearly, we need to engineer a new feature that informs our neural network of the pickup and drop off distance from the three major airports in NYC. When we train the neural network on this feature, it should then learn that pickups and drop offs near airports have a flat fare between **$40** and **$60**.

We can use the euc_distance function that we defined earlier to calculate the pickup and drop off distance from the three major airports in NYC:

```
airports = {'JFK_Airport': (-73.78,40.643),
            'Laguardia_Airport': (-73.87, 40.77),
            'Newark_Airport' : (-74.18, 40.69)}

for airport in airports:
    df['pickup_dist_' + airport] = euc_distance(df['pickup_latitude'],
                                                df['pickup_longitude'],
                                                airports[airport][1],
                                                airports[airport][0])
    df['dropoff_dist_' + airport] = euc_distance(df['dropoff_latitude'],
                                                 df['dropoff_longitude'],
                                                 airports[airport][1],
                                                 airports[airport][0])
```

Let's print out the first few rows, along with a few relevant columns to verify that the Euclidean distance function is functioning as intended:

```
print(df[['key', 'pickup_longitude', 'pickup_latitude',
          'dropoff_longitude', 'dropoff_latitude',
          'pickup_dist_JFK_Airport',
          'dropoff_dist_JFK_Airport']].head())
```

We get the following output:

	key	pickup_longitude	pickup_latitude	dropoff_longitude	dropoff_latitude	pickup_dist_JFK_Airport	dropoff_dist_JFK_Airport
0	2009-06-15 17:26:21.0000001	-73.844311	40.721319	-73.841610	40.712278	0.101340	0.092710
1	2010-01-05 16:52:16.0000002	-74.016048	40.711303	-73.979268	40.782004	0.245731	0.242961
2	2011-08-18 00:35:00.00000049	-73.982738	40.761270	-73.991242	40.750562	0.234714	0.237050
3	2012-04-21 04:30:42.0000001	-73.987130	40.733143	-73.991567	40.758092	0.225895	0.240846
4	2010-03-09 07:51:00.000000135	-73.968095	40.768008	-73.956655	40.783762	0.225847	0.225878

We can do a quick calculation on the preceding rows to verify that the Euclidean distance function works correctly. Lastly, notice that there is still a `key` column in the dataset. This column is similar to the `pickup_datetime` column, and it was probably used as a unique identifier in the database it was stored in. We can safely remove this column without any loss of information. To remove the `key` column, use this command:

```
df = df.drop(['key'], axis=1)
```

To recap, in this section, we used feature engineering to construct new features based on our own domain knowledge of the problem. From the raw datetime information provided, we extracted and constructed new features for the pickup year, month, day, day of the week, and hour. We also constructed distance-based features that are crucial to the prediction of fares, such as the distance between pickup and drop off points, as well as the pickup and drop off distance from the three main airports in NYC.

Similar to the previous *Data preprocessing* section, we're going to construct a helper function to summarize what we have done for feature engineering. This code modularization approach will help keep our code manageable:

```
def feature_engineer(df):
    # create new columns for year, month, day, day of week and hour
    def create_time_features(df):
        df['year'] = df['pickup_datetime'].dt.year
        df['month'] = df['pickup_datetime'].dt.month
        df['day'] = df['pickup_datetime'].dt.day
        df['day_of_week'] = df['pickup_datetime'].dt.dayofweek
        df['hour'] = df['pickup_datetime'].dt.hour
        df = df.drop(['pickup_datetime'], axis=1)
        return df

    # function to calculate euclidean distance
    def euc_distance(lat1, long1, lat2, long2):
        return(((lat1-lat2)**2 + (long1-long2)**2)**0.5)

    # create new column for the distance travelled
    def create_pickup_dropoff_dist_features(df):
```

```
    df['travel_distance'] = euc_distance(df['pickup_latitude'],
                                          df['pickup_longitude'],
                                          df['dropoff_latitude'],
                                          df['dropoff_longitude'])
    return df

# create new column for the distance away from airports
def create_airport_dist_features(df):
    airports = {'JFK_Airport': (-73.78,40.643),
                'Laguardia_Airport': (-73.87, 40.77),
                'Newark_Airport' : (-74.18, 40.69)}
    for k in airports:
        df['pickup_dist_'+k]=euc_distance(df['pickup_latitude'],
                                          df['pickup_longitude'],
                                          airports[k][1],
                                          airports[k][0])
        df['dropoff_dist_'+k]=euc_distance(df['dropoff_latitude'],
                                           df['dropoff_longitude'],
                                           airports[k][1],
                                           airports[k][0])
    return df

df = create_time_features(df)
df = create_pickup_dropoff_dist_features(df)
df = create_airport_dist_features(df)
df = df.drop(['key'], axis=1)
return df
```

Feature scaling

As a final preprocessing step, we should also scale our features before passing them to the neural network. Recall from the previous chapter, Chapter 2, *Predicting Diabetes with Multilayer Perceptrons*, that scaling ensures that all features have a uniform range of scale. This ensures that features with a greater scale (for example, year has a scale of > 2000) does not dominate features with a smaller scale (for example, passenger count has a scale between 1 to 6).

Before we scale the features in the DataFrame, it's a good idea to keep a copy of the prescaled DataFrame. The values of the features will be transformed after scaling (for example, year 2010 may be transformed to a value such as -0.134 after scaling), which can make it difficult for us to interpret the values. By keeping a copy of the prescaled DataFrame, we can easily reference the original values:

```
df_prescaled = df.copy()
```

We should also drop the `fare_amount` target variable before scaling, as we do not want to modify the target variable:

```
df_scaled = df.drop(['fare_amount'], axis=1)
```

Then, scale the features by calling the `scale` function from scikit-learn:

```
from sklearn.preprocessing import scale

df_scaled = scale(df_scaled)
```

Lastly, convert the object returned by the `scale` function into a pandas DataFrame and concatenate the original `fare_amount` column that was dropped before scaling:

```
cols = df.columns.tolist()
cols.remove('fare_amount')
df_scaled = pd.DataFrame(df_scaled, columns=cols, index=df.index)
df_scaled = pd.concat([df_scaled, df['fare_amount']], axis=1)
df = df_scaled.copy()
```

Deep feedforward networks

So far in this chapter, we have done an in-depth visualization of the dataset, cleaned up the dataset by handling outliers, and also performed feature engineering to create useful features for our model. For the rest of the chapter, we'll talk about the architecture of deep feedforward neural networks, and we'll train one in Keras for a regression task.

Model architecture

In the previous chapter, Chapter 2, *Predicting Diabetes with Multilayer Perceptrons*, we used a relatively simple MLP as our neural network. For this project, since there are more features, we shall use a deeper model to account for the additional complexity. The deep feedforward network will have four hidden layers. The first hidden layer will have 128 nodes, with each successive hidden layer having half the nodes of its predecessor. This neural network size is a good starting point for us and it should not take too long to train this neural network. A general rule of thumb is that we should start with a small neural network and only increase its complexity (size) as required.

In between each hidden layer, we will use the ReLU activation function to introduce non-linearity in the model. Since this is a regression problem, there will only be one node in the output layer (more on regression in the next sub-section). Note that we do not apply the ReLU activation function for the output layer as doing so would transform our predictions.

The following diagram illustrates the model architecture of the deep feedforward neural network:

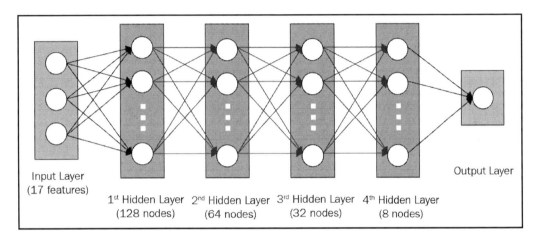

Input Layer
(17 features)

1st Hidden Layer   2nd Hidden Layer   3rd Hidden Layer   4th Hidden Layer
(128 nodes)   (64 nodes)   (32 nodes)   (8 nodes)

Output Layer

Loss functions for regression problems

It is important to understand what regression is, and how it affects the architecture of our neural network. Our task in this project is to predict taxi fares, which is a continuous variable. We can contrast this with the classification project that we did in the previous chapter, Chapter 2, *Predicting Diabetes with Multilayer Perceptrons*, where we designed a neural network to output a binary prediction (1 or 0), indicating whether the patient was at risk of diabetes.

Another way to think about regression and classification is that in regression, we are trying to predict the value of a continuous variable (for example, cost, time, or height), whereas in classification, we are trying to predict a class (for example, diabetes or no diabetes).

Recall that in the previous chapter, Chapter 2, *Predicting Diabetes with Multilayer Perceptrons*, we used percentage accuracy as a metric for measuring how strong our predictions are. In regression, the **root mean square error** (**RMSE**) is often used as the error metric.

The formula for *RMSE* is as follows:

$$RMSE = \sqrt{(prediction - actual)^2}$$

Notice how the formula takes the square of the difference between the predicted value and the actual value. This is to ensure that over estimations and under estimations are penalized equally (since the square of the error would be the same for both). We take the square-root to ensure that the magnitude of the error is similar to the actual values. The RMSE provides a loss function for our neural network, allowing it to tune its weights during the training process in order to reduce the error of its predictions.

Model building in Python using Keras

Now, let's implement our model architecture in Keras. Just like in the previous project, we're going to build our model layer by layer in Keras using the `Sequential` class.

First, split the DataFrame into the training features (`X`) and the target variable that we're trying to predict (`y`):

```
X = df.loc[:, df.columns != 'fare_amount']
y = df.loc[:, 'fare_amount']
```

Then, split the data into a training set (80%) and a testing set (20%):

```
from sklearn.model_selection import train_test_split

X_train, X_test, y_train, y_test = train_test_split(X, y, test_size=0.2)
```

Next, let's build our `Sequential` model in Keras according to the neural network architecture we outlined earlier:

```
from keras.models import Sequential
from keras.layers import Dense

model = Sequential()
model.add(Dense(128, activation= 'relu', input_dim=X_train.shape[1]))
model.add(Dense(64, activation= 'relu'))
model.add(Dense(32, activation= 'relu'))
model.add(Dense(8, activation= 'relu'))
model.add(Dense(1))
```

Before we start training our model, it is a good practice to verify the structure of our model:

```
model.summary()
```

The `summary()` function produces a table showing the number of layers and number of nodes in each layer, as well as the number of parameters in each layer (that is, the weights and biases). We can verify that this is consistent with the model architecture we outlined earlier.

Here's the table produced by the `summary()` function:

```
Layer (type)                 Output Shape              Param #
=================================================================
dense_1 (Dense)              (None, 128)               2304

dense_2 (Dense)              (None, 64)                8256

dense_3 (Dense)              (None, 32)                2080

dense_4 (Dense)              (None, 8)                 264

dense_5 (Dense)              (None, 1)                 9
=================================================================
Total params: 12,913
Trainable params: 12,913
Non-trainable params: 0
```

Finally, we can compile and train our neural network on the training data:

```
model.compile(loss='mse', optimizer='adam', metrics=['mse'])
model.fit(X_train, y_train, epochs=1)
```

Since there's a fair bit of data, it would take some time to train the neural network. After a few minutes, Keras would output the following at the end of the training epoch:

```
Epoch 1/1
386741/386741 [==============================] - 106s 275us/step - loss: 15.4968 - mean_squared_error: 15.4968
<keras.callbacks.History at 0x7fef288532b0>
```

Results analysis

Now that we have our neural network trained, let's use it to make some predictions to understand its accuracy.

We can create a function to make a prediction using a random sample from the testing set:

```
def predict_random(df_prescaled, X_test, model):
    sample = X_test.sample(n=1, random_state=np.random.randint(low=0,
                                                          high=10000))
    idx = sample.index[0]
    actual_fare = df_prescaled.loc[idx,'fare_amount']
    day_names = ['Monday', 'Tuesday', 'Wednesday', 'Thursday', 'Friday',
                'Saturday', 'Sunday']
    day_of_week = day_names[df_prescaled.loc[idx,'day_of_week']]
    hour = df_prescaled.loc[idx,'hour']
    predicted_fare = model.predict(sample)[0][0]
    rmse = np.sqrt(np.square(predicted_fare-actual_fare))

    print("Trip Details: {}, {}:00hrs".format(day_of_week, hour))
    print("Actual fare: ${:0.2f}".format(actual_fare))
    print("Predicted fare: ${:0.2f}".format(predicted_fare))
    print("RMSE: ${:0.2f}".format(rmse))
```

The `predict_random` function will pull a random row from the testing set and feed it to the model for prediction. The function will then calculate and display the RMSE of the prediction. Note that `df_prescaled` is required to provide us with the original values for day of week and hour, as the values in the testing set have already been transformed earlier and are no longer human-readable (for example, a day of week value of -0.018778 does not make much sense to us).

Let's run the `predict_random` function, shown as follows and see what kind of results we get:

```
predict_random(df_prescaled, X_test, model)
```

The trip details output by the `predict_random` function is as follows:

```
Trip Details: Sunday, 10:00hrs
Actual fare: $4.90
Predicted fare: $5.60
RMSE: $0.70
```

The following map depicts the travel details:

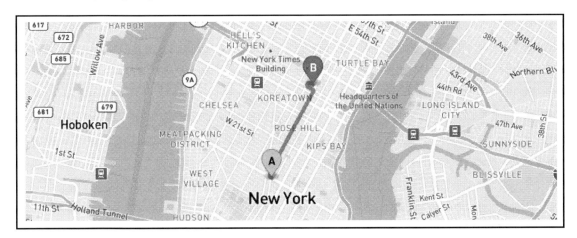

The pickup and drop off points are visualized in the preceding map. The `Actual fare` was $4.90, while the `Predicted fare` is $5.60, giving us an error of $0.70. It looks like our model is working well and the predictions are fairly accurate! Note that the map and route shown in the preceding screenshot is purely for visualization and is not part of the original dataset or code.

Let's run `predict_random` a few more times to get more results:

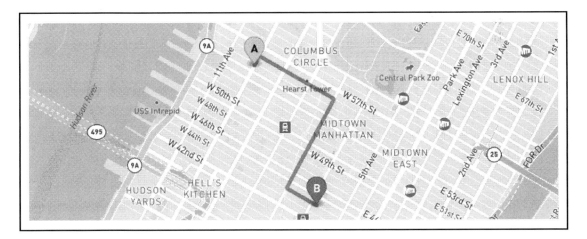

The trip details output by the `predict_random` function is as follows:

```
Trip Details: Wednesday, 7:00hrs
Actual fare: $6.10
Predicted fare: $6.30
RMSE: $0.20
```

Our prediction for this trip was almost spot on! The `Actual fare` was $6.10, while the fare predicted by our neural network is $6.30. It seems like our neural network makes really good predictions for short distance trips.

Let's see how well it does when the trip is further and more prone to traffic delays:

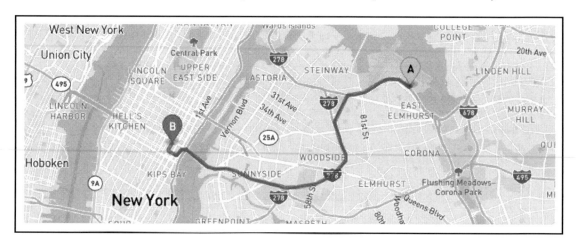

The trip details output by the `predict_random` function:

```
Trip Details: Monday, 10:00hrs
Actual fare: $35.80
Predicted fare: $38.11
RMSE: $2.31
```

As we can see from this sample, our neural network works really well even for long distance trips. The `Actual fare` was $35.80, while our neural network predicted a fare of $38.11. The error of $2.31 (~6% discrepancy) is pretty impressive given the distance of the trip.

As a final example, let's see how our neural network performs for fixed-rate trips. Recall that all trips to/from JFK airport incur a fixed fare of $52 plus tolls, no matter the distance traveled:

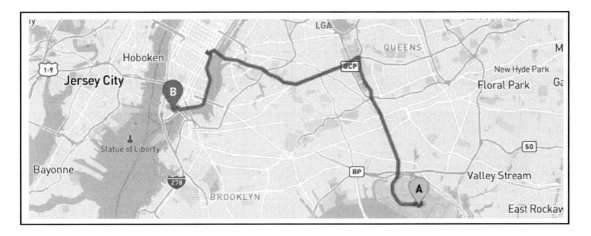

The trip details output by the `predict_random` function is as follows:

```
Trip Details: Saturday, 23:00hrs
Actual fare: $52.00
Predicted fare: $53.55
RMSE: $1.55
```

Nice! Our neural network understands that the trip started from JFK airport, and hence the fare should be close to $52. This was made possible through feature engineering, where we introduced new features that represents the pickup and drop off distance away from JFK airport. These new features allowed our neural network to learn that trips to/from JFK airport should have a fare close to $52. This shows the importance of feature engineering!

Finally, let's conclude the results by calculating the RMSE for the entire training and testing set:

```
from sklearn.metrics import mean_squared_error

train_pred = model.predict(X_train)
train_rmse = np.sqrt(mean_squared_error(y_train, train_pred))

test_pred = model.predict(X_test)
test_rmse = np.sqrt(mean_squared_error(y_test, test_pred))

print("Train RMSE: {:0.2f}".format(train_rmse))
print("Test RMSE: {:0.2f}".format(test_rmse))
```

We get the following output:

```
Train RMSE: 3.52
Test RMSE: 3.55
```

The RMSE values show that on average, our model predicts a fare that is accurate within ~$3.50.

Putting it all together

We have accomplished a lot in this chapter. Let's do a quick recap of the code that we have written so far.

We started off by defining a function for preprocessing. This `preprocess` function takes a DataFrame as an input and performs the following actions:

- Removing missing values
- Removing outliers in the fare amount
- Replacing outliers in passenger count with the mode
- Removing outliers in latitude and longitude (that is, only considering points within NYC)

This function is saved under `utils.py` in our project folder.

Next, we also defined a `feature_engineer` function for feature engineering. This function takes a DataFrame as an input and performs the following actions:

- Creating new columns for year, month, day, day of the week, and hour
- Creating new column for the Euclidean distance between the pickup and drop off points
- Creating new columns for the pickup and drop off distances away from JFK, Laguardia, and Newark airports

This function is also saved under `utils.py` in our project folder.

Now that we have defined our helper functions, we can proceed with our main neural network code. Let's create a new Python file, `main.py`, to house our main neural network code.

First, we import the necessary modules:

```
from utils import preprocess, feature_engineer
import pandas as pd
import numpy as np
from sklearn.preprocessing import scale
from sklearn.model_selection import train_test_split
from keras.models import Sequential
from keras.layers import Dense
from sklearn.metrics import mean_squared_error
```

Next, we import the first 500000 rows of the raw tabular data:

```
df = pd.read_csv('NYC_taxi.csv', parse_dates=['pickup_datetime'],
                                               nrows=500000)
```

We perform preprocessing and feature engineering using the functions that we defined previously:

```
df = preprocess(df)
df = feature_engineer(df)
```

Next, we scale the features:

```
df_prescaled = df.copy()
df_scaled = df.drop(['fare_amount'], axis=1)
df_scaled = scale(df_scaled)
cols = df.columns.tolist()
cols.remove('fare_amount')
df_scaled = pd.DataFrame(df_scaled, columns=cols, index=df.index)
df_scaled = pd.concat([df_scaled, df['fare_amount']], axis=1)
df = df_scaled.copy()
```

Next, we split the DataFrame into training and testing sets:

```
X = df.loc[:, df.columns != 'fare_amount']
y = df.fare_amount
X_train, X_test, y_train, y_test = train_test_split(X, y, test_size=0.2)
```

We build and train our deep feedforward neural network in Keras:

```
model=Sequential()
model.add(Dense(128, activation= 'relu', input_dim=X_train.shape[1]))
model.add(Dense(64, activation= 'relu'))
model.add(Dense(32, activation= 'relu'))
model.add(Dense(8, activation= 'relu'))
model.add(Dense(1))
model.compile(loss='mse', optimizer='adam', metrics=['mse'])
model.fit(X_train, y_train, epochs=1)
```

Finally, we analyze our results:

```
train_pred = model.predict(X_train)
train_rmse = np.sqrt(mean_squared_error(y_train, train_pred))
test_pred = model.predict(X_test)
test_rmse = np.sqrt(mean_squared_error(y_test, test_pred))
print("Train RMSE: {:0.2f}".format(train_rmse))
print("Test RMSE: {:0.2f}".format(test_rmse))

def predict_random(df_prescaled, X_test, model):
    sample = X_test.sample(n=1, random_state=np.random.randint(low=0,
                                                       high=10000))
    idx = sample.index[0]

    actual_fare = df_prescaled.loc[idx,'fare_amount']
    day_names = ['Monday','Tuesday','Wednesday','Thursday','Friday',
                'Saturday', 'Sunday']
    day_of_week = day_names[df_prescaled.loc[idx,'day_of_week']]
    hour = df_prescaled.loc[idx,'hour']
    predicted_fare = model.predict(sample)[0][0]
    rmse = np.sqrt(np.square(predicted_fare-actual_fare))

    print("Trip Details: {}, {}:00hrs".format(day_of_week, hour))
    print("Actual fare: ${:0.2f}".format(actual_fare))
    print("Predicted fare: ${:0.2f}".format(predicted_fare))
    print("RMSE: ${:0.2f}".format(rmse))

predict_random(df_prescaled, X_test, model)
```

That's all of our code! Notice how creating helper functions for preprocessing and feature engineering in utils.py allows our main code to be relatively short. By modularizing our code into separate helper functions, we can focus on the implementation of each step of the machine learning framework.

Summary

In this chapter, we designed and implemented a deep feedforward neural network capable of predicting taxi fares in NYC within an error of ~$3.50. We first performed exploratory data analysis, where we gained important insights on the factors that affect taxi fares. With these insights, we then performed feature engineering, which is the process of using your domain knowledge of the problem to create new features. We also introduced the concept of modularizing our functions in machine learning projects, which allowed us to keep our main code relatively short and neat.

We created our deep feedforward neural network in Keras, and trained it using the preprocessed data. Our results show that the neural network is able to make highly accurate predictions for both short and long distance trips. Even for fixed-rate trips, our neural network was able to produce highly accurate predictions.

This concludes the chapter on using a deep feedforward neural network for a regression prediction task. Together with the previous chapter, Chapter 2, *Predicting Diabetes with Multilayer Perceptrons*, we have seen how we can use neural networks for classification and regression. In the next chapter, Chapter 4, *Cats Versus Dogs – Image Classification Using CNNs*, we will introduce more complex neural networks for computer vision projects.

Questions

1. When reading a CSV file using pandas, how does pandas recognize that certain columns are datetime?

   We can use the `parse_dates` argument when reading the CSV file using the `read_csv` function in pandas.

2. How can we filter a DataFrame to only select rows within a certain range of values, assuming that we have a DataFrame, `df`, and we want to select rows with height values within the range of `160` and `180`?

   We can filter a DataFrame like so:

   ```
   df = df[(df['height'] >= 160) & (df['height'] <= 180)]
   ```

   This returns a new DataFrame with range of height values between `160` and `180`.

3. How can we use code modularization to organize our neural network projects?

   We can compartmentalize our functions using modular pieces of code. For example, in this project, we defined a `preprocess` and `feature_engineer` function in `utils.py`, which allows us to focus on the implementation of the preprocessing and feature engineering functions separately.

4. How is regression different from classification tasks?

   In regression, we are trying to predict the value of a continuous variable (for example, taxi fare) whereas in classification, we are trying to predict a class (for example, diabetes or no diabetes).

5. True or false? For regression tasks, we should apply an activation function for the output layer.

   False. For regression tasks, we should never apply an activation function for the output layer because doing so will transform our predictions, which then affects the model performance.

6. What loss function is typically used when training a neural network for regression tasks?

   The RMSE is a common loss function for regression tasks. The RMSE measures the absolute difference between the prediction and the actual target variable.

Cats Versus Dogs - Image
Classification Using CNNs

4

In this chapter, we will use **convolutional neural networks** (**CNNs**) to create a classifier that can predict whether a given image contains a cat or a dog.

This project marks the first in a series of projects where we will use neural networks for image recognition and computer vision problems. As we shall see, neural networks have proven to be an extremely effective tool for solving problems in computer vision.

In this chapter, we will cover the following topics:

- Motivation for the problem that we're trying to tackle: image recognition
- Neural networks and deep learning for computer vision
- Understanding convolution and max pooling
- Architecture of CNNs
- Training CNNs in Keras
- Using transfer learning to leverage on a state-of-the art neural network
- Analysis of our results

Technical requirements

The key Python libraries required for this chapter are:

- matplotlib 3.0.2
- Keras 2.2.4
- Numpy 1.15.2
- Piexif 1.1.2

 To download the dataset required for this project, please refer to the directions at `https://github.com/PacktPublishing/Neural-Network-Projects-with-Python/blob/master/Chapter04/how_to_download_the_dataset.txt`.

The code for this chapter can be found in the GitHub repository for the book at `https://github.com/PacktPublishing/Neural-Network-Projects-with-Python`.

To download the code into your computer, you may run the following `git clone` command:

```
$ git clone
https://github.com/PacktPublishing/Neural-Network-Projects-with-Python.git
```

After the process is complete, there will be a folder titled `Neural-Network-Projects-with-Python`. Enter the folder by running the following:

```
$ cd Neural-Network-Projects-with-Python
```

To install the required Python libraries in a virtual environment, run the following command:

```
$ conda env create -f environment.yml
```

Note that you should have installed Anaconda in your computer first, before running this command. To enter the virtual environment, run the following command:

```
$ conda activate neural-network-projects-python
```

 Important
This chapter requires an additional image processing library known as `Piexif`.

To download `Piexif`, please run the following command:

```
$ pip install piexif
```

Navigate to the folder `Chapter04` by running the following command:

```
$ cd Chapter04
```

The following files are located in the folder:

- `main_basic_cnn.py`: This is the main code for the basic CNN
- `main_vgg16.py`: This is the main code for the VGG16 network
- `utils.py`: This file contains auxiliary utility code that will help us in the implementation of our neural network
- `visualize_dataset.py`: This file contains the code for exploratory data analysis and data visualization
- `image_augmentation.py`: This file contains sample code for image augmentation

To run the code for the neural network, simply execute the `main_basic_cnn.py` and `main_vgg16.py` files:

```
$ python main_basic_cnn.py
$ python main_vgg16.py
```

Computer vision and object recognition

Computer vision is an engineering field where the objective is to create programs that can extract meaning from images. According to an urban legend, computer vision first started in the 1960s when Professor Marvin Minsky from MIT assigned a summer project to a group of undergraduates, with the requirement that they should attach a camera to a computer and to have the computer describe everything that it sees. The project was expected to be completed in just one summer. Needless to say, it wasn't completed within that summer as computer vision is an extremely complex field that scientists are continuously working on even today.

Early progression in computer vision was modest. In the 1960s, researchers started by creating algorithms to detect shapes, lines, and edges in photographs. The following decades saw the evolution of computer vision into several subfields. Computer vision researchers worked on signal processing, image processing, computer photometry, object recognition, and so on.

Object recognition is perhaps one of the most ubiquitous applications in computer vision. Researchers had worked on object recognition for a long time. The challenge faced by early object recognition researchers was that the dynamic appearance of objects made it difficult to teach computers to recognize them. Early computer vision researchers focused on template matching for object recognition, but often faced difficulties due to variations in angle, lighting, and occlusions.

The field of object recognition has grown exponentially in recent years, propelled by the advancements in neural networks and deep learning. In 2012, Alex Krizhevsky et al. won the **ImageNet Large Scale Visual Recognition Challenge (ILSVRC)** by a significant margin over other contenders. The winning idea proposed by Alex Krizhevsky et al. was to use a CNN (an architecture termed the AlexNet) for object recognition. AlexNet was a significant breakthrough for object recognition. Since then, neural networks have become the number one technique for object recognition and computer vision related tasks. In this project, you will create a CNN similar to AlexNet.

The breakthrough in object recognition also led to the rise of AI that we know today. Facebook uses facial recognition to automatically tag and classify photos of you and your friends. Security systems use facial recognition to detect intrusions and persons of interest. Self-driving cars use object recognition to detect pedestrians, traffic signs, and other road objects. In many ways, society is starting to view object recognition, computer vision, and AI as one entity, even though their roots are very much different.

Types of object recognition tasks

It is important to understand the different kinds of object recognition tasks, as the required neural network architecture greatly depends on the task. Object recognition tasks can be broadly classified into three different types:

- Image classification
- Object detection
- Instance segmentation

The following diagram depicts the difference between each task:

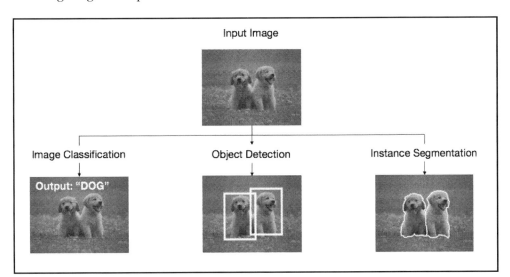

In **Image Classification**, the input to the problem is an image and the required output is simply a prediction of the class that the image belongs to. This is analogous to our first project, where we constructed a classifier to predict whether a patient is at risk of diabetes. In image classification, the problem is applied on pixels as our input data (specifically, the intensity value of each pixel), instead of tabular data represented by pandas DataFrames. In this project, we will focus on image classification.

In **Object Detection**, the input to the problem is an image and the required output are bounding boxes surrounding the detected objects. You can think of this as a step up from the image classification task. The neural network can no longer assume that there is only one class present in the image, and must assume that the image contains multiple classes. The neural network must then identify the presence of each class in the image, and to draw a bounding box around each of them. As you can imagine, this task is not trivial and object detection was a really difficult problem before neural networks came about. Today, neural networks can perform object detection efficiently. In 2014, 2 years after AlexNet was first developed, Girshick et al. showed that the results in image classification can be generalized to **Object Detection**. The intuitive idea behind their approach is to propose multiple boxes where objects of interest may exist, and then to use a CNN to predict the most likely class inside each bounding box. This approach is known as Regions with CNN (R-CNN).

Lastly, in **Instance Segmentation**, the input to the problem is an image and the output are pixel groupings that correspond to each class. You can think of instance segmentation as a refinement of object detection. Instance segmentation is especially useful and prevalent in technology today. The portrait mode function in many smartphone cameras relies on instance segmentation to separate objects in the foreground from the background, creating a nice depth of field (bokeh) effect. Instance segmentation is also crucial in self-driving cars, as the location of each object around the car must be identified with pinpoint precision. In 2017, an adaption of R-CNN, known as Mask R-CNN, was shown to be extremely effective at instance segmentation.

As we can see, recent advancements in object recognition are driven by CNNs. In this project, we will gain an in-depth understanding of CNNs, and we will train and create one from scratch in Keras.

Digital images as neural network input

Recall that in previous chapters, we made the distinction that neural networks require numerical inputs. We saw how we can encode categorical features, such as day of week, into numerical features using one-hot encoding. How then do we use an image as input for our neural network? Well, the short answer is that all digital images are numerical in nature!

To see why this is so, consider a 28 x 28 image of a handwritten digit 3, as shown in the following screenshot. Let's assume for now that the image is in grayscale (black and white). If we look at the intensity of each pixel that makes up the image, we can see that certain pixels are totally white, while some pixels are gray and black. In a computer, white pixels are represented with the value **0** and black pixels are represented with a value of **255**. Everything else in between white and black (that is, shades of gray) has a value in between **0** and **255**. Therefore, digital images are essentially numerical data and neural networks are perfectly able to learn from them:

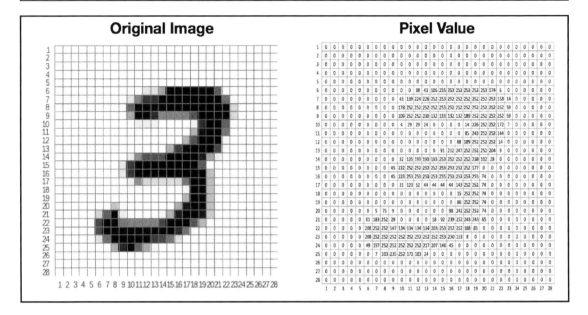

What about color images? Color images are simply images with three channels—red, green, and blue (commonly known as RGB). The pixel values in each channel then represent the red intensity, green intensity, and blue intensity. Another way to think about it is, that for a pure red image, the pixels value will be 255 in the red channel and 0 for the green and blue channels.

The following depicts a color image, and the separation of the color image into its RGB channels. Notice how a color image is stacked in a three-dimensional manner. In contrast, a grayscale image has only two dimensions:

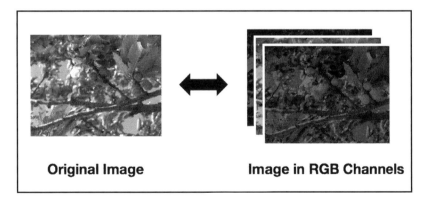

Building blocks of CNNs

One of the challenges faced in image classification is that the appearance of objects is dynamic. Just as there are many different breeds of cats and dogs, there are an infinite number of ways cats and dogs can appear in images. This makes it difficult for rudimentary image classification techniques, as it is impossible to show an infinite number of photos of cats and dogs to a computer.

However, this really shouldn't be a problem at all. Humans don't require an infinite number of photos of cats and dogs to differentiate between the two. A toddler can easily differentiate cats and dogs once he has seen just a few of them. If we think about how humans approach image classification, we notice that humans tend to look for landmark features while trying to identify an object. For example, we know that cats tend to be smaller in size compared to dogs, cats tend to have pointy ears, and cats have a shorter snout compared to dogs. Instinctively, humans look for these features while classifying an image.

Can we then teach a computer to look for these features within the entire image? The answer is a resounding yes! and the key lies in **convolution**.

Filtering and convolution

Before we can understand what convolution is, it is important to first understand filtering.

Suppose we have a 9 x 9 image as our input, and we need to classify the image as an X or an O. The following diagram illustrates some sample input images.

A perfectly drawn O is shown in the leftmost box in the following diagram, while the other two boxes show badly drawn Os:

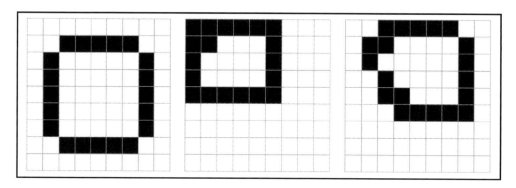

A perfectly drawn X is shown in the leftmost box, while the other two boxes show badly drawn Xs:

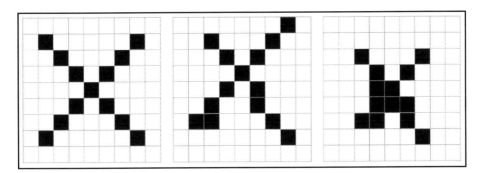

In either case, we cannot expect the figures to be drawn perfectly. This is no problem for human beings, as we can all differentiate between Os and Xs even for the badly drawn cases.

Let's think about what makes it easy for human beings to differentiate between the two. What are the characteristic features in the images that allows us to differentiate them easily? Well, we know that Os tend to have flat horizontal edges, while Xs tend to have diagonal lines.

The following diagram depicts one such characteristic feature for Os:

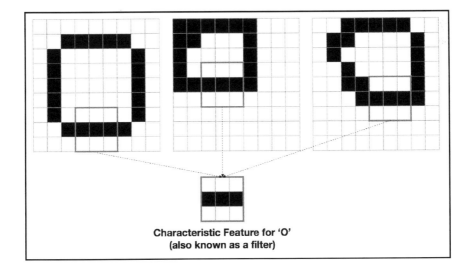

Characteristic Feature for 'O'
(also known as a filter)

And the following diagram depicts one such characteristic feature for Xs:

Characteristic Feature for 'X'
(also known as a filter)

In this case, the characteristic feature (also known as the filter) is of size 3 × 3. The presence of the characteristic feature in an image gives us a big hint on the class of the image. For example, if an image contains an horizontal edge, the characteristic feature for O, then the image is probably an O.

How then do we search for the presence of the characteristic feature in an image? We can simply do a brute force search by taking the 3 x 3 filter, before sliding it through every single pixel in the image to look for a match.

Let's start from the top left-hand corner of the image. The mathematical function performed by the filter (known as filtering) is the element-wise multiplication of the sliding window with the filter. In the top left-hand corner, the output from the filter is **2** (notice that this is a perfect match since the window is identical to the filter).

The following diagram shows the filtering operation on the top left-hand corner of the image. Note that for simplicity, we assume that pixel intensity values are **0** or **1** (instead of 0-255 in real digital images):

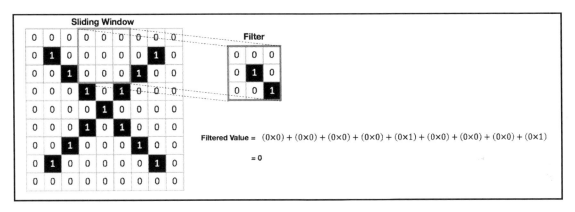

Next, we slide the window toward the right to cover the next 3 x 3 section in the image. The following diagram shows the filtering operation on the next 3 x 3 section:

The process of sliding the window through the entire image and calculating the filtered value is known as **convolution**. The layer in the neural network that performs convolution is known as the convolutional layer. Essentially, convolution provides us with a map to the areas where the characteristic feature is found in each image. This ensures that our neural network is able to perform intelligent, dynamic object recognition just like a human being!

In the preceding example, we handcrafted the filter based on our own knowledge of Os and Xs. Note that, when we train a neural network, it will automatically learn the most appropriate filter to use. Recall that in previous chapters, the fully connected layer (dense layer) was used and the weights of the layers were tuned during training. Similarly, the weights of a convolutional layer will be tuned during training.

Lastly, note that there are two main hyperparameters in a convolutional layer:

- **Number of filters**: In the preceding example, we have used just one filter. We can increase the number of filters to find multiple characteristic features.
- **Filter size**: In the preceding example, we have used a 3 x 3 filter size. We can tune the filter size to represent larger characteristic features.

We will talk about these hyperparameters in further detail when we construct our neural network later on in the chapter.

Max pooling

In CNNs, it is common to place a max pooling layer immediately after a convolution layer. The objective of the max pooling layer is to reduce the number of weights after each convolution layer, thereby reducing model complexity and avoiding overfitting.

The max pooling layer does this simply by looking at each subset of the input passed to it, and throwing out all but the maximum value in the subset. Let's take a look at an example to see what this means. Assume that our input to the max pooling layer is a 4 x 4 tensor (a tensor is just an n-dimensional array, such as those output by a convolutional layer), and we are using a 2 x 2 max pooling layer. The following diagram illustrates the **Max Pooling** operation:

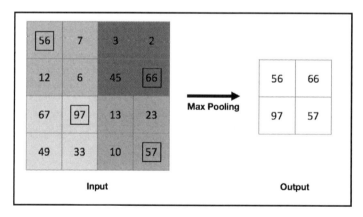

As we can see from the preceding diagram, **Max Pooling** simply looks at each 2 x 2 region of the input, and discards all but the maximum value in that region (boxed up in the preceding diagram). This effectively halves the height and width of the original input, reducing the number of parameters before passing it to the next layer.

Basic architecture of CNNs

We have seen the basic building blocks of CNNs in the previous section. Now, we'll put these building blocks together and see what a complete CNN looks like.

CNNs are almost always stacked together in a block of convolution and pooling pattern. The activation function used for the convolution layer is usually ReLU, as discussed in the previous chapters.

The following diagram shows the first few layers in a typical CNN, made up of a series of convolution and pooling layers:

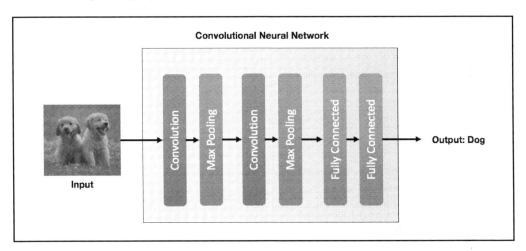

The final layers in a CNN will always be **Fully Connected** layers (dense layers) with a sigmoid or softmax activation function. Note that the sigmoid activation function is used for binary classification problems, whereas the softmax activation function is used for multiclass classification problems.

The **Fully Connected** layer is identical to those that we have seen in the first two chapters: Chapter 1, *Machine Learning and Neural Networks 101* and Chapter 2, *Diabetes Prediction with Multilayer Perceptrons*. At this point, you might be wondering what is the rationale for placing the fully connected layer at the end of a CNN? In CNNs, the early layers learn and extract the characteristic features of the data they are trying to predict. For example, we have seen how a convolutional layer learns the characteristic spatial features of Os and Xs. The convolutional layers then pass this information on to the fully connected layers, which then learn how to make accurate predictions, just like in an MLP.

Essentially, the early layers of a CNN are responsible for identifying the characteristic spatial features, and the fully connected layers at the end are responsible for making predictions. The implication of this is significant. Instead of handcrafting features (that is, day of week, distance, and so on) for the machine learning algorithm, as we did in the previous chapter, Chapter 3, *Predicting Taxi Fares with Deep Feedforward Nets*, we're simply providing all the data to the CNN as it is. The CNN then automatically learns the best characteristic features to differentiate the classes. This is true AI!

A review of modern CNNs

Now that we've seen the basic architecture of CNNs, let's take a look at modern, state-of-the-art CNNs. We'll do a walk-through of the evolution of CNNs, and see how they have changed over the years. We'll not go into the technical and mathematical details behind the implementation. Instead, we'll provide an intuitive overview of some of the most important CNNs.

LeNet (1998)

The first CNN was developed by Yann LeCun in 1998, with the architecture known as LeNet. LeCun was the first to prove that CNNs were effective in image recognition, particularly in the domain of handwritten digits recognition. However, throughout the 2000s, few scientists managed to build on the work done by LeCun and there were few breakthroughs in CNNs (and AI in general).

AlexNet (2012)

As we mentioned earlier, AlexNet was developed by Alex Krizhevsky et al. and it was used to win the ILSVRC in 2012. AlexNet was built on the same principles as LeNet, although AlexNet used a much deeper architecture. The overall number of trainable parameters in AlexNet is around 60 million, over 1,000 times more than LeNet.

VGG16 (2014)

VGG16 was developed by Oxford's **Visual Geometry Group** (**VGG**) and it was considered to be a very important neural network. VGG16 was one of the first CNNs to deviate from large filter sizes, instead using a convolution filter size of 3 x 3.

VGG16 finished second in the image recognition task in the ILSVRC in 2014. A downside to VGG16 is that there are many more parameters to be trained, leading to a significant training time.

Inception (2014)

The Inception network was developed by researchers from Google and it won the ILSVRC in 2014. The guiding principle for the Inception network was to provide highly accurate predictions efficiently. Google's interest was to create a CNN that could be trained and deployed in real time across their network of servers. To do that, the researchers developed something known as the Inception module, that vastly improved training time while maintaining its accuracy. In fact, in the 2014 ILSVRC, the Inception network managed to achieve a higher accuracy than VGG16, despite having far fewer parameters.

The Inception network has been continuously improved upon. At the time of writing, the latest Inception network is at its 4th version (commonly known as Inception-v4).

ResNet (2015)

The **residual neural network** (**ResNet**) was introduced by Kaiming He et al. at the 2015 ILSVRC (by now, you should notice that this competition is extremely important for neural networks and computer vision, and new state-of-the-art techniques are revealed during the annual competition).

The salient feature of ResNet was the residual block technique, which allowed the neural network to be deeper while keeping the number of parameters moderate.

Where we stand today

As we have seen, CNNs have progressed and improved exponentially in the past few years. In fact, recent CNNs can outperform humans at certain image recognition tasks. The recurring theme in recent years is to use innovative techniques to improve model performance, while preserving the model complexity. Clearly, the speed of the neural network is just as important as the accuracy.

The cats and dogs dataset

Now that we understand the theory behind CNNs, let's dive into data exploration. The cats and dogs dataset is provided by Microsoft. The instructions for the downloading and setting up of the dataset can be found in the *Technical requirements* section of this chapter.

Let's plot the images to better understand the kind of data we're working with. To do that, we can simply run the following code:

```
from matplotlib import pyplot as plt
import os
import random

# Get list of file names
_, _, cat_images = next(os.walk('Dataset/PetImages/Cat'))

# Prepare a 3x3 plot (total of 9 images)
fig, ax = plt.subplots(3,3, figsize=(20,10))

# Randomly select and plot an image
for idx, img in enumerate(random.sample(cat_images, 9)):
    img_read = plt.imread('Dataset/PetImages/Cat/'+img)
    ax[int(idx/3), idx%3].imshow(img_read)
    ax[int(idx/3), idx%3].axis('off')
    ax[int(idx/3), idx%3].set_title('Cat/'+img)
plt.show()
```

We'll see the following output:

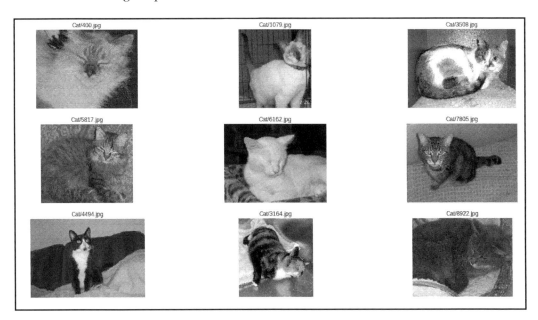

We can make some observations about our data:

- The images have different dimensions.
- The subjects (cat/dog) are mostly centered in the image.
- The subjects (cat/dog) have different orientations, and they may be occluded in the image. In other words, there's no guarantee that we'll always see the tail of the cat in the image.

Now, let's do the same for the dog images:

```
# Get list of file names
_, _, dog_images = next(os.walk('Dataset/PetImages/Dog'))

# Prepare a 3x3 plot (total of 9 images)
fig, ax = plt.subplots(3,3, figsize=(20,10))

# Randomly select and plot an image
for idx, img in enumerate(random.sample(dog_images, 9)):
    img_read = plt.imread('Dataset/PetImages/Dog/'+img)
    ax[int(idx/3), idx%3].imshow(img_read)
    ax[int(idx/3), idx%3].axis('off')
    ax[int(idx/3), idx%3].set_title('Dog/'+img)
plt.show()
```

We'll see the following output:

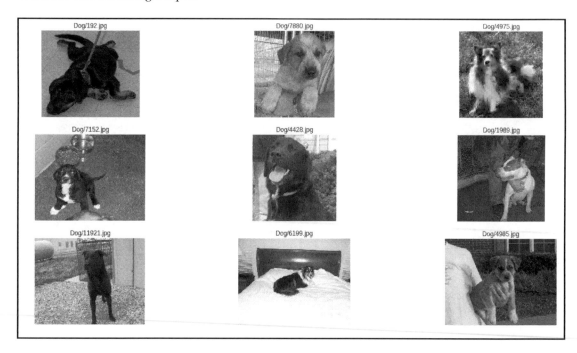

Managing image data for Keras

One common problem encountered in neural network projects for image classification is that most computers do not have sufficient RAM to load the entire set of data into memory. Even for relatively modern and powerful computers, it would be far too slow to load the entire set of images into memory and to train a CNN from there.

To alleviate this problem, Keras provides a useful `flow_from_directory` method that takes as an input the path to the images, and generates batches of data as output. The batches of data are loaded into memory, as required before model training. This way, we can train a deep neural network on a huge number of images without worrying about memory issues. Furthermore, the `flow_from_directory` method allows us to perform image preprocessing steps such as resizing and other image augmentation techniques by simply passing an argument. The `flow_from_directory` method would then perform the necessary image preprocessing steps in real time before passing the data for model training.

To do all these, there are certain schemas for file and folder management that we must abide by, in order for `flow_from_directory` to work. In particular, we are required to create subdirectories for training and testing data, and within the training and testing subdirectories, we need to further create one subdirectory per class. The following diagram illustrates the required folder structure:

```
/data
    ... /train
        ... /cat
            ... 0.jpg
            ... 1.jpg
            ... 2.jpg
        ... /dog
            ... 0.jpg
            ... 1.jpg
            ... 2.jpg
    ... /test
        ... /cat
            ... 0.jpg
            ... 1.jpg
            ... 2.jpg
        ... /dog
            ... 0.jpg
            ... 1.jpg
            ... 2.jpg
```

The `flow_from_directory` method would then infer the class of the images from the folder structure.

The raw data is provided in a `Cat` and `Dog` folder, without separation of training and testing data. Therefore, we need to split the data into a `Train` and `Test` folder as per the preceding schema. To do that, we need to perform the following steps:

1. Create `/Train/Cat`, `/Train/Dog`, `/Test/Cat`, and `/Test/Dog` folders.
2. Randomly assign 80% of the the images as train images and 20% of the images as test images.
3. Copy those images into the respective folders.

We have provided a helper function in utils.py to do these steps. We simply need to invoke the function, as follows:

```
from utils import train_test_split

src_folder = 'Dataset/PetImages/'
train_test_split(src_folder)
```

 If you run into an error while executing this code block, with the error message **ImportError: No Module Named Piexif**, it means that you have not installed Piexif in your Python virtual environment. This chapter requires an additional library for image processing. To download Piexif, please follow the instructions in the *Technical requirements section* at the start of this chapter.

Great! Our images are now placed in the appropriate folders for Keras.

Image augmentation

Before we start building our CNN, let's take a look at image augmentation, which is an important technique in image classification projects. Image augmentation is the creation of additional training data by making minor alterations to images in certain ways in order to create new images. For example, we can do the following:

- Image rotation
- Image translation
- Horizontal flip
- Zooming into the image

The motivation for image augmentation is that CNNs require a huge amount of training data before they can generalize well. However, it is often difficult to collect data, more so for images. With image augmentation, we can artificially create new training data based on the existing images.

As always, Keras provides a handy `ImageDataGenerator` class to help us easily perform image augmentation. Let's create a new instance of the class:

```
from keras.preprocessing.image import ImageDataGenerator

image_generator = ImageDataGenerator(rotation_range = 30,
                                     width_shift_range = 0.2,
                                     height_shift_range = 0.2,
                                     zoom_range = 0.2,
                                     horizontal_flip=True,
                                     fill_mode='nearest')
```

As we can see from this code snippet, there are several arguments that we can provide to the `ImageDataGenerator` class. Each of the arguments control how much of a modification is done to the existing image. We should avoid extreme transformations, as those extremely distorted images do not represent images from the real world and may introduce noise into our model.

Next, let's use it to augment a randomly selected image from the `/Train/Dog/` folder. Then, we can plot it to compare the augmented images with the original image. We can do this by running the following code:

```
fig, ax = plt.subplots(2,3, figsize=(20,10))
all_images = []

_, _, dog_images = next(os.walk('Dataset/PetImages/Train/Dog/'))
random_img = random.sample(dog_images, 1)[0]
random_img = plt.imread('Dataset/PetImages/Train/Dog/'+random_img)
all_images.append(random_img)

random_img = random_img.reshape((1,) + random_img.shape)
sample_augmented_images = image_generator.flow(random_img)

for _ in range(5):
    augmented_imgs = sample_augmented_images.next()
    for img in augmented_imgs:
        all_images.append(img.astype('uint8'))

for idx, img in enumerate(all_images):
    ax[int(idx/3), idx%3].imshow(img)
    ax[int(idx/3), idx%3].axis('off')
    if idx == 0:
        ax[int(idx/3), idx%3].set_title('Original Image')
    else:
        ax[int(idx/3), idx%3].set_title('Augmented Image {}'.format(idx))

plt.show()
```

We'll see the following output:

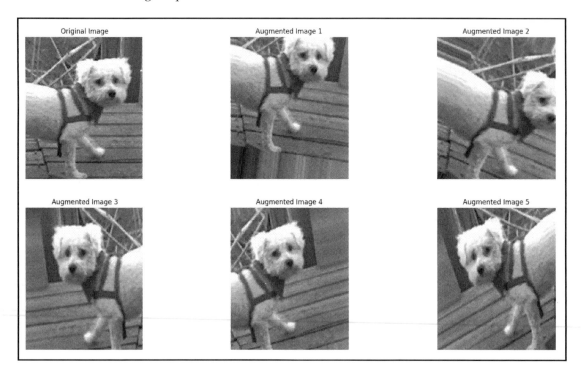

As we can see, each augmented image is randomly shifted or rotated by a certain amount as controlled by the arguments passed into the `ImageDataGenerator` class. These augmented images will provide supplemental training data for our CNN, increasing the robustness of our model.

Model building

We're finally ready to start building our CNN in Keras. In this section, we'll take two different approaches to model building. First, we'll start by building a relatively simple CNN consisting of a few layers. We'll take a look at the performance of the simple model, and discuss its pros and cons. Next, we'll use a model that was considered state-of-the art just a few years ago—the VGG16 model. We'll see how we can leverage on the pre-trained weights to adapt the VGG16 model for cats versus dogs image classification.

Building a simple CNN

In an earlier section, we showed how the fundamental building blocks of a CNN consist of a series of convolutional and pooling layers. In this section, we're going to build a basic CNN consisting of this repeating pattern, as shown in the following diagram:

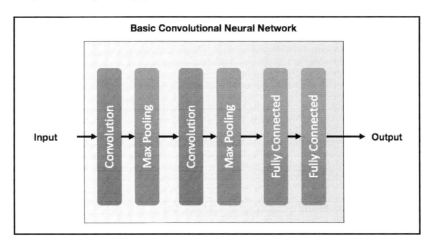

This basic CNN consists of two repeated blocks of **Convolution** and **Max Pooling**, following by two **Fully Connected** layers. As discussed in a previous section, the convolution and max pooling layers are responsible for learning the spatial characteristics of the classes (for example, identifying the ears of cats), whereas the **Fully Connected** layers learn to make predictions using these spatial characteristics. We can thus represent the architecture of our basic CNN in another manner (we shall see why it is useful to visualize our neural network in this manner in the next subsection):

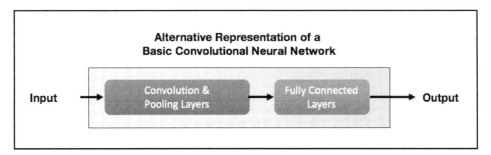

Building a CNN is similar to building an MLP or a feedforward neural network, as we've done in the previous chapters. We'll start off by declaring a new `Sequential` model instance:

```
from keras.models import Sequential
from keras.layers import Conv2D, MaxPooling2D
from keras.layers import Dropout, Flatten, Dense
from keras.preprocessing.image import ImageDataGenerator

model = Sequential()
```

Before we add any convolutional layers, it is useful to think about the hyperparameters that we are going to use. For a CNN, there are several hyperparameters:

- **Convolutional layer filter size**: Most modern CNNs use a small filter size of 3 x 3.
- **Number of filters**: Let's use a filter number of 32. This is a good balance between speed and performance.
- **Input size**: As we've seen in an earlier section, the input images have different sizes, with their width and height approximately 150 px. Let's use an input size of 32 x 32 pixels. This compresses the original image, which can result in some information loss, but helps to speed up the training of our neural network.
- **Max pooling size**: A common max pooling size is 2 x 2. This will halve the input layer dimensions.
- **Batch size**: This corresponds to the number of training samples to use in each mini batch during gradient descent. A large batch size results in more accurate training but longer training time and memory usage. Let's use a batch size of 16.
- **Steps per epoch**: This is the number of iterations in each training epoch. Typically, this is equal to the number of training samples divided by the batch size.
- **Epochs**: The number of epochs to train our data. Note that, in neural networks, the number of epochs refers to the number of times the model sees each training sample during training. Multiple epochs are usually needed, as gradient descent is an iterative optimization method. Let's train our model for 10 epochs. This means that each training sample will be passed to the the model 10 times during training.

Let's declare variables for these hyperparameters so that they are constant throughout our code:

```
FILTER_SIZE = 3
NUM_FILTERS = 32
INPUT_SIZE  = 32
MAXPOOL_SIZE = 2
BATCH_SIZE = 16
STEPS_PER_EPOCH = 20000//BATCH_SIZE
EPOCHS = 10
```

We can now add the first convolutional layer, with 32 filters, each of size (3 x 3):

```
model.add(Conv2D(NUM_FILTERS, (FILTER_SIZE, FILTER_SIZE),
                input_shape = (INPUT_SIZE, INPUT_SIZE, 3),
                activation = 'relu'))
```

Next, we add a max pooling layer:

```
model.add(MaxPooling2D(pool_size = (MAXPOOL_SIZE, MAXPOOL_SIZE)))
```

This is the basic convolution-pooling pattern of our CNN. Let's repeat this once more according to our model architecture:

```
model.add(Conv2D(NUM_FILTERS, (FILTER_SIZE, FILTER_SIZE),
                input_shape = (INPUT_SIZE, INPUT_SIZE, 3),
                activation = 'relu'))

model.add(MaxPooling2D(pool_size = (MAXPOOL_SIZE, MAXPOOL_SIZE)))
```

We are now done with the convolution and pooling layers. Before we move on to the fully connected layers, we need to flatten its input. Flatten is a function in Keras that transforms a multidimensional vector into a single dimensional vector. For example, if the vector is of shape (5,5,3) before passing to Flatten, the output vector will be of shape (75) after passing to Flatten.

To add a Flatten layer, we simply run the following code:

```
model.add(Flatten())
```

We can now add a fully connected layer with 128 nodes:

```
model.add(Dense(units = 128, activation = 'relu'))
```

Before we add our last fully connected layer, it is a good practice to add a dropout layer. The dropout layer randomly sets a certain fraction of its input to 0. This helps to reduce overfitting, by ensuring that the model does not place too much emphasis on certain weights:

```
# Set 50% of the weights to 0
model.add(Dropout(0.5))
```

We add one last fully connected layer to our model:

```
model.add(Dense(units = 1, activation = 'sigmoid'))
```

 Note that the last fully connected layer should have only one node, as we're doing binary classification (cat or dog) in this project.

We'll compile our model using the `adam` optimizer. The `adam` optimizer is a generalization of the **stochastic gradient descent (SGD)** algorithm that we've seen in Chapter 1, *Machine Learning and Neural Networks 101* and it is widely used to train CNNs. The loss function is `binary_crossentropy` since we're doing a binary classification:

```
model.compile(optimizer = 'adam', loss = 'binary_crossentropy',
              metrics = ['accuracy'])
```

 In general, we use `binary_crossentropy` for binary classification problems and `categorical_crossentropy` for multiclass classification problems.

We're now ready to train our CNN. Notice that we have not loaded any of the data into memory. We'll use the `ImageDataGenerator` and `flow_from_directory` method to train our model in real time, which loads batches of the dataset into memory only as required:

```
training_data_generator = ImageDataGenerator(rescale = 1./255)

training_set = training_data_generator. \
               flow_from_directory('Dataset/PetImages/Train/',
                                   target_size=(INPUT_SIZE,INPUT_SIZE),
                                   batch_size=BATCH_SIZE,
                                   class_mode='binary')

model.fit_generator(training_set, steps_per_epoch = STEPS_PER_EPOCH,
                    epochs=EPOCHS, verbose=1)
```

This will start the training and once it is complete, you will see the following output:

```
Epoch 1/10
1250/1250 [==============================] - 79s 63ms/step - loss: 0.6347 - acc: 0.6247
Epoch 2/10
1250/1250 [==============================] - 85s 68ms/step - loss: 0.5540 - acc: 0.7175
Epoch 3/10
1250/1250 [==============================] - 81s 65ms/step - loss: 0.5066 - acc: 0.7511
Epoch 4/10
1250/1250 [==============================] - 87s 69ms/step - loss: 0.4778 - acc: 0.7696
Epoch 5/10
1250/1250 [==============================] - 80s 64ms/step - loss: 0.4478 - acc: 0.7858
Epoch 6/10
1250/1250 [==============================] - 85s 68ms/step - loss: 0.4247 - acc: 0.8054
Epoch 7/10
1250/1250 [==============================] - 81s 65ms/step - loss: 0.4007 - acc: 0.8141
Epoch 8/10
1250/1250 [==============================] - 82s 65ms/step - loss: 0.3835 - acc: 0.8241
Epoch 9/10
1250/1250 [==============================] - 85s 68ms/step - loss: 0.3635 - acc: 0.8371
Epoch 10/10
1250/1250 [==============================] - 81s 65ms/step - loss: 0.3395 - acc: 0.8486
```

We can clearly see that the loss decreases while the accuracy increases with each epoch.

Now that our model is trained, let's evaluate it on the testing set. We'll create a new `ImageDataGenerator` and call `flow_from_directory` on the images in the `test` folder:

```
testing_data_generator = ImageDataGenerator(rescale = 1./255)

test_set = testing_data_generator. \
            flow_from_directory('Dataset/PetImages/Test/',
                                target_size=(INPUT_SIZE, INPUT_SIZE),
                                batch_size=BATCH_SIZE,
                                class_mode = 'binary')
score = model.evaluate_generator(test_set, steps=len(test_set))
for idx, metric in enumerate(model.metrics_names):
    print("{}: {}".format(metric, score[idx]))
```

We'll get the following output:

```
loss: 0.8116428855985403
acc: 0.8054
```

We obtained an accuracy of 80%! That's pretty impressive considering that we only used a basic CNN. This shows the power of CNNs; we obtained an accuracy close to human performance from just a few lines of code.

Leveraging on pre-trained models using transfer learning

Can we take our model further? Can we achieve close to 90%, reaching human level performance? As we shall see in this section, we can obtain better performance by leveraging on transfer learning.

Transfer learning is a technique in machine learning where a model trained for a certain task is modified to make predictions for another task. For example, we may use a model trained to classify cars to classify trucks instead, since they are similar. In the context of CNN, transfer learning involves freezing the convolution-pooling layers, and only retraining the final fully connected layers. The following diagram illustrates this process:

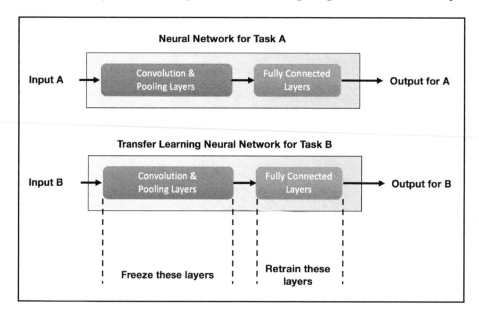

How does transfer learning work? Intuitively, the purpose of the convolution and pooling layers is to learn the spatial characteristics of the classes. We can therefore reuse these layers since the spatial characteristics are similar in both tasks. We just need to retrain the final fully connected layers to re-purpose the neural network to make predictions for the new class. Naturally, a crucial requirement for transfer learning is that tasks A and B must be similar to one another.

In this section, we're going to re-purpose the VGG16 model to make predictions on images of cats and dogs. The VGG16 model was originally developed for the ILSVRC, which required the model to make a 1,000 class multiclass classification. Among the 1,000 classes are specific breeds of cats and dogs. In other words, VGG16 knows how to recognize specific breeds of cats and dogs, and not just cats and dogs in general. It is therefore a viable approach to use transfer learning using the VGG16 model for our cats and dogs image classification problem.

The VGG16 model and its trained weights are provided directly in Keras. Let's create a new VGG16 model, as shown in the following code:

```
from keras.applications.vgg16 import VGG16

INPUT_SIZE = 128 # Change this to 48 if the code takes too long to run
vgg16 = VGG16(include_top=False, weights='imagenet',
              input_shape=(INPUT_SIZE,INPUT_SIZE,3))
```

Note that we used `include_top=False` when we created a new VGG16 model. This argument tells Keras not to import the fully connected layers at the end of the VGG16 network.

We're now going to freeze the rest of the layers in the VGG16 model, since we're not going to retrain them from scratch. We can freeze the layers by running the following code snippet:

```
for layer in vgg16.layers:
    layer.trainable = False
```

Next, we're going to add a fully connected layer with 1 node right at the end of the neural network. The syntax to do this is slightly different, since the VGG16 model is not a Keras `Sequential` model that we're used to. In any case, we can add the layers by running the following code:

```
from keras.models import Model

input_ = vgg16.input
output_ = vgg16(input_)
last_layer = Flatten(name='flatten')(output_)
last_layer = Dense(1, activation='sigmoid')(last_layer)
model = Model(input=input_, output=last_layer)
```

This is just a manual way of adding layers in Keras, which the .add() function in Sequential model has simplified for us so far. The rest of the code is similar to what we have seen in the previous section. We declare a training data generator, and we train the model (only the newly added layers) by calling flow_from_directory(). Since we only need to train the final layer, we'll just train the model for 3 epochs:

Caution

The following code block takes around an hour to run if you are not running Keras on a GPU (graphics card). If the code takes too long to run on your computer, you may reduce the INPUT_SIZE parameter to speed up model training. However, note that this will lower the accuracy of your model.

```
# Define hyperparameters
BATCH_SIZE = 16
STEPS_PER_EPOCH = 200
EPOCHS = 3

model.compile(optimizer = 'adam', loss = 'binary_crossentropy',
              metrics = ['accuracy'])

training_data_generator = ImageDataGenerator(rescale = 1./255)
testing_data_generator = ImageDataGenerator(rescale = 1./255)

training_set = training_data_generator. \
             flow_from_directory('Dataset/PetImages/Train/',
                            target_size=(INPUT_SIZE,INPUT_SIZE),
                            batch_size = BATCH_SIZE,
                            class_mode = 'binary')

test_set = testing_data_generator. \
             flow_from_directory('Dataset/PetImages/Test/',
                            target_size=(INPUT_SIZE,INPUT_SIZE),
                            batch_size = BATCH_SIZE,
                            class_mode = 'binary')

model.fit_generator(training_set, steps_per_epoch = STEPS_PER_EPOCH,
                    epochs = EPOCHS, verbose=1)
```

We'll get the following output:

```
Epoch 1/3
200/200 [==============================] - 381s 2s/step - loss: 0.3808 - acc: 0.8253
Epoch 2/3
200/200 [==============================] - 418s 2s/step - loss: 0.2903 - acc: 0.8731
Epoch 3/3
200/200 [==============================] - 404s 2s/step - loss: 0.2941 - acc: 0.8754
```

The training accuracy doesn't look much different to the basic CNN in the previous section. This is expected, since both neural networks do really well in the training set. However, the testing accuracy is ultimately the metric which we will use to evaluate the performance of our model. Let's see how well it does on the testing set:

```
score = model.evaluate_generator(test_set, len(test_set))

for idx, metric in enumerate(model.metrics_names):
    print("{}: {}".format(metric, score[idx]))
```

We'll see the following output:

```
loss: 0.23026393374204635
acc: 0.905
```

That's amazing! By making use of transfer learning, we managed to obtain a testing accuracy of 90.5%. Note that the training time here is much shorter than training a VGG16 model from scratch (it would probably take days to train a VGG16 model from scratch, even with a powerful GPU!), since we are only training the last layer. This shows that we can leverage on a pre-trained state-of-the art model like VGG16 to make predictions for our own projects.

Results analysis

Let's take a deeper look into our results. In particular, we would like to know what kind of images our CNN does well in, and what kind of images it gets wrong.

Recall that the output of the sigmoid activation function in the last layer of our CNN is a list of values between 0 and 1 (one value/prediction per image). If the output value is < 0.5, then the prediction is class 0 (that is, cat) and if the output value is $>= 0.5$, then the prediction is class 1 (that is, dog). Therefore, an output value close to 0.5 means that the model isn't so sure, while an output value very close to 0.0 or 1.0 means that the model is very sure about its predictions.

Let's run through the images in the testing set one by one, using our model to make predictions on the class of the image, and classify the images according to three categories:

- **Strongly right predictions**: The model predicted these images correctly, and the output value is > 0.8 or < 0.2
- **Strongly wrong predictions**: The model predicted these images wrongly, and the output value is > 0.8 or < 0.2
- **Weakly wrong predictions**: The model predicted these images wrongly, and the output value is between 0.4 and 0.6

The following code snippet will do this for us:

```
# Generate test set for data visualization
test_set = testing_data_generator. \
            flow_from_directory('Dataset/PetImages/Test/',
                                target_size = (INPUT_SIZE, INPUT_SIZE),
                                batch_size = 1,
                                class_mode = 'binary')

strongly_wrong_idx = []
strongly_right_idx = []
weakly_wrong_idx = []

for i in range(test_set.__len__()):
    img = test_set.__getitem__(i)[0]
    pred_prob = model.predict(img)[0][0]
    pred_label = int(pred_prob > 0.5)
    actual_label = int(test_set.__getitem__(i)[1][0])
    if pred_label != actual_label and (pred_prob > 0.8 or
        pred_prob < 0.2): strongly_wrong_idx.append(i)
    elif pred_label != actual_label and (pred_prob > 0.4 and
        pred_prob < 0.6): weakly_wrong_idx.append(i)
    elif pred_label == actual_label and (pred_prob > 0.8 or
        pred_prob < 0.2): strongly_right_idx.append(i)
    # stop once we have enough images to plot
    if (len(strongly_wrong_idx)>=9 and len(strongly_right_idx)>=9
        and len(weakly_wrong_idx)>=9): break
```

Let's visualize the images from these three groups by randomly selecting 9 of the images in each group, and plot them on a 3×3 grid. The following helper function allows us to do that:

```
from matplotlib import pyplot as plt
import random

def plot_on_grid(test_set, idx_to_plot, img_size=INPUT_SIZE):
```

```
fig, ax = plt.subplots(3,3, figsize=(20,10))
for i, idx in enumerate(random.sample(idx_to_plot,9)):
    img = test_set.__getitem__(idx)[0].reshape(img_size, img_size ,3)
    ax[int(i/3), i%3].imshow(img)
    ax[int(i/3), i%3].axis('off')
```

We can now plot 9 randomly selected images from the strongly right predictions group:

```
plot_on_grid(test_set, strongly_right_idx)
```

We'll see the following output:

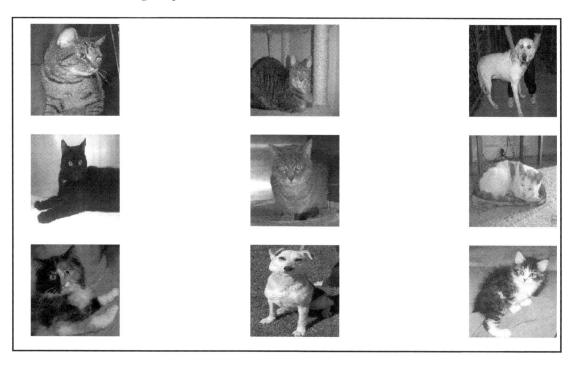

Selected images that have strong predictions, and are correct

No surprises there! These are almost classical images of cats and dogs. Notice that the pointy ears of cats and the dark eyes of dogs can all be seen in the preceding images. These characteristic features allow our CNN to easily identify them.

Let's now take a look at the strongly wrong predictions group:

```
plot_on_grid(test_set, strongly_wrong_idx)
```

We'll get the following output:

Selected images that have strong predictions, but are wrong

We notice a few commonalities among these strongly wrong predictions. The first thing we notice is that certain dogs do resemble cats with their pointy ears. Perhaps our neural network placed too much emphasis on the pointy ears and classified these dogs as cats. Another thing we notice is that some of the subjects were not facing the camera, making it really difficult to identify them. No wonder our neural network got them wrong.

Finally, let's take a look at the weakly wrong predictions group:

```
plot_on_grid(test_set, weakly_wrong_idx)
```

We'll get the following output:

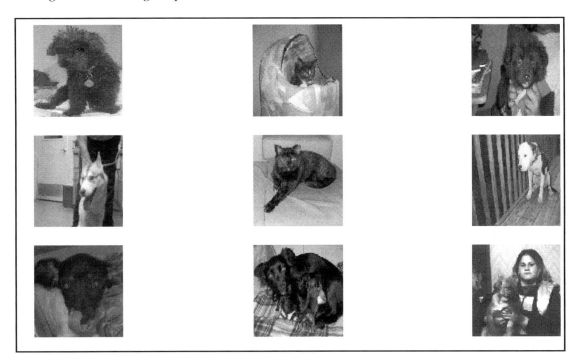

Selected images that have weak predictions, and are wrong

These images are ones that our model is on the fence with. Perhaps there is an equal number of characteristics to suggest that the object could be a dog or a cat. This is perhaps the most obvious with the images in the first row, where the puppies in the first row have a small frame like a cat, which could have confused the neural network.

Summary

In this chapter, we built a classifier that can predict whether an image contains a cat or a dog by using two different CNNs. We first went through the theory behind CNNs, and we understood that the fundamental building blocks of a CNN are the convolution, pooling, and fully connected layers. In particular, the front of the CNN consists of a block of convolution-pooling layers, repeated an arbitrary number of times. This block is responsible for identifying spatial characteristics in the images, which can be used to classify the images. The back of the CNN consists of fully connected layers, similar to an MLP. This block is responsible for making the final predictions.

In the first CNN, we used a basic architecture that achieved 80% accuracy on the testing set. This basic CNN consists of two convolutional-max pooling layers, followed by two fully connected layers. In the second CNN, we used transfer learning to leverage on the pre-trained VGG16 network for our classification. We removed the final fully connected layer with 1,000 nodes in the pre-trained network, and added our own fully connected layer with one node (for our binary classification task). We managed to obtain an accuracy of 90% using the fine-tuned VGG16 model.

Lastly, we visualized the images that our model did well in, as well as the images that our model struggled with. We saw that our model could not be certain when the subject is not facing the camera or when the subject has characteristics resembling both a cat and a dog (for example, a small puppy with pointy ears).

That concludes the chapter on using CNNs for image recognition. In the next chapter, `Chapter 5`, *Removing Noise from Images Using Autoencoders*, we'll use an autoencoder neural network to remove noise from images.

Questions

1. How are images represented in computers?

    Images are represented in computers as a group of pixels, with each pixel having its own intensity (value between 0 and 255). Color images have three channels (red, green, and blue) while grayscale images have only one channel.

2. What are the fundamental building blocks of a CNN?

    All convolutional neural network consists of convolution layers, pooling layers, and fully connected layers.

3. What is the role of the convolutional and pooling layers?

    The convolutional and pooling layers are responsible for extracting spatial characteristics from the images. For example, when training a CNN to identify images of cats, one such spatial characteristic would be the pointy ears of cats.

4. What is the role of the fully connected layers?

   The fully connected layers are similar to the those in MLPs and feedforward neural networks. Their role is to use the spatial characteristics as input, and to output predicted classes.

5. What is transfer learning, and how is it useful?

   Transfer learning is a technique in machine learning where a model trained for a certain task is modified to make predictions for another task. Transfer learning allows us to leverage on state-of-the art models, such as VGG16, for our own purposes, with minimal training time.

Removing Noise from Images Using Autoencoders

5

In this chapter, we will study a class of neural networks known as autoencoders, which have gained traction in recent years. In particular, the ability of autoencoders to remove noise from images has been greatly studied. In this chapter, we will build and train an autoencoder that is able to denoise and restore corrupted images.

In this chapter, we'll cover the following topics:

- What are autoencoders?
- Unsupervised learning
- Types of autoencoders—basic autoencoders, deep autoencoders and convolutional autoencoders
- Autoencoders for image compression
- Autoencoders for image denoising
- Step-by-step guide to build and train an autoencoder in Keras
- Analysis of our results

Technical requirements

The Python libraries required for this chapter are:

- matplotlib 3.0.2
- Keras 2.2.4
- Numpy 1.15.2
- PIL 5.4.1

The code and dataset for this chapter can be found in the GitHub repository for the book at `https://github.com/PacktPublishing/Neural-Network-Projects-with-Python`:

To download the code into your computer, you may run the following `git clone` command:

```
$ git clone
https://github.com/PacktPublishing/Neural-Network-Projects-with-Python.git
```

After the process is complete, there will be a folder titled `Neural-Network-Projects-with-Python`. Enter the folder by running:

```
$ cd Neural-Network-Projects-with-Python
```

To install the required Python libraries in a virtual environment, run the following command:

```
$ conda env create -f environment.yml
```

Note that you should have installed Anaconda in your computer first, before running this command. To enter the virtual environment, run the following command:

```
$ conda activate neural-network-projects-python
```

Navigate to the `Chapter05` folder by running the following command:

```
$ cd Chapter05
```

The following files are located in the folder:

- `autoencoder_image_compression.py`: This is the code for the *Building a simple autoencoder* section in this chapter
- `basic_autoencoder_denoise_MNIST.py` and `conv_autoencoder_denoise_MNIST.py`: These are the code for the *Denoising autoencoder* section in this chapter
- `basic_autoencoder_denoise_documents.py` and `deep_conv_autoencoder_denoise_documents.py`: These are the code for the *Denoising documents with autoencoders* section in this chapter

To run the code in each file, simply execute each Python file, as follows:

```
$ python autoencoder_image_compression.py
```

What are autoencoders?

So far in this book, we have looked at the applications of neural networks for supervised learning. Specifically, in each project, we have a labeled dataset (that is, features **x** and label **y**) and our goal is to train a neural network using this dataset, so that the neural network is able to predict label **y** from any new instance **x**.

A typical feedforward neural network is shown in the following diagram:

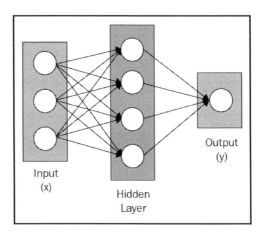

In this chapter, we will study a different class of neural networks, known as autoencoders. Autoencoders represent a paradigm shift from the conventional neural networks we have seen so far. The goal of autoencoders is to learn a **Latent Representation** of the input. This representation is usually a compressed representation of the original input.

All autoencoders have an **Encoder** and a **Decoder.** The role of the encoder is to encode the input to a learned, compressed representation, and the role of the decoder is to reconstruct the original input using the compressed representation.

The following diagram illustrates the architecture of a typical autoencoder:

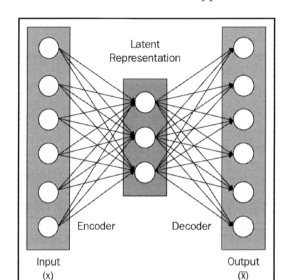

Notice that, in the preceding diagram, we do not require a label *y*, unlike in CNNs. This distinction means that autoencoders are a form of unsupervised learning, while CNNs fall within the realm of supervised learning.

Latent representation

At this point, you might wonder what is the purpose of autoencoders. Why do we bother learning a representation of the original input, only to reconstruct a similar output? The answer lies in the learned representation of the input. By forcing the learned representation to be compressed (that is, having smaller dimensions compared to the input), we essentially force the neural network to learn the most salient representation of the input. This ensures that the learned representation only captures the most relevant characteristics of the input, known as the **latent representation**.

As a concrete example of latent representations, take, for example, an autoencoder trained on the cats and dogs dataset, as shown in the following diagram:

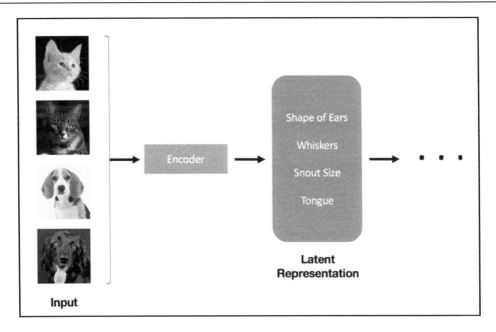

An autoencoder trained on this dataset will eventually learn that the salient characteristics of cats and dogs are the the shape of the ears, the length of whiskers, the snout size, and the length of the tongue visible. These salient characteristics are captured by the latent representation.

With this latent representation learned by the autoencoder, we can then do the following:

- Reduce the dimensionality of the input data. The latent representation is a natural reduced representation of the input data.
- Remove any noise from the input data (known as denoising). Noise is not a salient characteristic and therefore should be easily identifiable by using the latent representation.

In the sections to follow, we shall create and train autoencoders for each of the preceding purposes.

Note that, in the previous example, we have used examples such as shape of ears and snout size as descriptions for the latent representation. In reality, latent representations are simply a matrix of numbers and it is impossible to assign meaningful labels for them (nor do we need to). The descriptions that we used here simply provide an intuitive explanation for latent representations.

Autoencoders for data compression

So far, we have seen how autoencoders are able to learn a reduced representation of the input data. It is natural to think that autoencoders can do a good job at generalized data compression. However, that is not the case. Autoencoders are poor at generalized data compression, such as image compression (that is, JPEG) and audio compression (that is, MP3), because the learned latent representation only represents the data on which it was trained. In other words, autoencoders only work well for images similar to those on which it was trained.

Furthermore, autoencoders are a "lossy" form of data compression, which means that the output from autoencoders will have less information when compared to the original input. These characteristics mean that autoencoders are poor at being generalized data compression techniques. Other forms of data compression, such as JPEG and MP3, are superior when compared to autoencoders.

The MNIST handwritten digits dataset

One of the datasets that we'll use for this chapter is the MNIST handwritten digits dataset. The MNIST dataset contains 70,000 samples of handwritten digits, each of size 28 x 28 pixels. Each sample contains only one digit within the image, and all samples are labeled.

The MNIST dataset is provided directly in Keras, and we can import it by simply running the following code:

```
from keras.datasets import mnist

training_set, testing_set = mnist.load_data()
X_train, y_train = training_set
X_test, y_test = testing_set
```

Let's plot out each of the digits to better visualize our data. The following code snippet uses `matplotlib` to plot the data:

```
from matplotlib import pyplot as plt
fig, ((ax1, ax2, ax3, ax4, ax5), (ax6, ax7, ax8, ax9, ax10)) =
plt.subplots(2, 5, figsize=(10,5))

for idx, ax in enumerate([ax1,ax2,ax3,ax4,ax5, ax6,ax7,ax8,ax9,ax10]):
    for i in range(1000):
        if y_test[i] == idx:
            ax.imshow(X_test[i], cmap='gray')
            ax.grid(False)
            ax.set_xticks([])
            ax.set_yticks([])
            break
plt.tight_layout()
plt.show()
```

We get the following output:

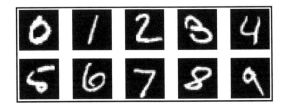

We can see that the digits are definitely handwritten, and each 28 x 28 image captures only one digit. The autoencoder should be able to learn the compressed representation of these digits (smaller than 28 x 28), and to reproduce the images using this compressed representation.

The following diagram illustrates this:

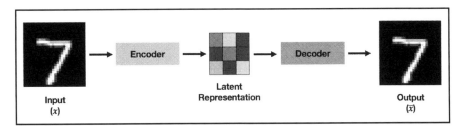

Building a simple autoencoder

To cement our understanding, let's start off by building the most basic autoencoder, as shown in the following diagram:

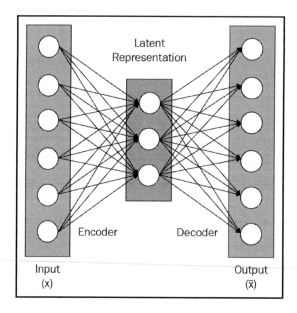

So far, we have emphasized that the hidden layer (**Latent Representation**) should be of a smaller dimension than the input data. This ensures that the latent representation is a compressed representation of the salient features of the input. But how small should it be?

Ideally, the size of the hidden layer should balance between being:

- Sufficiently *small* enough to represent a compressed representation of the input features
- Sufficiently *large* enough for the decoder to reconstruct the original input without too much loss

In other words, the size of the hidden layer is a hyperparameter that we need to select carefully to obtain the best results. We shall see how we can define the size of the hidden layer in Keras.

Building autoencoders in Keras

First, let's start building our basic autoencoder in Keras. As always, we'll use the `Sequential` class in Keras to build our model.

We'll start by importing and defining a new `Sequential` class in Keras:

```
from keras.models import Sequential

model = Sequential()
```

Next, we'll add the hidden layer to our model. From the previous diagram, we can clearly see that the hidden layer is a fully connected layer (that is, a `Dense` layer). From the `Dense` class in Keras, we can define the size of the hidden layer through the `units` parameter. The number of units is a hyperparameter that we will be experimenting with. For now, let's use a single node (units=1) as the hidden layer. The `input_shape` to the `Dense` layer is a vector of size `784` (since we are using 28 x 28 images) and the `activation` function is the `relu` activation function.

The following code adds a `Dense` layer with a single node to our model:

```
from keras.layers import Dense

hidden_layer_size = 1
model.add(Dense(units=hidden_layer_size, input_shape=(784,),
                activation='relu'))
```

Lastly, we'll add the output layer. The output layer is also a fully connected layer (that is, a `Dense` layer), and the size of the output layer should naturally be `784`, since we are trying to output the original 28 x 28 image. We use a `Sigmoid` activation function for the output to constrain the output values (value per pixel) between 0 and 1.

The following code adds an output `Dense` layer with `784` units to our model:

```
model.add(Dense(units=784, activation='sigmoid'))
```

Before we train our model, let's check the structure of our model and make sure that it is consistent with our diagram.

We can do this by calling the `summary()` function:

```
model.summary()
```

We get the following output:

```
Layer (type)                    Output Shape                Param #
=================================================================
dense_1 (Dense)                 (None, 1)                   785
_____
dense_2 (Dense)                 (None, 784)                 1568
=================================================================
Total params: 2,353
Trainable params: 2,353
Non-trainable params: 0
_____
```

Before we move on to the next step, let's create a function that encapsulates the model creation process that we just went through. Having such a function is useful, as it allows us to easily create different models with different hidden layer sizes.

The following code defines a function that creates a basic autoencoder with a `hidden_layer_size` variable:

```
def create_basic_autoencoder(hidden_layer_size):
    model = Sequential()
    model.add(Dense(units=hidden_layer_size, input_shape=(784,),
                  activation='relu'))
    model.add(Dense(units=784, activation='sigmoid'))
    return model

model = create_basic_autoencoder(hidden_layer_size=1)
```

The next step is to preprocess our data. There are two preprocessing steps required:

1. Reshape the images from a 28 x 28 vector to a 784 x 1 vector.
2. Normalize the values of the vector between 0 and 1 from the current 0 to 255. This smaller range of values makes it easier to train our neural network using the data.

To reshape the images from 28 x 28 to 784 x 1, we simply run the following code:

```
X_train_reshaped = X_train.reshape((X_train.shape[0],
                                     X_train.shape[1]*X_train.shape[2]))
X_test_reshaped = X_test.reshape((X_test.shape[0],
                                  X_test.shape[1]*X_test.shape[2]))
```

Note that first dimension, `X_train.shape[0]`, refers to the number of samples.

To normalize the values of the vector between 0 and 1 (from the original range of 0 to 255), we run the following code:

```
X_train_reshaped = X_train_reshaped/255.
X_test_reshaped = X_test_reshaped/255.
```

With that done, we can start to train our model. We'll first compile our model using the adam optimizer and `mean_squared_error` as the `loss` function. The `mean_squared_error` is useful in this case because we need a `loss` function that quantifies the pixel-wise discrepancy between the input and the output.

The following code compiles our model using the aforementioned parameters:

```
model.compile(optimizer='adam', loss='mean_squared_error')
```

Finally, let's train our model for 10 epochs. Note that we use `X_train_reshaped` as both the input (*x*) and output (*y*). This makes sense because we are trying to train the autoencoder to produce output that is identical to the input.

We train our autoencoder with the following code:

```
model.fit(X_train_reshaped, X_train_reshaped, epochs=10)
```

We'll see the following output:

```
Epoch 1/10
60000/60000 [==============================] - 3s 51us/step - loss: 0.0750
Epoch 2/10
60000/60000 [==============================] - 3s 43us/step - loss: 0.0653
Epoch 3/10
60000/60000 [==============================] - 3s 47us/step - loss: 0.0641
Epoch 4/10
60000/60000 [==============================] - 3s 47us/step - loss: 0.0635
Epoch 5/10
60000/60000 [==============================] - 3s 44us/step - loss: 0.0632
Epoch 6/10
60000/60000 [==============================] - 3s 44us/step - loss: 0.0629
Epoch 7/10
60000/60000 [==============================] - 3s 43us/step - loss: 0.0625
Epoch 8/10
60000/60000 [==============================] - 3s 43us/step - loss: 0.0620
Epoch 9/10
60000/60000 [==============================] - 3s 43us/step - loss: 0.0616
Epoch 10/10
60000/60000 [==============================] - 3s 43us/step - loss: 0.0613
<keras.callbacks.History at 0x7fe7b2cadb00>
```

With our model trained, let's apply it on our testing set:

```
output = model.predict(X_test_reshaped)
```

We would like to plot the output, and see how closely it matches with the original input. Remember, the autoencoder should produce output images that are close to the original input images.

The following code selects five random images from the testing set and plots them on the top row. It then plots the output images for these five randomly selected inputs on the bottom row:

```
import random
fig, ((ax1, ax2, ax3, ax4, ax5),
      (ax6, ax7, ax8, ax9, ax10)) = plt.subplots(2, 5, figsize=(20,7))

# randomly select 5 images
randomly_selected_imgs = random.sample(range(output.shape[0]),5)

# plot original images (input) on top row
for i, ax in enumerate([ax1,ax2,ax3,ax4,ax5]):
    ax.imshow(X_test[randomly_selected_imgs[i]], cmap='gray')
```

```
        if i == 0:
            ax.set_ylabel("INPUT",size=40)
        ax.grid(False)
        ax.set_xticks([])
        ax.set_yticks([])

    # plot output images from our autoencoder on the bottom row
    for i, ax in enumerate([ax6,ax7,ax8,ax9,ax10]):
        ax.imshow(output[randomly_selected_imgs[i]].reshape(28,28),
                cmap='gray')
        if i == 0:
            ax.set_ylabel("OUTPUT",size=40)
        ax.grid(False)
        ax.set_xticks([])
        ax.set_yticks([])

    plt.tight_layout()
    plt.show()
```

We'll see the following output:

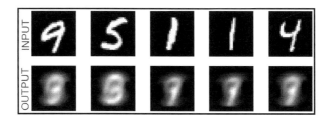

Top: Original images provided to the autoencoder as input; bottom: images output from the autoencoder

Wait a minute: the output images look terrible! They look like a blurry white scribble and they look nothing like our original input images. Clearly, an autoencoder with a hidden layer size of one node is insufficient to encode this dataset. This latent representation is too small for our autoencoder to sufficiently capture the salient features of our data.

Effect of hidden layer size on autoencoder performance

Let's try training more autoencoders with different hidden layer sizes and see how they fare.

The following code creates and trains five different models with 2, 4, 8, 16, and 32 nodes in the hidden layer:

```
hiddenLayerSize_2_model = create_basic_autoencoder(hidden_layer_size=2)
hiddenLayerSize_4_model = create_basic_autoencoder(hidden_layer_size=4)
hiddenLayerSize_8_model = create_basic_autoencoder(hidden_layer_size=8)
hiddenLayerSize_16_model = create_basic_autoencoder(hidden_layer_size=16)
hiddenLayerSize_32_model = create_basic_autoencoder(hidden_layer_size=32)
```

Notice how each successive model has twice the number of nodes in the hidden layer as the preceding model.

Now, let's train all five of our models together. We use the `verbose=0` argument in the `fit()` function to hide the output, as shown in the following code snippet:

```
hiddenLayerSize_2_model.compile(optimizer='adam',
                                loss='mean_squared_error')
hiddenLayerSize_2_model.fit(X_train_reshaped, X_train_reshaped,
                            epochs=10, verbose=0)

hiddenLayerSize_4_model.compile(optimizer='adam',
                                loss='mean_squared_error')
hiddenLayerSize_4_model.fit(X_train_reshaped, X_train_reshaped,
                            epochs=10, verbose=0)

hiddenLayerSize_8_model.compile(optimizer='adam',
                                loss='mean_squared_error')
hiddenLayerSize_8_model.fit(X_train_reshaped, X_train_reshaped,
                            cpochs=10, verbose=0)

hiddenLayerSize_16_model.compile(optimizer='adam',
                                 loss='mean_squared_error')
hiddenLayerSize_16_model.fit(X_train_reshaped, X_train_reshaped,
                             epochs=10, verbose=0)

hiddenLayerSize_32_model.compile(optimizer='adam',
                                 loss='mean_squared_error')
hiddenLayerSize_32_model.fit(X_train_reshaped, X_train_reshaped,
                             epochs=10, verbose=0)
```

Once training is complete, we apply the trained models on the testing set:

```
output_2_model = hiddenLayerSize_2_model.predict(X_test_reshaped)
output_4_model = hiddenLayerSize_4_model.predict(X_test_reshaped)
output_8_model = hiddenLayerSize_8_model.predict(X_test_reshaped)
output_16_model = hiddenLayerSize_16_model.predict(X_test_reshaped)
output_32_model = hiddenLayerSize_32_model.predict(X_test_reshaped)
```

Now, let's plot five randomly selected outputs from each model and see how they compare to the original input image:

```
fig, axes = plt.subplots(7, 5, figsize=(15,15))

randomly_selected_imgs = random.sample(range(output.shape[0]),5)
outputs = [X_test, output, output_2_model, output_4_model, output_8_model,
          output_16_model, output_32_model]

# Iterate through each subplot and plot accordingly
for row_num, row in enumerate(axes):
    for col_num, ax in enumerate(row):
        ax.imshow(outputs[row_num][randomly_selected_imgs[col_num]]. \
                  reshape(28,28), cmap='gray')
        ax.grid(False)
        ax.set_xticks([])
        ax.set_yticks([])
plt.tight_layout()
plt.show()
```

We get the following output:

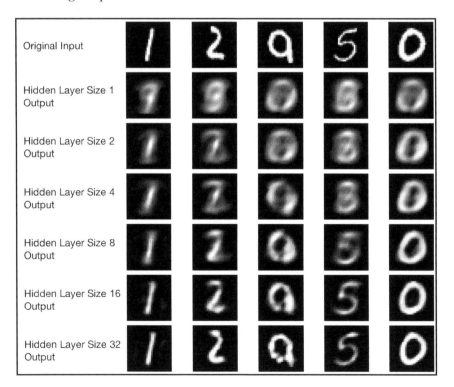

Isn't it beautiful? We can clearly see a nice transition as we double the number of nodes in the hidden layer. Gradually, we see that the output images become clearer and closer to the original input as we increase the number of nodes in the hidden layer.

At 32 nodes in the hidden layer, the output becomes very close (though not perfect) to the original input. Interestingly, we have shrunk the original input by 24.5 times ($784 \div 32$) and still managed to produce a satisfactory output. That's a pretty impressive compression ratio!

Denoising autoencoders

Another interesting application of autoencoders is image denoising. Image noise is defined as a random variations of brightness in an image. Image noise may originate from the sensors of digital cameras. Although digital cameras these days are capable of capturing high quality images, image noise may still occur, especially in low light conditions.

Denoising images has been a challenge for researchers for many years. Early methods include applying some sort of image filter (that is, mean averaging filter, where the pixel value is replaced with the average pixel value of its neighbors) over the image. However, such methods can sometimes fall short and the effects can be less than ideal.

A few years ago, researchers discovered that we can train autoencoders for image denoising. The idea is simple. Instead of using the same input and output when training conventional autoencoders (as described in the previous section), we use a noisy image as the input and a clean reference image for the autoencoder to compare its output against. This is illustrated in the following diagram:

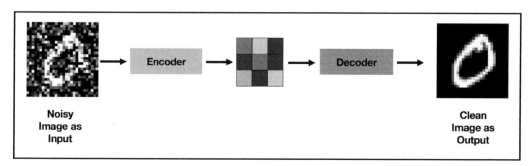

During the training process, the autoencoder will learn that the noises in the image should not be part of the output, and will learn to output a clean image. Essentially, we are training our autoencoder to remove noise from images!

Let's start by introducing noise to the MNIST dataset. We'll add a random value between -0.5 and 0.5 to each pixel in the original images. This has the effect of increasing and decreasing the intensity of pixels at random. The following code does this using numpy:

```
import numpy as np

X_train_noisy = X_train_reshaped + np.random.normal(0, 0.5,
                                  size=X_train_reshaped.shape)
X_test_noisy = X_test_reshaped + np.random.normal(0, 0.5,
                                  size=X_test_reshaped.shape)
```

Finally, we clip the noisy images between 0 and 1 to normalize the images:

```
X_train_noisy = np.clip(X_train_noisy, a_min=0, a_max=1)
X_test_noisy = np.clip(X_test_noisy, a_min=0, a_max=1)
```

Let's define a basic autoencoder just like we did in the previous section. This basic autoencoder has a single hidden layer with 16 nodes.

The following code creates this autoencoder using the function that we defined in the previous section:

```
basic_denoise_autoencoder = create_basic_autoencoder(hidden_layer_size=16)
```

Next, we train our denoising autoencoder. Remember, the input to the denoising autoencoder is a noisy image and the output is a clean image. The following code trains our basic denoising autoencoder:

```
basic_denoise_autoencoder.compile(optimizer='adam',
                                  loss='mean_squared_error')
basic_denoise_autoencoder.fit(X_train_noisy, X_train_reshaped, epochs=10)
```

Once training is done, we apply our denoising autoencoder on the test images:

```
output = basic_denoise_autoencoder.predict(X_test_noisy)
```

We plot the output and compare it with the original image and the noisy image:

```
fig, ((ax1, ax2, ax3, ax4, ax5), (ax6, ax7, ax8, ax9, ax10),
(ax11,ax12,ax13,ax14,ax15)) = plt.subplots(3, 5, figsize=(20,13))
randomly_selected_imgs = random.sample(range(output.shape[0]),5)

# 1st row for original images
for i, ax in enumerate([ax1,ax2,ax3,ax4,ax5]):
    ax.imshow(X_test_reshaped[randomly_selected_imgs[i]].reshape(28,28),
              cmap='gray')
    if i == 0:
        ax.set_ylabel("Original \n Images", size=30)
```

```
        ax.grid(False)
        ax.set_xticks([])
        ax.set_yticks([])

    # 2nd row for input with noise added
    for i, ax in enumerate([ax6,ax7,ax8,ax9,ax10]):
        ax.imshow(X_test_noisy[randomly_selected_imgs[i]].reshape(28,28),
                  cmap='gray')
        if i == 0:
            ax.set_ylabel("Input With \n Noise Added", size=30)
        ax.grid(False)
        ax.set_xticks([])
        ax.set_yticks([])

    # 3rd row for output images from our autoencoder
    for i, ax in enumerate([ax11,ax12,ax13,ax14,ax15]):
        ax.imshow(output[randomly_selected_imgs[i]].reshape(28,28),
                  cmap='gray')
        if i == 0:
            ax.set_ylabel("Denoised \n Output", size=30)
        ax.grid(False)
        ax.set_xticks([])
        ax.set_yticks([])

plt.tight_layout()
plt.show()
```

We get the following output:

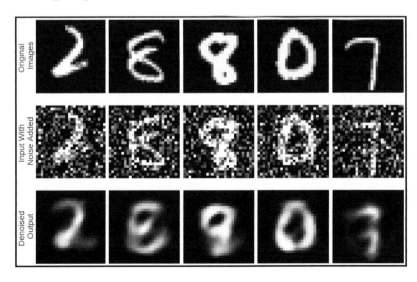

How does it do? Well, it could definitely be better! This basic denoising autoencoder is perfectly capable of removing noise, but it doesn't do a very good job at reconstructing the original image. We can see that this basic denoising autoencoder sometimes fails to separate noise from the digits, especially near the center of the image.

Deep convolutional denoising autoencoder

Can we do better than the basic, one-hidden layer autoencoder? We saw in the previous chapter, Chapter 4, *Cats Versus Dogs – Image Classification Using CNNs*, that deep CNNs perform well for image classification tasks. Naturally, we can apply the same concept for autoencoders too. Instead of using only one hidden layer, we use multiple layers (that is, a deep network) and instead of a fully connected dense layer, we use convolutional layers.

The following diagram illustrates the architecture of a deep convolutional autoencoder:

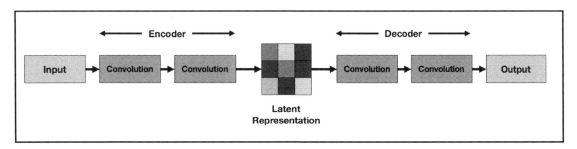

Constructing a deep convolutional autoencoder in Keras is simple. Once again, we'll use the Sequential class in Keras to construct our model.

First, we define a new Sequential class:

```
conv_autoencoder = Sequential()
```

Next, let's add the first two convolutional layers, which act as the encoder in our model. There are several parameters we need to define while using the Conv2D class in Keras:

- **Number of filters**: Typically, we use a decreasing number of filters for each layer in the encoder. Conversely, we use an increasing number of filters for each layer in the decoder. Let's use 16 filters for the first convolutional layer in the encoder and eight filters for the second convolutional layer in the encoder. Conversely, let's use eight filters for the first convolutional layer in the decoder and 16 filters for the second convolutional layer in the decoder.

- **Filter size:** As shown in the previous chapter, Chapter 4, *Cats Versus Dogs – Image Classification Using CNNs*, a filter size of 3 x 3 is typical for convolutional layers.
- **Padding:** For autoencoders, we use a same padding. This ensures that the height and width of successive layers remains the same. This is useful because we need to ensure that the dimensions of the final output is the same as the input.

The following code snippet adds the first two convolutional layers with the aforementioned parameters to our model:

```
from keras.layers import Conv2D
conv_autoencoder.add(Conv2D(filters=16, kernel_size=(3,3),
                            activation='relu', padding='same',
                            input_shape=(28,28,1)))
conv_autoencoder.add(Conv2D(filters=8, kernel_size=(3,3),
                            activation='relu', padding='same'))
```

Next, we'll add the decoder layers onto our model. Just like the encoder layers, the decoder layers are also convolutional layers. The only difference is that, in the decoder layers, we use an increasing number of filters after each successive layer.

The following code snippet adds the next two convolutional layers as the decoder:

```
conv_autoencoder.add(Conv2D(filters=8, kernel_size=(3,3),
                            activation='relu', padding='same'))
conv_autoencoder.add(Conv2D(filters=16, kernel_size=(3,3),
                            activation='relu', padding='same'))
```

Finally, we add the output layer to our model. The output layer should be a convolutional layer with only one filter, as we are trying to output a 28 x 28 x 1 image. The Sigmoid function is used as the activation function for the output layer.

The following code adds the final output layer:

```
conv_autoencoder.add(Conv2D(filters=1, kernel_size=(3,3),
                            activation='sigmoid', padding='same'))
```

Let's take a look at the structure of the model to make sure that it is consistent with what was shown in the diagram earlier. We can do so by calling the summary() function:

```
conv_autoencoder.summary()
```

We get the following output:

```
Layer (type)                 Output Shape             Param #
=================================================================
conv2d_1 (Conv2D)            (None, 28, 28, 16)         160

conv2d_2 (Conv2D)            (None, 28, 28, 8)          1160

conv2d_3 (Conv2D)            (None, 28, 28, 8)          584

conv2d_4 (Conv2D)            (None, 28, 28, 16)         1168

conv2d_5 (Conv2D)            (None, 28, 28, 1)          145
=================================================================
Total params: 3,217
Trainable params: 3,217
Non-trainable params: 0
```

We are now ready to train our deep convolutional autoencoder. As usual, we define the training process under the `compile` function and call the `fit` function, as shown in the following code:

```
conv_autoencoder.compile(optimizer='adam', loss='binary_crossentropy')
conv_autoencoder.fit(X_train_noisy.reshape(60000,28,28,1),
                     X_train_reshaped.reshape(60000,28,28,1),
                     epochs=10)
```

Once training is done, we'll get the following output:

```
Epoch 1/10
60000/60000 [==============================] - 17s 286us/step - loss: 0.1251
Epoch 2/10
60000/60000 [==============================] - 17s 279us/step - loss: 0.1039
Epoch 3/10
60000/60000 [==============================] - 17s 279us/step - loss: 0.1022
Epoch 4/10
60000/60000 [==============================] - 17s 280us/step - loss: 0.1012
Epoch 5/10
60000/60000 [==============================] - 17s 279us/step - loss: 0.1004
Epoch 6/10
60000/60000 [==============================] - 17s 279us/step - loss: 0.0998
Epoch 7/10
60000/60000 [==============================] - 17s 280us/step - loss: 0.0994
Epoch 8/10
60000/60000 [==============================] - 17s 280us/step - loss: 0.0990
Epoch 9/10
60000/60000 [==============================] - 17s 279us/step - loss: 0.0987
Epoch 10/10
60000/60000 [==============================] - 17s 282us/step - loss: 0.0985
```

Let's use the trained model on the testing set:

```
output = conv_autoencoder.predict(X_test_noisy.reshape(10000,28,28,1))
```

It will be interesting to see how this deep convolutional autoencoder performs on the testing set. Remember, the testing set represents images that the model has never seen before.

We plot the output and compare it with the original image and the noisy image:

```
fig, ((ax1, ax2, ax3, ax4, ax5), (ax6, ax7, ax8, ax9, ax10),
(ax11,ax12,ax13,ax14,ax15)) = plt.subplots(3, 5, figsize=(20,13))
randomly_selected_imgs = random.sample(range(output.shape[0]),5)

# 1st row for original images
for i, ax in enumerate([ax1,ax2,ax3,ax4,ax5]):
    ax.imshow(X_test_reshaped[randomly_selected_imgs[i]].reshape(28,28),
            cmap='gray')
    if i == 0:
        ax.set_ylabel("Original \n Images", size=30)
    ax.grid(False)
    ax.set_xticks([])
    ax.set_yticks([])

# 2nd row for input with noise added
for i, ax in enumerate([ax6,ax7,ax8,ax9,ax10]):
    ax.imshow(X_test_noisy[randomly_selected_imgs[i]].reshape(28,28),
            cmap='gray')
    if i =- 0:
        ax.set_ylabel("Input With \n Noise Added", size=30)
    ax.grid(False)
    ax.set_xticks([])
    ax.set_yticks([])

# 3rd row for output images from our autoencoder
for i, ax in enumerate([ax11,ax12,ax13,ax14,ax15]):
    ax.imshow(output[randomly_selected_imgs[i]].reshape(28,28),
            cmap='gray')
    if i == 0:
        ax.set_ylabel("Denoised \n Output", size=30)
    ax.grid(False)
    ax.set_xticks([])
    ax.set_yticks([])

plt.tight_layout()
plt.show()
```

We get the following output:

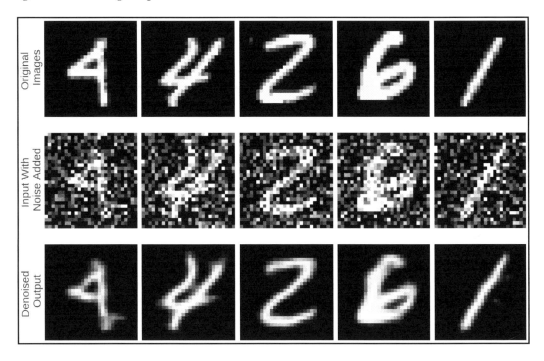

Isn't that amazing? The denoised output from our deep convolutional autoencoder is so good that we can barely differentiate the original images and the denoised output.

Despite the impressive results, it is important to keep in mind that the convolutional model that we used is pretty simple. The advantage of deep neural networks is that we can always increase the complexity of the model (that is, more layers and more filters per layer) and use it on more complex datasets. This ability to scale is one of the main advantages of deep neural networks.

Denoising documents with autoencoders

So far, we have applied our denoising autoencoder on the MNIST dataset, which is a pretty simple dataset. Let's take a look now at a more complicated dataset, which better represents the challenges of denoising documents in real life.

The dataset that we will be using is provided for free by the **University of California Irvine (UCI)**. For more information on the dataset, you can visit UCI's website at `https://archive.ics.uci.edu/ml/datasets/NoisyOffice`.

The dataset can be found in the accompanying GitHub repository for this book. For more information on downloading the code and dataset for this chapter from the GitHub repository, please refer to the *Technical requirements* section earlier in the chapter.

The dataset consists of 216 different noisy images. The noisy images are scanned office documents that are tainted by coffee stains, wrinkled marks, and other sorts of defects that are typical in office documents. For every noisy image, a corresponding reference clean image is provided, which represents the office document in an ideal noiseless state.

Let's take a look at the dataset to have a better idea of what we are working with. The dataset is located at the following folder:

```
noisy_imgs_path = 'Noisy_Documents/noisy/'
clean_imgs_path = 'Noisy_Documents/clean/'
```

The `Noisy_Documents` folder contains two subfolders (`noisy` and `clean`), which contains the noisy and clean images, respectively.

To load the `.png` images into Python, we can use the `load_img` function provided by Keras. To convert the loaded images into a `numpy` array, we use the `img_to_array` function in Keras.

The following code imports the noisy `.png` images in the `/Noisy_Documents/noisy/` folder into a `numpy` array:

```
import os
import numpy as np
from keras.preprocessing.image import load_img, img_to_array

X_train_noisy = []

for file in sorted(os.listdir(noisy_imgs_path)):
    img = load_img(noisy_imgs_path+file, color_mode='grayscale',
                target_size=(420,540))
    img = img_to_array(img).astype('float32')/255
    X_train_noisy.append(img)

# convert to numpy array
X_train_noisy = np.array(X_train_noisy)
```

To verify that our images are loaded properly into the `numpy` array, let's print the dimensions of the array:

```
print(X_train_noisy.shape)
```

We get the following output:

```
(216, 420, 540, 1)
```

We can see that there are **216** images in the array, each with dimensions 420 x 540 x 1 (width x height x number of channels for each image).

Let's do the same for the clean images. The following code imports the clean `.png` images in the `/Noisy_Documents/clean/` folder into a `numpy` array:

```
X_train_clean = []

for file in sorted(os.listdir(clean_imgs_path)):
    img = load_img(clean_imgs_path+file, color_mode='grayscale',
                   target_size=(420,540))
    img = img_to_array(img).astype('float32')/255
    X_train_clean.append(img)

# convert to numpy array
X_train_clean = np.array(X_train_clean)
```

Let's display the loaded images to have a better idea of the kind of images we are working with. The following code randomly selects 3 images and plots them, as shown in the following code:

```
import random
fig, ((ax1,ax2), (ax3,ax4),
      (ax5,ax6)) = plt.subplots(3, 2, figsize=(10,12))

randomly_selected_imgs = random.sample(range(X_train_noisy.shape[0]),3)

# plot noisy images on the left
for i, ax in enumerate([ax1,ax3,ax5]):
    ax.imshow(X_train_noisy[i].reshape(420,540), cmap='gray')
    if i == 0:
        ax.set_title("Noisy Images", size=30)
    ax.grid(False)
    ax.set_xticks([])
    ax.set_yticks([])

# plot clean images on the right
for i, ax in enumerate([ax2,ax4,ax6]):
    ax.imshow(X_train_clean[i].reshape(420,540), cmap='gray')
    if i == 0:
        ax.set_title("Clean Images", size=30)
    ax.grid(False)
```

```
        ax.set_xticks([])
        ax.set_yticks([])

    plt.tight_layout()
    plt.show()
```

We get the output as shown in the following screenshot:

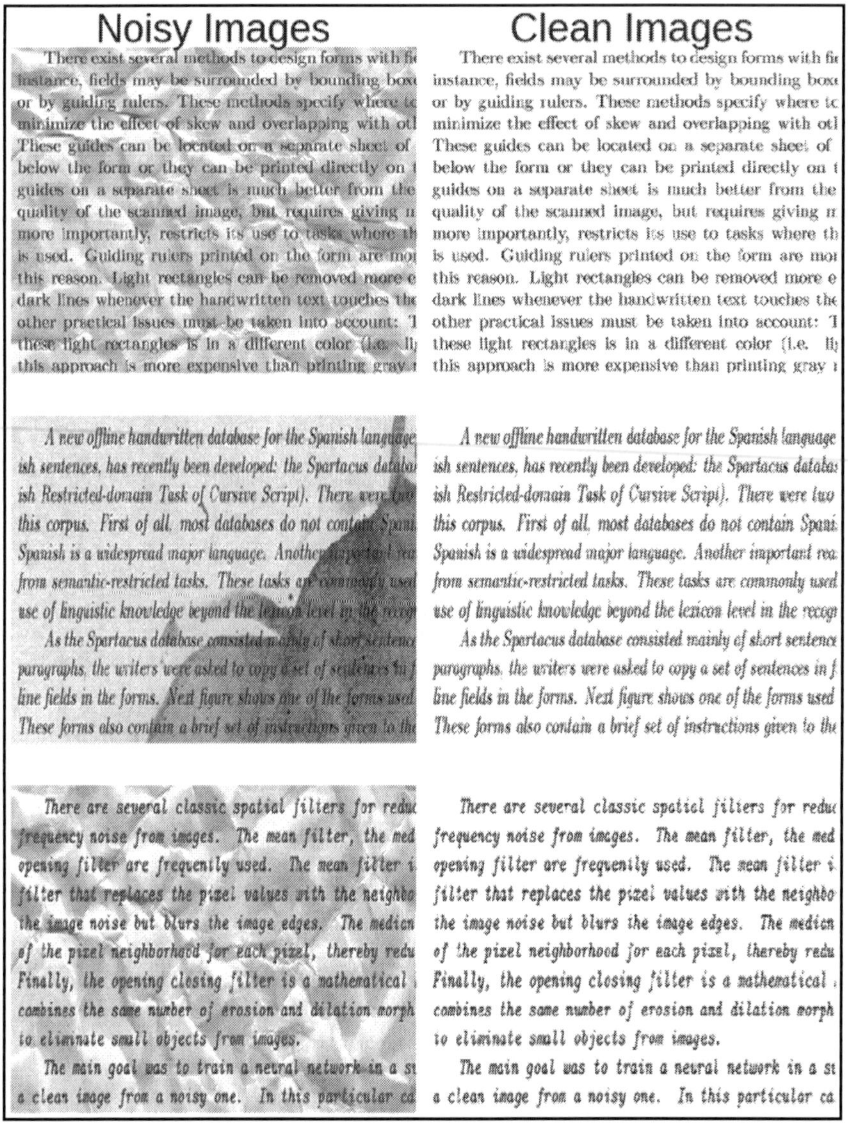

We can see that the kind of noise in this dataset is markedly different from what we saw in the MNIST dataset. The noise in this dataset are random artifacts that appear throughout the image. Our autoencoder model needs to have a strong understanding of signal versus noise in order to successfully denoise this dataset.

Before we proceed to train our model, let's split our dataset into a training and testing set, as shown in the following code:

```
# use the first 20 noisy images as testing images
X_test_noisy = X_train_noisy[0:20,]
X_train_noisy = X_train_noisy[21:,]

# use the first 20 clean images as testing images
X_test_clean = X_train_clean[0:20,]
X_train_clean = X_train_clean[21:,]
```

Basic convolutional autoencoder

We're now ready to tackle the problem. Let's start with a basic model to see how far we can go with it.

As always, we define a new `Sequential` class:

```
basic_conv_autoencoder = Sequential()
```

Next, we add a single convolutional layer as our encoder layer:

```
basic_conv_autoencoder.add(Conv2D(filters=8, kernel_size=(3,3),
                                  activation='relu', padding='same',
                                  input_shape=(420,540,1)))
```

We add a single convolutional layer as our decoder layer:

```
basic_conv_autoencoder.add(Conv2D(filters=8, kernel_size=(3,3),
                                  activation='relu', padding='same'))
```

Finally, we add an output layer:

```
basic_conv_autoencoder.add(Conv2D(filters=1, kernel_size=(3,3),
                                  activation='sigmoid', padding='same'))
```

Let's check the structure of the model:

```
basic_conv_autoencoder.summary()
```

We get the output as shown in the following screenshot:

```
Layer (type)                    Output Shape             Param #
=================================================================
conv2d_26 (Conv2D)              (None, 420, 540, 8)      80
_____
conv2d_27 (Conv2D)              (None, 420, 540, 8)      584
_____
conv2d_28 (Conv2D)              (None, 420, 540, 1)      73
=================================================================
Total params: 737
Trainable params: 737
Non-trainable params: 0
```

Here's the code to train our basic convolutional autoencoder:

```
basic_conv_autoencoder.compile(optimizer='adam',
                               loss='binary_crossentropy')
basic_conv_autoencoder.fit(X_train_noisy, X_train_clean, epochs=10)
```

Once the training is done, we apply our model on the testing set:

```
output = basic_conv_autoencoder.predict(X_test_noisy)
```

Let's plot the output and see what kind of results we got. The following code plots the original noisy images in the left column, the original clean images in the middle column, and the denoised image output from our model in the right column:

```
fig, ((ax1,ax2,ax3),(ax4,ax5,ax6)) = plt.subplots(2,3, figsize=(20,10))

randomly_selected_imgs = random.sample(range(X_test_noisy.shape[0]),2)

for i, ax in enumerate([ax1, ax4]):
    idx = randomly_selected_imgs[i]
    ax.imshow(X_test_noisy[idx].reshape(420,540), cmap='gray')
    if i == 0:
        ax.set_title("Noisy Images", size=30)
    ax.grid(False)
    ax.set_xticks([])
    ax.set_yticks([])

for i, ax in enumerate([ax2, ax5]):
    idx = randomly_selected_imgs[i]
    ax.imshow(X_test_clean[idx].reshape(420,540), cmap='gray')
    if i == 0:
        ax.set_title("Clean Images", size=30)
    ax.grid(False)
```

```
    ax.set_xticks([])
    ax.set_yticks([])

for i, ax in enumerate([ax3, ax6]):
    idx = randomly_selected_imgs[i]
    ax.imshow(output[idx].reshape(420,540), cmap='gray')
    if i == 0:
        ax.set_title("Output Denoised Images", size=30)
    ax.grid(False)
    ax.set_xticks([])
    ax.set_yticks([])

plt.tight_layout()
plt.show()
```

We get the output as shown in the following screenshot:

Well, our model can certainly do a better job. The denoised images tend to have a gray background rather than a white background in the true `Clean Images`. The model also does a poor job at removing the coffee stains from the `Noisy Images`. Furthermore, the words in the denoised images are faint, showing that the model struggles at this task.

Deep convolutional autoencoder

Let's try denoising the images with a deeper model and more filters in each convolutional layer.

We start by defining a new `Sequential` class:

```
conv_autoencoder = Sequential()
```

Next, we add three convolutional layers as our encoder, with 32, 16, and 8 filters:

```
conv_autoencoder.add(Conv2D(filters=32, kernel_size=(3,3),
                          input_shape=(420,540,1),
                          activation='relu', padding='same'))
conv_autoencoder.add(Conv2D(filters=16, kernel_size=(3,3),
                          activation='relu', padding='same'))
conv_autoencoder.add(Conv2D(filters=8, kernel_size=(3,3),
                          activation='relu', padding='same'))
```

Similarly for the decoder, we add three convolutional layers with 8, 16, and 32 filters:

```
conv_autoencoder.add(Conv2D(filters=8, kernel_size=(3,3),
                          activation='relu', padding='same'))
conv_autoencoder.add(Conv2D(filters=16, kernel_size=(3,3),
                          activation='relu', padding='same'))
conv_autoencoder.add(Conv2D(filters=32, kernel_size=(3,3),
                          activation='relu', padding='same'))
```

Finally, we add an output layer:

```
conv_autoencoder.add(Conv2D(filters=1, kernel_size=(3,3),
                          activation='sigmoid', padding='same'))
```

Let's check the structure of our model:

```
conv_autoencoder.summary()
```

We get the following output:

```
Layer (type)                Output Shape              Param #
=================================================================
conv2d_29 (Conv2D)          (None, 420, 540, 32)       320

conv2d_30 (Conv2D)          (None, 420, 540, 16)       4624

conv2d_31 (Conv2D)          (None, 420, 540, 8)        1160

conv2d_32 (Conv2D)          (None, 420, 540, 8)        584

conv2d_33 (Conv2D)          (None, 420, 540, 16)       1168

conv2d_34 (Conv2D)          (None, 420, 540, 32)       4640

conv2d_35 (Conv2D)          (None, 420, 540, 1)        289
=================================================================
Total params: 12,785
Trainable params: 12,785
Non-trainable params: 0
```

From the preceding output, we can see that there are **12,785** parameters in our model, which is approximately 17 times more than the basic model we used in the previous section.

Let's train the model and apply it on the testing images:

Caution

The following code may take some time to run if you are not using Keras with a GPU. If the model is taking too long to train, you may reduce the number of filters in each convolutional layer in the model.

```
conv_autoencoder.compile(optimizer='adam', loss='binary_crossentropy')
conv_autoencoder.fit(X_train_noisy, X_train_clean, epochs=10)

output = conv_autoencoder.predict(X_test_noisy)
```

Finally, we plot the output to see the kind of results we get. The following code plots the original noisy images in the left column, the original clean images in the middle column, and the denoised image output from our model in the right column:

```
fig, ((ax1,ax2,ax3),(ax4,ax5,ax6)) = plt.subplots(2,3, figsize=(20,10))

randomly_selected_imgs = random.sample(range(X_test_noisy.shape[0]),2)

for i, ax in enumerate([ax1, ax4]):
    idx = randomly_selected_imgs[i]
    ax.imshow(X_test_noisy[idx].reshape(420,540), cmap='gray')
    if i == 0:
        ax.set_title("Noisy Images", size=30)
    ax.grid(False)
    ax.set_xticks([])
    ax.set_yticks([])

for i, ax in enumerate([ax2, ax5]):
    idx = randomly_selected_imgs[i]
    ax.imshow(X_test_clean[idx].reshape(420,540), cmap='gray')
    if i == 0:
        ax.set_title("Clean Images", size=30)
    ax.grid(False)
    ax.set_xticks([])
    ax.set_yticks([])

for i, ax in enumerate([ax3, ax6]):
    idx = randomly_selected_imgs[i]
    ax.imshow(output[idx].reshape(420,540), cmap='gray')
    if i == 0:
        ax.set_title("Output Denoised Images", size=30)
    ax.grid(False)
    ax.set_xticks([])
    ax.set_yticks([])

plt.tight_layout()
plt.show()
```

We get the following output:

The result looks amazing! In fact, the output denoised images look so good that we can barely differentiate them from the true clean images. We can see that the coffee stain has been almost entirely removed and the noise from the crumpled paper is non-existent in the denoised image. Furthermore, the words in the denoised images look sharp and clear, and we can easily read the words in the denoised images.

This dataset truly demonstrates the power of autoencoders. By adding on additional complexity in the form of deeper convolutional layers and more filters, the model is able to differentiate the signal from the noise, allowing it to successfully denoise images that are heavily corrupted.

Summary

In this chapter, we looked at autoencoders, a class of neural networks that learn the latent representation of input images. We saw that all autoencoders have an encoder and decoder component. The role of the encoder is to encode the input to a learned, compressed representation and the role of the decoder is to reconstruct the original input using the compressed representation.

We first looked at autoencoders for image compression. By training an autoencoder with identical input and output, the autoencoder learns the most salient features of the input. Using MNIST images, we constructed an autoencoder with a 24.5 times compression rate. Using this learned 24.5x compressed representation, the autoencoder is able to successfully reconstruct the original input.

Next, we looked at denoising autoencoders. By training an autoencoder with noisy images as input and clean images as output, the autoencoder is able to pick out the signal from the noise, and is able to successfully denoise the noisy image. We trained a deep convolutional autoencoder, and the autoencoder was able to successfully denoise documents with coffee stains and other sorts of image corruptions. The results were impressive, with the autoencoder removing almost all of the noise in the noisy documents, producing an output that is almost identical to the true clean images.

In the next chapter, `Chapter 6`, *Sentiment Analysis of Movie Reviews Using LSTM* we'll use a **long short-term memory** (**LSTM**) neural network to predict the sentiment of movie reviews.

Questions

1. How are autoencoders different from a conventional feed forward neural network?

   Autoencoders are neural networks that learn a compressed representation of the input, known as the latent representation. They are different from conventional feed forward neural networks because their structure consists of an encoder and a decoder component, which is not present in CNNs.

2. What happens when the latent representation of the autoencoder is too small?

   The size of the latent representation should be sufficiently *small* enough to represent a compressed representation of the input, and also be sufficiently *large* enough for the decoder to reconstruct the original image without too much loss.

3. What are the input and output when training a denoising autoencoder?

   The input to a denoising autoencoder should be a noisy image and the output should be a reference clean image. During the training process, the autoencoder learns that the output should not contain any noise (through the `loss` function), and the latent representation of the autoencoder should only contain the signals (that is, non-noise elements)

4. What are some of the ways we can improve the complexity of denoising autoencoders?

   For denoising autoencoders, convolutional layers always work better than dense layers, just as CNNs work better than conventional feed forward neural networks for image classification tasks. We can also improve the complexity of our model by building a deeper network with more layers, and by using more filters in each convolutional layer.

6
Sentiment Analysis of Movie Reviews Using LSTM

In previous chapters, we looked at neural network architectures, such as the basic MLP and feedforward neural networks, for classification and regression tasks. We then looked at CNNs, and we saw how they are used for image recognition tasks. In this chapter, we will turn our attention to **recurrent neural networks** (**RNNs**) (in particular, to **long short-term memory** (**LSTM**) networks) and how they can be used in sequential problems, such as **Natural Language Processing** (**NLP**). We will develop and train a LSTM network to predict the sentiment of movie reviews on IMDb.

In this chapter, we'll cover the following topics:

- Sequential problems in machine learning
- NLP and sentiment analysis
- Introduction to RNNs and LSTM networks
- Analysis of the IMDb movie reviews dataset
- Word embeddings
- A step-by-step guide to building and training an LSTM network in Keras
- Analysis of our results

Technical requirements

The Python libraries required for this chapter are as follows:

- matplotlib 3.0.2
- Keras 2.2.4
- seaborn 0.9.0
- scikit-learn 0.20.2

The code for this chapter can be found in the GitHub repository for the book.

To download the code onto your computer, you may run the following `git clone` command:

```
$ git clone
https://github.com/PacktPublishing/Neural-Network-Projects-with-Python.git
```

After the process is complete, there will be a folder entitled `Neural-Network-Projects-with-Python`. Enter the folder by running the following:

```
$ cd Neural-Network-Projects-with-Python
```

To install the required Python libraries in a virtual environment, run the following command:

```
$ conda env create -f environment.yml
```

Note that you should have installed Anaconda on your computer first, before running this command. To enter the virtual environment, run the following command:

```
$ conda activate neural-network-projects-python
```

Navigate to the `Chapter06` folder by running the following command:

```
$ cd Chapter06
```

The following file is located in the folder:

- `lstm.py`: This is the main code for this chapter

To run the code, simply execute the `lstm.py` file:

```
$ python lstm.py
```

Sequential problems in machine learning

Sequential problems are a class of problem in machine learning in which the order of the features presented to the model is important for making predictions. Sequential problems are commonly encountered in the following scenarios:

- NLP, including sentiment analysis, language translation, and text prediction
- Time series predictions

For example, let's consider the text prediction problem, as shown in the following screenshot, which falls under NLP:

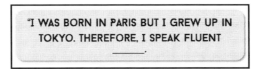

Human beings have an innate ability for this, and it is trivial for us to know that the word in the blank is probably the word *Japanese*. The reason for this is that as we read the sentence, we process the words as a sequence. The sequence of the words captures the information required to make the prediction. By contrast, if we discard the sequential information and only consider the words individually, we get a *bag of words*, as shown in the following diagram:

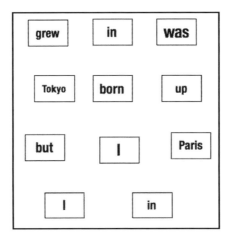

We can see that our ability to predict the word in the blank is now severely impacted. Without knowing the sequence of words, it is impossible to predict the word in the blank.

Besides text predictions, sentiment analysis and language translation are also sequential problems. In fact, many NLP problems are sequential problems, because the languages that we speak are sequential in nature, and the sequence conveys context and other subtle nuances.

Sequential problems also occur naturally in time series problems. Time series problems are common in stock markets. Often, we wish to know whether a particular stock will rise or fall on a certain day. This problem is accurately defined as a time series problem, because knowing the movement of the stocks in the preceding hours or minutes is often crucial to predicting whether the stock will rise or fall. Today, machine learning methods are being heavily applied in this domain, with algorithmic trading strategies driving the buying and selling of stocks.

In this chapter, we will focus on NLP problems. In particular, we will create a neural network for sentiment analysis.

NLP and sentiment analysis

NLP is a subfield in **artificial intelligence** (**AI**) that is concerned with the interaction of computers and human languages. As early as the 1950s, scientists were interested in designing intelligent machines that could understand human languages. Early efforts to create a language translator focused on the rule-based approach, where a group of linguistic experts handcrafted a set of rules to be encoded in machines. However, this rule-based approach produced results that were sub-optimal, and, often, it was impossible to convert these rules from one language to another, which meant that scaling up was difficult. For many decades, not much progress was made in NLP, and human language was a goal that AI couldn't reach—until the resurgence of deep learning.

With the proliferation of deep learning and neural networks in the image classification domain, scientists began to wonder whether the powers of neural networks could be applied to NLP. In the late '00s, tech giants, including Apple, Amazon, and Google, applied LSTM networks to NLP problems, and the results were astonishing. The ability of AI assistants, such as Siri and Alexa, to understand multiple languages spoken in different accents was the result of deep learning and LSTM networks. In recent years, we have also seen a massive improvement in the abilities of text translation software, such as Google Translate, which is capable of producing translations as good as human language experts.

Sentiment analysis is also an area of NLP that benefited from the resurgence of deep learning. Sentiment analysis is defined as the prediction of the positivity of a text. Most sentiment analysis problems are classification problems (positive/neutral/negative) and not regression problems.

There are many practical applications of sentiment analysis. For example, modern customer service centers use sentiment analysis to predict the satisfaction of customers through the reviews they provide on platforms such as Yelp or Facebook. This allows businesses to step in immediately whenever customers are dissatisfied, allowing the problem to be addressed as soon as possible, and preventing customer churn.

Sentiment analysis has also been applied in the domain of stocks trading. In 2010, scientists showed that by sampling the sentiment in Twitter (positive versus negative tweets), we can predict whether the stock market will rise. Similarly, high-frequency trading firms use sentiment analysis to sample the sentiment of news related to certain companies, and execute trades automatically, based on the positivity of the news.

Why sentiment analysis is difficult

Early efforts in sentiment analysis faced many hurdles, due to the presence of subtle nuances in human languages. The same word can often covey a different meaning, depending on the context. Take for example the following two sentences:

We know that the sentiment of the first sentence is negative, as it probably means that the building is literally on fire. On the other hand, we know that the sentiment of the second sentence is positive, since it is unlikely that the person is literally on fire. Instead, it probably means that the person is on a *hot streak*, and this is positive. The rule-based approach toward sentiment analysis suffers because of these subtle nuances, and it is incredibly complex to encode this knowledge in a rule-based manner.

Another reason sentiment analysis is difficult is because of sarcasm. Sarcasm is commonly used in many cultures, especially in an online medium. Sarcasm is difficult for computers to understand. In fact, even humans fail to detect sarcasm at times. Take for example the following sentence:

"THANKS FOR LOSING MY LUGGAGE! WHAT A WAY TO TREAT A LOYAL CUSTOMER"

You can probably detect sarcasm in the preceding sentence, and come to the conclusion that the sentiment is negative. However, it is not easy for a program to understand that.

In the next section, we will look at RNNs and LSTM nets, and how they have been used to tackle sentiment analysis.

RNN

Up until now, we have used neural networks such as the MLP, feedforward neural network, and CNN in our projects. The constraint faced by these neural networks is that they only accept a fixed input vector such as an image, and output another vector. The high-level architecture of these neural networks can be summarized by the following diagram:

This restrictive architecture makes it difficult for CNNs to work with sequential data. To work with sequential data, the neural network needs to take in specific bits of the data at each time step, in the sequence that it appears. This provides the idea for an RNN. An RNN has high-level architecture, as shown in the following diagram:

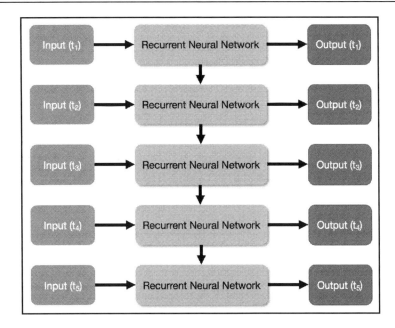

From the previous diagram, we can see that an RNN is a multi-layered neural network. We can break up the raw input, splitting it into time steps. For example, if the raw input is a sentence, we can break up the sentence into individual words (in this case, every word represents a time step). Each word will then be provided in the corresponding layer in the RNN as **Input**. More importantly, each layer in an RNN passes its output to the next layer. The intermediate output passed from layer to layer is known as the hidden state. Essentially, the hidden state allows an RNN to maintain a memory of the intermediate states from the sequential data.

What's inside an RNN?

Let's now take a closer look at what goes on inside each layer of an RNN. The following diagram depicts the mathematical function inside each layer of an RNN:

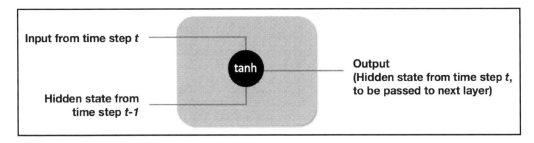

The mathematical function of an RNN is simple. Each layer *t* within an RNN has two inputs:

- The input from the time step *t*
- The hidden state passed from the previous layer *t-1*

Each layer in an RNN simply sums up the two inputs and applies a *tanh* function to the sum. It then outputs the result, to be passed as a hidden state to the next layer. It's that simple! More formally, the output hidden state of layer *t* is this:

$$s_t = tanh(s_{t-1} + x_t)$$

But what exactly is the *tanh* function? The *tanh* function is the hyperbolic tangent function, and it simply squashes a value between **1** and **-1**. The following graph illustrates this:

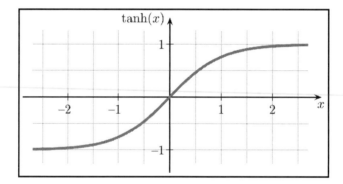

The tanh function is a good choice as a non-linear transformation of the combination of the current input and the previous hidden state, because it ensures that the weights don't diverge too rapidly. It has also other nice mathematical properties, such as being easily differentiable.

Finally, to get the final output from the last layer in the RNN, we simply apply a *sigmoid* function to it:

$$O_n = sigmoid(s_n)$$

In the previous equation, n is the index of the last layer in the RNN. Recall from previous chapters that the *sigmoid* function produces an output between 0 and 1, hence providing the probabilities for each class as a prediction.

We can see that if we stack these layers together, the final output from an RNN depends on the non-linear combination of the inputs at different time steps.

Long- and short-term dependencies in RNNs

The architecture of an RNN makes it ideal for handling sequential data. Let's take a look at some concrete examples, to understand how an RNN handles different lengths of sequential data.

Let's first take a look at a short piece of text as our sequential data:

"THE WEATHER IS HOT TODAY"

We can treat this short sentence as sequential data by breaking it down into five different inputs, with each word at each time step. This is illustrated in the following diagram:

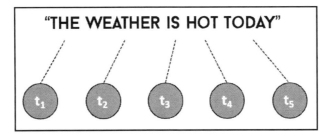

Now, suppose that we are building a simple RNN to predict whether is it snowing based on this sequential data. The RNN would look something like this:

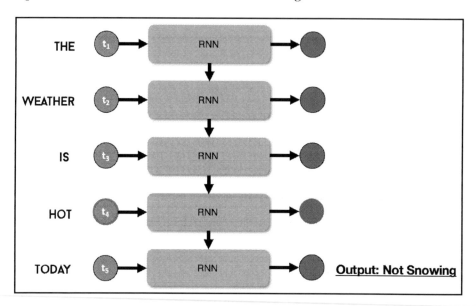

The critical piece of information in the sequence is the word **HOT**, at time step 4 (t_4 circled in red). With this piece of information, the RNN is able to easily predict that it is not snowing today. Notice that the critical piece of information came just shortly before the final output. In other words, we would say that there is a short-term dependency in this sequence.

Clearly, RNNs have no problems with short-term dependencies. But what about long-term dependencies? Let's take a look now at a longer sequence of text. Let's use the following paragraph as an example:

> "I really liked the movie but I was disappointed in the service and cleanliness of the cinema. The cinema should be better maintained in order to provide a better experience for customers."

Our goal is to predict whether the customer liked the movie. Clearly, the customer liked the movie but not the cinema, which was the main complaint in the paragraph. Let's break up the paragraph into a sequence of inputs, with each word at each time step (32 time steps for 32 words in the paragraph). The RNN would look this:

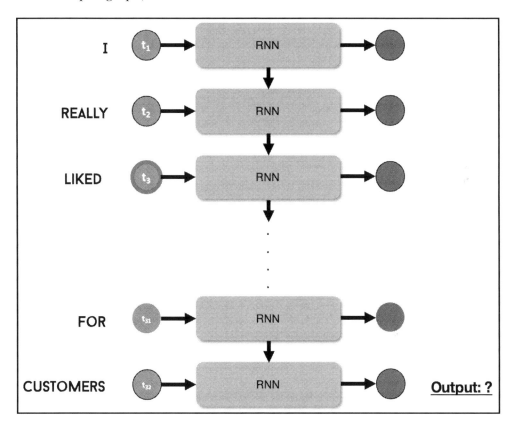

The critical words **liked the movie** appeared between time steps 3 and 5. Notice that there is a significant gap between the critical time steps and the output time step, as the rest of the text was largely irrelevant to the prediction problem (whether the customer liked the movie). In other words, we say that there is a long-term dependency in this sequence. Unfortunately, RNNs do not work well with long-term dependency sequences. RNNs have a good short-term memory, but a bad long-term memory. To understand why this is so, we need to understand the **vanishing gradient problem** when training neural networks.

The vanishing gradient problem

The vanishing gradient problem is a problem when training deep neural networks using gradient-based methods such as backpropagation. Recall in previous chapters, we discussed the backpropagation algorithm in training neural networks. In particular, the `loss` function provides information on the accuracy of our predictions, and allows us to adjust the weights in each layer, to reduce the loss.

So far, we have assumed that backpropagation works perfectly. Unfortunately, that is not true. When the loss is propagated backward, the loss tends to decrease with each successive layer:

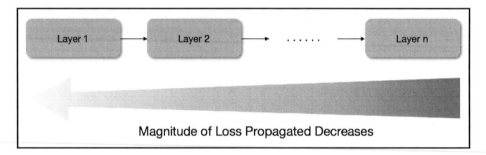

As a result, by the time the loss is propagated back toward the first few layers, the loss has already diminished so much that the weights do not change much at all. With such a small loss being propagated backward, it is impossible to adjust and train the weights of the first few layers. This phenomenon is known as the vanishing gradient problem in machine learning.

Interestingly, the vanishing gradient problem does not affect CNNs in computer vision problems. However, when it comes to sequential data and RNNs, the vanishing gradient can have a significant impact. The vanishing gradient problem means that RNNs are unable to learn from early layers (early time steps), which causes it to have poor long-term memory.

To address this problem, Hochreiter and others proposed a clever variation of the RNN, known as the **long short-term memory (LSTM)** network.

The LSTM network

LSTMs are a variation of RNNs, and they solve the long-term dependency problem faced by conventional RNNs. Before we dive into the technicalities of LSTMs, it is useful to understand the intuition behind them.

LSTMs – the intuition

As we explained in the previous section, LSTMs were designed to overcome the problem with long-term dependencies. Let's assume we have this movie review:

> "I loved this movie! The action sequences were on point and the acting was terrific. Highly recommended!"

Our task is to predict whether the reviewer liked the movie. As we read this review, we immediately understand that this review is positive. In particular, the following words (highlighted) are the most important:

> "I loved this movie! The action sequences were on point and the acting was terrific. Highly recommended!"

If we think about it, only the highlighted words are important, and we can ignore the rest of the words. This is an important strategy. By selectively remembering certain words, we can ensure that our neural network does not get bogged down by too many unnecessary words that do not provide much predictive power. This is an important distinction of LSTMs over conventional RNNs. Conventional RNNs have a tendency to remember everything (even unnecessary inputs) that results in the inability to learn from long sequences. By contrast, LSTMs selectively remember important inputs (such as the preceding highlighted text), and this allows them to handle both short- and long-term dependencies.

The ability of LSTMs to learn from both short- and long-term dependencies gives it its name, **long short-term memory** (**LSTM**).

What's inside an LSTM network?

LSTMs have the same repeating structure of RNNs that we have seen previously. However, LSTMs differ in their internal structure.

The following diagram shows a high-level overview of the repeating unit of an LSTM:

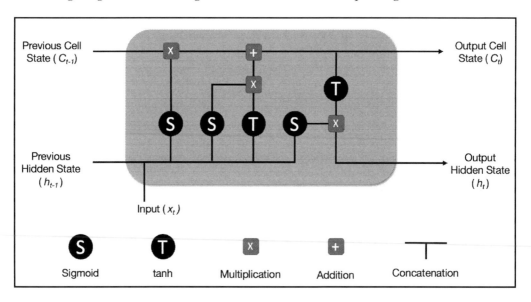

The preceding diagram might look complicated to you now, but, don't worry, as we'll go through everything step by step. As we mentioned in the previous section, LSTMs have the ability to selectively remember important inputs and to forget the rest. The internal structure of an LSTM allows it to do that.

An LSTM differs from a conventional RNN in that it has a cell state, in addition to the hidden state. You can think of the cell state as the current memory of the LSTM. It flows from one repeating structure to the next, conveying important information that has to be retained at the moment. In contrast, the hidden state is the overall memory of the entire LSTM. It contains everything that we have seen so far, both important and unimportant information.

How does the LSTM release information between the hidden state and the cell state? It does so via three important gates:

- Forget gate
- Input gate
- Output gate

Just like physical gates, the three gates restrict the flow of information from the hidden state to the cell state.

Forget gate

The **Forget gate (f)** of an LSTM is highlighted in the following diagram:

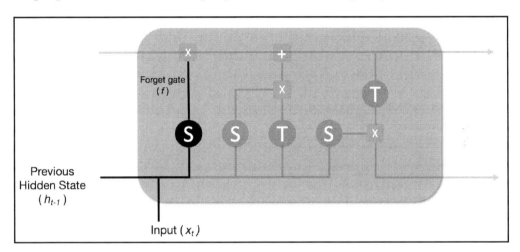

The **Forget gate (f)** forms the first part of the LSTM repeating unit, and its role is to decide how much data we should forget or remember from the previous cell state. It does so by first concatenating the **Previous Hidden State (h_{t-1})** and the current **Input (x_t)**, then passing the concatenated vector through a sigmoid function. Recall that the sigmoid function outputs a vector with values between 0 and 1. A value of 0 means to stop the information from passing through (forget), and a value of 1 means to pass the information through (remember).

The output of the forget gate, *f*, is as follows:

$$f = \sigma(concatenate(h_{t-1}, x_t))$$

Input gate

The next gate is the **Input gate (i)**. The **Input gate (i)** controls how much information to pass to the current cell state. The input gate of an LSTM is highlighted in the following diagram:

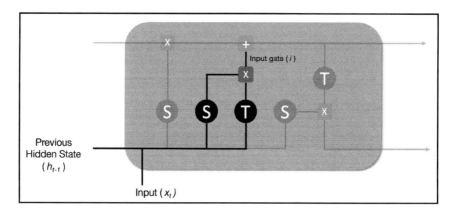

Just like the forget gate, the **Input gate (i)** takes as input the concatenation of the **Previous Hidden State (h$_{t-1}$)** and the current **Input (x$_t$)**. It then passes two copies of the concatenated vector through a sigmoid function and a tanh function, before multiplying them together.

The output of the input gate, *i*, is as follows:

$$i = \sigma(concatenate(h_{t-1}, x_t)) * tanh(concatenate(h_{t-1}, x_t))$$

At this point, we have what is required to compute the current cell state (**C$_t$**) to be output. This is illustrated in the following diagram:

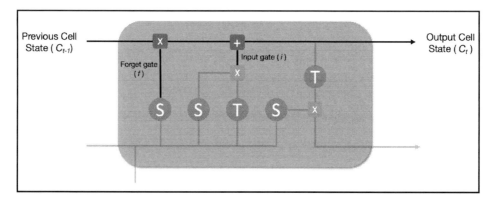

The current cell state C_t is as follows:

$$C_t = (f * C_t) + i$$

Output gate

Finally, the output gate controls how much information is to be retained in the hidden state. The output gate is highlighted in the following diagram:

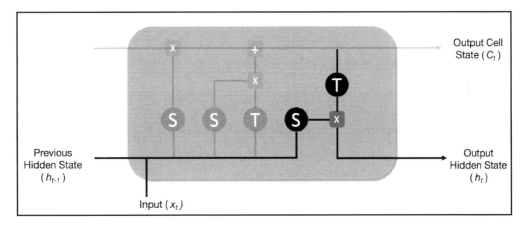

First, we concatenate the **Previous Hidden State (h_{t-1})** and the current **Input (x_t)**, and pass it through a sigmoid function. Then, we take the current cell state (C_t) and pass it through a tanh function. Finally, we take the multiplication of the two, which is passed to the next repeating unit as the hidden state (h_t). This process is summarized by the following equation:

$$h_t = \sigma(concatenate(h_{t-1}, x_t)) * tanh(C_t)$$

Making sense of this

Many beginners to LSTMs often get intimidated by the mathematical formulas involved. Although it is useful to understand the mathematical functions behind LSTMs, it is often difficult (and not very useful) to try to relate the intuition behind LSTMs and the mathematical formulas. Instead, it is more useful to understand LSTMs at a high level, and then to apply a black box algorithm, as we shall see in the later sections.

The IMDb movie reviews dataset

At this point, let's take a quick look at the IMDb movie reviews dataset before we start building our model. It is always a good practice to understand our data before we build our model.

The IMDb movie reviews dataset is a corpus of movie reviews posted on the popular movie reviews website `https://www.imdb.com/`. Each movie review has a label indicating whether the review is positive (1) or negative (0).

The IMDb movie reviews dataset is provided in Keras, and we can import it by simply calling the following code:

```
from keras.datasets import imdb
training_set, testing_set = imdb.load_data(index_from = 3)
X_train, y_train = training_set
X_test, y_test = testing_set
```

We can print out the first movie review as follows:

```
print(X_train[0])
```

We'll see the following output:

```
[1, 14, 22, 16, 43, 530, 973, 1622, 1385, 65, 458, 4468, 66, 3941, 4, 173,
36, 256, 5, 25, 100, 43, 838, 112, 50, 670, 22665, 9, 35, 480, 284, 5, 150,
4, 172, 112, 167, 21631, 336, 385, 39, 4, 172, 4536, 1111, 17, 546, 38, 13,
447, 4, 192, 50, 16, 6, 147, 2025, 19, 14, 22, 4, 1920, 4613, 469, 4, 22,
71, 87, 12, 16, 43, 530, 38, 76, 15, 13, 1247, 4, 22, 17, 515, 17, 12, 16,
626, 18, 19193, 5, 62, 386, 12, 8, 316, 8, 106, 5, 4, 2223, 5244, 16, 480,
66, 3785, 33, 4, 130, 12, 16, 38, 619, 5, 25, 124, 51, 36, 135, 48, 25,
1415, 33, 6, 22, 12, 215, 28, 77, 52, 5, 14, 407, 16, 82, 10311, 8, 4, 107,
117, 5952, 15, 256, 4, 31050, 7, 3766, 5, 723, 36, 71, 43, 530, 476, 26,
400, 317, 46, 7, 4, 12118, 1029, 13, 104, 88, 4, 381, 15, 297, 98, 32,
2071, 56, 26, 141, 6, 194, 7486, 18, 4, 226, 22, 21, 134, 476, 26, 480, 5,
144, 30, 5535, 18, 51, 36, 28, 224, 92, 25, 104, 4, 226, 65, 16, 38, 1334,
88, 12, 16, 283, 5, 16, 4472, 113, 103, 32, 15, 16, 5345, 19, 178, 32]
```

We see a sequence of numbers, because Keras has already encoded the words as numbers as part of the preprocessing. We can convert the review back to words, using the built-in word-to-index dictionary provided by Keras as part of the dataset:

```
word_to_id = imdb.get_word_index()
word_to_id = {key:(value+3) for key,value in word_to_id.items()}
word_to_id["<PAD>"] = 0
word_to_id["<START>"] = 1
id_to_word = {value:key for key,value in word_to_id.items()}
```

Now, we can show the original review in words:

```
print(' '.join(id_to_word[id] for id in X_train[159] ))
```

We'll see the following output:

```
<START> a rating of 1 does not begin to express how dull depressing and
relentlessly bad this movie is
```

Clearly, the sentiment of this review is negative! Let's make sure by printing the y value:

```
print(y_train[159])
```

We'll see the following output:

```
0
```

A y value of 0 refers to a negative review and a y value of 1 refers to a positive review. Let's take a look at an example of a positive review:

```
print(' '.join(id_to_word[id] for id in X_train[6]))
```

We'll get the following output:

```
<START> lavish production values and solid performances in this
straightforward adaption of jane austen's satirical classic about the
marriage game within and between the classes in provincial 18th century
england northam and paltrow are a salutory mixture as friends who must pass
through jealousies and lies to discover that they love each other good
humor is a sustaining virtue which goes a long way towards explaining the
accessability of the aged source material which has been toned down a bit
in its harsh scepticism i liked the look of the film and how shots were set
up and i thought it didn't rely too much on successions of head shots like
most other films of the 80s and 90s do very good results
```

To check the sentiment of the review, try this:

```
print(y_train[6])
```

We get the following output:

```
1
```

Representing words as vectors

So far, we have looked at what RNNs and LSTM networks represent. There remains an important question we need to address: how do we represent words as input data for our neural network? In the case of CNNs, we saw how images are essentially three-dimensional vectors/matrixes, with dimensions represented by the image width, height, and the number of channels (three channels for color images). The values in the vectors represent the intensity of each individual pixel.

One-hot encoding

How do we create a similar vector/matrix for words so that they can be used as input to our neural network? In earlier chapters, we saw how categorical variables such as the day of week can be one-hot encoded to numerical variables by creating a new feature for each variable. It may be tempting to think that we can also one-hot encode our sentences in this manner, but such a method has significant disadvantages.

Let's consider phrases such as the following:

- Happy, excited
- Happy
- Excited

The following diagram shows a one-hot encoded two-dimensional representation of these phrases:

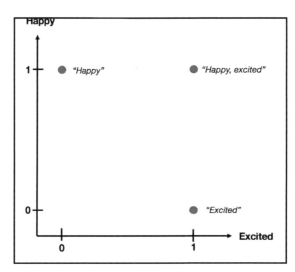

In this vector representation, the phrase "**Happy, excited**" has a value of **1** for both axes, because both the words "**Happy**" and "**Excited**" are present in the phrase. Similarly, the phrase **Happy** has a value of **1** for the **Happy** axis and a value of **0** for the **Excited** axis, because it only contains the word **Happy**.

The full two-dimensional vector representation is shown in the following table:

Happy	Excited
1	1
1	0
0	1

There are several problems with this one-hot encoded representation. Firstly, the number of axes depends on the number of unique words in our dataset. As we can imagine, there are tens of thousands of unique words in the English dictionary. If we were to create an axis for each word, then the size of our vector would quickly grow out of hand. Secondly, such a vector representation would be extremely sparse (full of zeros). This is because most words appear only once in each sentence/paragraph. It is difficult to train a neural network on such a sparse vector.

Finally, and perhaps most importantly, such a vector representation does not take into consideration the similarity of words. In our preceding example, **Happy** and **Excited** are both words that convey positive emotions. However, this one-hot encoded representation does not take this similarity into consideration. Thus, important information is lost when words are represented in this form.

As we can see, there are significant disadvantages associated with one-hot encoded vectors. In the next section, we'll look at **word embeddings**, which overcome these disadvantages.

Word embeddings

Word embeddings are a learned form of vector representation for words. The main advantage of word embeddings is that they have fewer dimensions than the one-hot encoded representation, and they place similar words close to one another.

The following diagram shows an example of a word embedding:

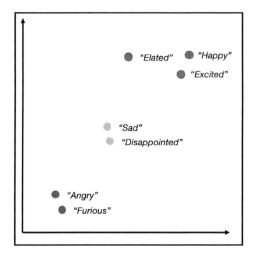

Notice that the learned word embedding knows that the words **"Elated"**, **"Happy"**, and **"Excited"** are similar words, and hence should be placed near each other. Similarly, the words **"Sad"**, **"Disappointed"**, **"Angry"**, and **"Furious"** are on the opposite ends of the spectrum, and should be placed far away.

We won't go into detail regarding the creation of the word embeddings, but essentially they are trained using supervised learning algorithms. Keras also provides a convenient API for training our own word embeddings. In this project, we will train our word embeddings on the IMDb movie reviews dataset.

Model architecture

Let's take a look at the model architecture of our IMDb movie review sentiment analyzer, shown in the following diagram:

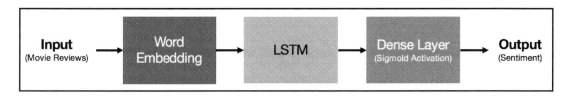

This should be fairly familiar to you by now! Let's go through each component briefly.

Input

The input to our neural network shall be IMDb movie reviews. The reviews will be in the form of English sentences. As we've seen, the dataset provided in Keras has already encoded the English words into numbers, as neural networks require numerical inputs. However, there remains a problem we need to address. As we know, movie reviews have different lengths. If we were to represent the reviews as a vector, then different reviews would have different vector lengths, which is not acceptable for a neural network. Let's keep this in mind for now, and we'll see how we can address this issue as we build our neural network.

Word embedding layer

The first layer in our neural network is the word embedding layer. As we've seen earlier, word embeddings are a learned form of vector representation for words. The word embedding layer takes in words as input, and then outputs a vector representation of these words. The vector representation should place similar words close to one another, and dissimilar words distant from one another. The word embedding layer learns this vector representation during training.

LSTM layer

The LSTM layer takes as input the vector representation of the words from the word embedding layer, and learns how to classify the vector representation as positive or negative. As we've seen earlier, LSTMs are a variation of RNNs, which we can think of as multiple neural networks stacked on top of one another.

Dense layer

The next layer is the dense layer (fully connected layer). The dense layer takes as input the output from the LSTM layer, and transforms it into a fully connected manner. Then, we apply a sigmoid activation on the dense layer, so that the final output is between 0 and 1.

Output

The output is a probability between 0 and 1, representing the probability that the movie review is positive or negative. A probability near to 1 means that the movie review is positive, while a probability near to 0 means that the movie review is negative.

Model building in Keras

We're finally ready to start building our model in Keras. As a reminder, the model architecture that we're going to use is shown in the previous section.

Importing data

First, let's import the dataset. The IMDb movie reviews dataset is already provided in Keras, so we can import it directly:

```
from keras.datasets import imdb
```

The `imdb` class has a `load_data` main function, which takes in the following important argument:

- `num_words`: This is defined as the maximum number of unique words to be loaded. Only the *n* most common unique words (as they appear in the dataset) will be loaded. If *n* is small, the training time will be faster at the expense of accuracy. Let's set `num_words = 10000`.

The `load_data` function returns two tuples as the output. The first tuple holds the training set, while the second tuple holds the testing set. Note that the `load_data` function splits the data equally and randomly into training and testing sets.

The following code imports the data, with the previously mentioned parameters:

```
training_set, testing_set = imdb.load_data(num_words = 10000)
X_train, y_train = training_set
X_test, y_test = testing_set
```

Let's do a quick check to see the amount of data we have:

```
print("Number of training samples = {}".format(X_train.shape[0]))
print("Number of testing samples = {}".format(X_test.shape[0]))
```

We'll see the following output:

```
Number of training samples = 25000
Number of testing samples = 25000
```

We can see that we have 25000 training and testing samples each.

Zero padding

Before we can use the data as input to our neural network, we need to address an issue. Recall that in the previous section, we mentioned that movie reviews have different lengths, and therefore the input vectors have different sizes. This is an issue, as neural networks only accept fixed-size vectors.

To address this issue, we are going to define a `maxlen` parameter. The `maxlen` parameter shall be the maximum length of each movie review. Reviews that are longer than `maxlen` will be truncated, and reviews that are shorter than `maxlen` will be padded with zeros.

The following diagram illustrates the zero padding process:

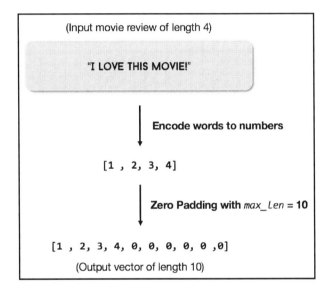

Using zero padding, we ensure that the input will have a fixed vector length.

As always, Keras provides a handy function to perform zero padding. Under the Keras `preprocessing` module, there's a `sequence` class that allows us to perform preprocessing for sequential data. Let's import the `sequence` class:

```
from keras.preprocessing import sequence
```

The `sequence` class has a `pad_sequences` function that allows us to perform zero padding on our sequential data. Let's truncate and pad our training and testing data using a `maxlen` of `100`. The following code shows how we can do this:

```
X_train_padded = sequence.pad_sequences(X_train, maxlen= 100)
X_test_padded = sequence.pad_sequences(X_test, maxlen= 100)
```

Now, let's verify the vector length after zero padding:

```
print("X_train vector shape = {}".format(X_train_padded.shape))
print("X_test vector shape = {}".format(X_test_padded.shape))
```

We'll see the following output:

```
X_train vector shape = (25000, 100)
X_test vector shape = (25000, 100)
```

Word embedding and LSTM layers

With our input preprocessed, we can now turn our attention to model building. As always, we will use the `Sequential` class in Keras to build our model. Recall that the `Sequential` class allows us to stack layers on top of one another, making it really easy to build complex models layer by layer.

As always, let's define a new `Sequential` class:

```
from keras.models import Sequential
model = Sequential()
```

We can now add the word embedding layer to our model. The word embedding layer can be constructed directly from the `keras.layers` as follows:

```
from keras.layers import Embedding
```

The `Embedding` class takes the following important arguments:

- `input_dim`: The input dimensions of the word embedding layer. This should be the same as the `num_words` parameter that we used when we loaded in our data. Essentially, this is the maximum number of unique words in our dataset.
- `output_dim`: The output dimensions of the word embedding layer. This should be a hyperparameter to be fine-tuned. For now, let's use a value of `128`.

We can add an embedding layer with the previously mentioned parameters to our sequential model as follows:

```
model.add(Embedding(input_dim = 10000, output_dim = 128))
```

Similarly, we can add a `LSTM` layer directly from `keras.layers` as follows:

```
from keras.layers import LSTM
```

The `LSTM` class takes the following important arguments:

- `units`: This refers to the number of recurring units in the `LSTM` layer. A larger number of units results in a more complex model, at the expense of training time and overfitting. For now, let's use a typical value of `128` for the number of units.
- `activation`: This refers to the type of activation function applied to the cell state and the hidden state. The default value is the tanh function.
- `recurrent_activation`: This refers to the type of activation function applied to the forget, input, and output gates. The default value is the `sigmoid` function.

You might notice that the kind of activation function is rather limited in Keras. Instead of selecting individual activations for the forget, input, and output gates, we are limited to choosing a single activation function for all three gates. This is unfortunately a limitation that we need to work with. However, the good news is that this deviation from theory does not significantly affect our results. The LSTM that we build in Keras is perfectly able to learn from the sequential data.

We can add an `LSTM` layer with the previously mentioned parameters to our sequential model as follows:

```
model.add(LSTM(units=128))
```

Finally, we add a `Dense` layer with `sigmoid` as the `activation` function. Recall that the purpose of this layer is to ensure that the output of our model has a value between 0 and 1, representing the probability that the movie review is positive. We can add a `Dense` layer as follows:

```
from keras.layers import Dense
model.add(Dense(units=1, activation='sigmoid'))
```

The `Dense` layer is the final layer in our neural network. Let's verify the structure of our model by calling the `summary()` function:

```
model.summary()
```

We get the following output:

```
Layer (type)                 Output Shape              Param #
=================================================================
embedding_3 (Embedding)      (None, None, 128)         1280000
_____
lstm_3 (LSTM)                (None, 128)               131584
_____
dense_3 (Dense)              (None, 1)                 129
=================================================================
Total params: 1,411,713
Trainable params: 1,411,713
Non-trainable params: 0
```

Nice! We can see that the structure of our Keras model matches the model architecture in the diagram that we introduced at the start of the previous section.

Compiling and training models

With the model building complete, we're ready to compile and train our model. By now, you should be familiar with the model compilation in Keras. As always, there are certain parameters we need to decide when we compile our model. They are as follows:

- **Loss function**: We use a `binary_crossentropy` loss function when the target output is binary and a `categorical_crossentropy` loss function when the target output is multi-class. Since the sentiment of movie reviews in this project is **binary** (that is, positive or negative), we will use a `binary_crossentropy` loss function.
- **Optimizer**: The choice of optimizer is an interesting problem in LSTMs. Without getting into the technicalities, certain optimizers may not work for certain datasets, due to the vanishing gradient and the **exploding gradient problem** (the opposite of the vanishing gradient problem). It is often impossible to know beforehand which optimizer works better for the dataset. Therefore, the best way to know is to train different models using different optimizers, and to use the optimizer that gives the best results. Let's try the `SGD`, `RMSprop`, and the `adam` optimizer.

We can compile our model as follows:

```
# try the SGD optimizer first
Optimizer = 'SGD'

model.compile(loss='binary_crossentropy', optimizer = Optimizer)
```

Now, let's train our model for 10 epochs, using the testing set as the validation data. We can do so as follows:

```
scores = model.fit(x=X_train_padded, y=y_train,
                   batch_size = 128, epochs=10,
                   validation_data=(X_test_padded, y_test))
```

The `scores` object returned is a Python dictionary that provides the training and validation accuracy and the loss per epoch.

Before we go on to analyze our results, let's put all our code into a single function. This allows us to easily test and compare the performance of different optimizers.

We define a `train_model()` function that takes in an `Optimizer` as an argument:

```
def train_model(Optimizer, X_train, y_train, X_val, y_val):
    model = Sequential()
    model.add(Embedding(input_dim = 10000, output_dim = 128))
    model.add(LSTM(units=128))
    model.add(Dense(units=1, activation='sigmoid'))
    model.compile(loss='binary_crossentropy', optimizer = Optimizer,
                  metrics=['accuracy'])
    scores = model.fit(X_train, y_train, batch_size=128,
                       epochs=10,
                       validation_data=(X_val, y_val),
                       verbose=0)
    return scores, model
```

Using this function, let's train three different models using three different optimizers, the SGD, RMSprop, and the `adam` optimizer:

```
SGD_score, SGD_model = train_model(Optimizer = 'sgd',
                                   X_train=X_train_padded,
                                   y_train=y_train,
                                   X_val=X_test_padded,
                                   y_val=y_test)

RMSprop_score, RMSprop_model = train_model(Optimizer = 'RMSprop',
                                           X_train=X_train_padded,
                                           y_train=y_train,
                                           X_val=X_test_padded,
```

```
                                       y_val=y_test)

Adam_score, Adam_model = train_model(Optimizer = 'adam',
                                     X_train=X_train_padded,
                                     y_train=y_train,
                                     X_val=X_test_padded,
                                     y_val=y_test)
```

Analyzing the results

Let's plot the validation accuracy per epoch for the three different models. First, we plot for the model trained using the sgd optimizer:

```
from matplotlib import pyplot as plt

plt.plot(range(1,11), SGD_score.history['acc'], label='Training Accuracy')
plt.plot(range(1,11), SGD_score.history['val_acc'],
         label='Validation Accuracy')
plt.axis([1, 10, 0, 1])
plt.xlabel('Epoch')
plt.ylabel('Accuracy')
plt.title('Train and Validation Accuracy using SGD Optimizer')
plt.legend()
plt.show()
```

We get the following output:

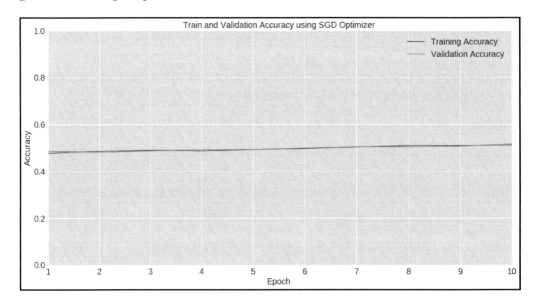

Did you notice anything wrong? The training and validation accuracy is stuck at 50%! Essentially, this shows that the training has failed and our neural network performs no better than a random coin toss for this binary classification task. Clearly, the `sgd` optimizer is not suitable for this dataset and this LSTM network. Can we do better if we use another optimizer? Let's try the `RMSprop` optimizer.

We plot the training and validation accuracy for the model trained using the `RMSprop` optimizer, as shown in the following code:

```
plt.plot(range(1,11), RMSprop_score.history['acc'],
        label='Training Accuracy')
plt.plot(range(1,11), RMSprop_score.history['val_acc'],
        label='Validation Accuracy')
plt.axis([1, 10, 0, 1])
plt.xlabel('Epoch')
plt.ylabel('Accuracy')
plt.title('Train and Validation Accuracy using RMSprop Optimizer')
plt.legend()
plt.show()
```

We get the following output:

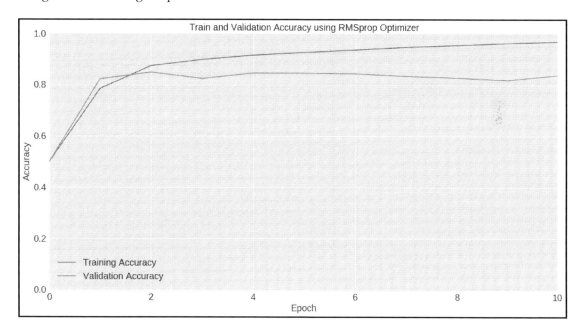

That's much better! Within 10 epochs, our model is able to achieve a training accuracy of more than 95% and a validation accuracy of around 85%. That's not bad at all. Clearly, the RMSprop optimizer performs better than the sgd optimizer for this task.

Finally, let's try the adam optimizer and see how it performs. We plot the training and validation accuracy for the model trained using the adam optimizer, as shown in the following code:

```
plt.plot(range(1,11), Adam_score.history['acc'], label='Training Accuracy')
plt.plot(range(1,11), Adam_score.history['val_acc'],
        label='Validation Accuracy')
plt.axis([1, 10, 0, 1])
plt.xlabel('Epoch')
plt.ylabel('Accuracy')
plt.title('Train and Validation Accuracy using Adam Optimizer')
plt.legend()
plt.show()
```

We get the following output:

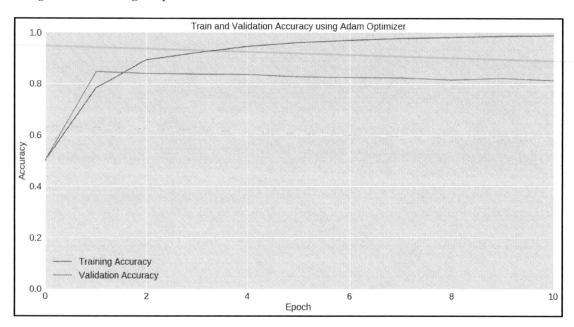

The adam optimizer does pretty well. From the preceding graph, we can see that the Training Accuracy is almost 100% after 10 epochs, while the Validation Accuracy is around 80%. This gap of 20% suggests that overfitting is happening when the adam optimizer is used.

By contrast, the gap between training and validation accuracy is smaller for the RMSprop optimizer. Hence, we conclude that the RMSprop optimizer is the most optimal for this dataset and the LSTM network, and we shall use the model built using the RMSprop optimizer from this point onward.

Confusion matrix

In `Chapter 2`, *Diabetes Prediction with Multilayer Perceptrons*, we saw how the confusion matrix is a useful visualization tool to evaluate the performance of our model. Let's also use the confusion matrix to evaluate the performance of our model in this project.

To recap, these are the definitions of the terms in the confusion matrix:

- **True negative**: The actual class is negative (negative sentiment), and the model also predicted negative
- **False positive**: The actual class is negative (negative sentiment), but the model predicted positive
- **False negative**: The actual class is positive (positive sentiment), but the model predicted negative
- **True positive**: The actual class is positive (positive sentiment), and the model predicted positive

We want our false positive and false negative numbers to be as low as possible, and for the true negative and true positive numbers to be as high as possible.

We can construct a confusion matrix using the `confusion_matrix` class from `sklearn`, using `seaborn` for visualization:

```
from sklearn.metrics import confusion_matrix
import seaborn as sns

plt.figure(figsize=(10,7))
sns.set(font_scale=2)
y_test_pred = RMSprop_model.predict_classes(X_test_padded)
c_matrix = confusion_matrix(y_test, y_test_pred)
ax = sns.heatmap(c_matrix, annot=True, xticklabels=['Negative Sentiment',
                 'Positive Sentiment'], yticklabels=['Negative Sentiment',
                 'Positive Sentiment'], cbar=False, cmap='Blues', fmt='g')
ax.set_xlabel("Prediction")
ax.set_ylabel("Actual")
```

We get the following output:

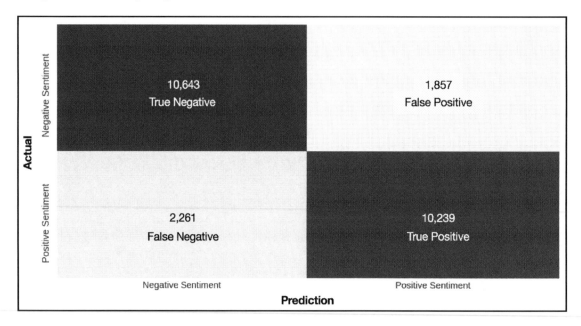

From the preceding confusion matrix, we can see that most of the testing data was classified correctly, with the number of true negatives and true positives at around 85%. In other words, our model is 85% accurate at predicting sentiment for movie reviews. That's pretty impressive!

Let's take a look at some of the wrongly classified samples, and see where the model got it wrong. The following code captures the index of the wrongly classified samples:

```
false_negatives = []
false_positives = []

for i in range(len(y_test_pred)):
    if y_test_pred[i][0] != y_test[i]:
        if y_test[i] == 0: # False Positive
            false_positives.append(i)
        else:
            false_negatives.append(i)
```

Let's first take a look at the false positives. As a reminder, false positives refer to movie reviews that were negative but that our model wrongly classified as positive.

We have selected an interesting false positive; this is shown as follows:

```
"The sweet is never as sweet without the sour". This quote was essentially
the theme for the movie in my opinion ..... It is a movie that really makes
you step back and look at your life and how you live it. You cannot really
appreciate the better things in life (the sweet) like love until you have
experienced the bad (the sour). ..... Only complaint is that the movie gets
very twisted at points and is hard to really understand...... I recommend
you watch it and see for yourself.
```

Even as a human, it is hard to predict the sentiment of this movie review! The first sentence of the movie probably sets the tone of the reviewer. However, it is written in a really subtle manner, and it is difficult for our model to pick out the intention of the sentence. Furthermore, the middle of the review praises the movie, before ending with the conclusion that the `movie gets very twisted at points and is hard to really understand`.

Now, let's take a look at some false negatives:

```
I hate reading reviews that say something like 'don't waste your time this
film stinks on ice'. It does to that reviewer yet for me it may have some
sort of naïve charm ..... This film is not as good in my opinion as any of
the earlier series entries ... But the acting is good and so is the
lighting and the dialog. It's just lacking in energy and you'll likely
figure out exactly what's going on and how it's all going to come out in
the end not more than a quarter of the way through ..... But still I'll
recommend this one for at least a single viewing. I've watched it at least
twice myself and got a reasonable amount of enjoyment out of it both times
```

This review is definitely on the fence, and it looked pretty neutral, with the reviewer presenting the good and bad of the movie. Another point to note is that, at the start of the review, the reviewer quoted another reviewer (`I hate reading reviews that say something like 'don't waste your time this film stinks on ice'`). Our model probably didn't understand that this quote is not the opinion of this reviewer. Quoted text is definitely a challenge for most NLP models.

Let's take a look at another false negative:

```
I just don't understand why this movie is getting beat up in here jeez. It
is mindless, it isn't polished ..... I just don't get it. The jokes work on
more then one level. If you didn't get it, I know what level you're at.
```

This movie review can be considered a *rant* against other movie reviews, similar to the previous review that we showed. The presence of multiple negative words in the movie probably misled our model, and our model did not understand that the review was ranting against all the other negative reviews. Statistically speaking, such reviews are relatively rare, and it is difficult for our model to learn the true sentiment of such reviews.

Putting it all together

We have covered a lot in this chapter. Let's consolidate all our code here:

```python
from keras.datasets import imdb
from keras.preprocessing import sequence
from keras.models import Sequential
from keras.layers import Embedding
from keras.layers import Dense, Embedding
from keras.layers import LSTM
from matplotlib import pyplot as plt
from sklearn.metrics import confusion_matrix
import seaborn as sns

# Import IMDB dataset
training_set, testing_set = imdb.load_data(num_words = 10000)
X_train, y_train = training_set
X_test, y_test = testing_set

print("Number of training samples = {}".format(X_train.shape[0]))
print("Number of testing samples = {}".format(X_test.shape[0]))

# Zero-Padding
X_train_padded = sequence.pad_sequences(X_train, maxlen= 100)
X_test_padded = sequence.pad_sequences(X_test, maxlen= 100)

print("X_train vector shape = {}".format(X_train_padded.shape))
print("X_test vector shape = {}".format(X_test_padded.shape))

# Model Building
def train_model(Optimizer, X_train, y_train, X_val, y_val):
    model = Sequential()
    model.add(Embedding(input_dim = 10000, output_dim = 128))
    model.add(LSTM(units=128))
    model.add(Dense(units=1, activation='sigmoid'))
    model.compile(loss='binary_crossentropy', optimizer = Optimizer,
                  metrics=['accuracy'])
    scores = model.fit(X_train, y_train, batch_size=128, epochs=10,
                       validation_data=(X_val, y_val))
```

```
        return scores, model

# Train Model
RMSprop_score, RMSprop_model = train_model(Optimizer = 'RMSprop',
X_train=X_train_padded, y_train=y_train, X_val=X_test_padded, y_val=y_test)

# Plot accuracy per epoch
plt.plot(range(1,11), RMSprop_score.history['acc'],
         label='Training Accuracy')
plt.plot(range(1,11), RMSprop_score.history['val_acc'],
         label='Validation Accuracy')
plt.axis([1, 10, 0, 1])
plt.xlabel('Epoch')
plt.ylabel('Accuracy')
plt.title('Train and Validation Accuracy using RMSprop Optimizer')
plt.legend()
plt.show()

# Plot confusion matrix
y_test_pred = RMSprop_model.predict_classes(X_test_padded)
c_matrix = confusion_matrix(y_test, y_test_pred)
ax = sns.heatmap(c_matrix, annot=True, xticklabels=['Negative Sentiment',
                 'Positive Sentiment'], yticklabels=['Negative Sentiment',
                 'Positive Sentiment'], cbar=False, cmap='Blues', fmt='g')
ax.set_xlabel("Prediction")
ax.set_ylabel("Actual")
plt.show()
```

Summary

In this chapter, we created an LSTM-based neural network that can predict the sentiment of movie reviews with 85% accuracy. We first looked at the theory behind recurrent neural networks and LSTMs, and we understood that they are a special class of neural network designed to handle sequential data, where the order of the data matters.

We also looked at how we can convert sequential data such as a paragraph of text into a numerical vector, as input for neural networks. We saw how word embeddings can reduce the dimensionality of such a numerical vector into something more manageable for training neural networks, without necessarily losing information. A word embedding layer does this by learning which words are similar to one another, and it places such words in a cluster, in the transformed vector.

We also looked at how we can easily construct a LSTM neural network in Keras, using the `Sequential` model. We also investigated the effect of different optimizers on the LSTM, and we saw how the LSTM is unable to learn from the data when certain optimizers are used. More importantly, we saw that tuning and experimenting is an essential part of the machine learning process, in order to maximize our results.

Lastly, we analyzed our results, and we saw how LSTM-based neural networks fail to detect sarcasm and other subtleties in our language. NLP is an extremely challenging subfield of machine learning that researchers are still working on today.

In the next chapter, `Chapter 7`, *Implementing a Facial Recognition System with Neural Networks*, we'll look at **Siamese neural networks**, and how they can be used to create a face recognition system.

Questions

1. What are sequential problems in machine learning?

   Sequential problems are a class of problem in machine learning in which the order of the features presented to the model is important for making predictions. Examples of sequential problems include NLP problems (for example, speech and text) and time series problems.

2. What are some reasons that make it challenging for AI to solve sentiment analysis problems?

   Human languages often contain words that have different meanings, depending on the context. It is therefore important for a machine learning model to fully understand the context before making a prediction. Furthermore, sarcasm is common in human languages, which is difficult for an AI-based model to comprehend.

3. How is an RNN different than a CNN?

   RNNs can be thought of as multiple, recursive copies of a single neural network. Each layer in an RNN passes its output to the next layer as input. This allows an RNN to use sequential data as input.

4. What is the hidden state of an RNN?

The intermediate output passed from layer to layer in an RNN is known as the hidden state. The hidden state allows an RNN to maintain a memory of the intermediate states from the sequential data.

5. What are the disadvantages of using an RNN for sequential problems?

RNNs suffer from the vanishing gradient problem, which results in features early on in the sequence being "forgotten" due to the small weights assigned to them. Therefore, we say that RNNs have a long-term dependency problem.

6. How is an LSTM network different than a conventional RNN?

LSTM networks are designed to overcome the long-term dependency problem in conventional RNNs. An LSTM network contains three gates (input, output, and forget gates), which allows it to place emphasis on certain features (that is, words), regardless of when the feature appears in the sequence.

7. What is the disadvantage of one-hot encoding words to transform them to numerical inputs?

The dimensionality of a one-hot encoded word vector tends to be huge (due to the amount of different words in a language), which makes it difficult for the neural network to learn from the vector. Furthermore, a one-hot encoded vector does not take into consideration the relationships between similar words in a language.

8. What are word embeddings?

Word embeddings are a learned formed of vector representation for words. The main advantage of word embeddings is that they have smaller dimensions than the one-hot encoded representation, and they place similar words close to one another. Word embeddings are usually the first layer in an LSTM-based neural network.

9. What important preprocessing step is required when working with textual data?

Textual data often has uneven lengths, which results in vectors of different sizes. Neural networks are unable to accept vectors of different sizes as input. Therefore, we apply zero padding as a preprocessing step, to truncate and pad vectors evenly.

10. Tuning and experimenting is often an essential part of the machine learning process. What experimenting have we done in this project?

In this project, we experimented with different optimizers (the SGD, RMSprop, and adam optimizers) for training our neural network. We found that the SGD optimizer was unable to train the LSTM network, while the RMSprop optimizer had the best accuracy.

7
Implementing a Facial Recognition System with Neural Networks

In this chapter, we will implement a facial recognition system using a **Siamese neural network**. Such facial recognition systems are prevalent in smartphones and other smart security systems in modern buildings and facilities. We will go through the theory behind Siamese neural networks, and why facial recognition problems are a special class of problems in image recognition, making it difficult for a conventional **convolutional neural networks (CNNs)** to solve them. We will train and implement a robust model that can recognize faces, even when the subject has different expressions and when the photo is taken from different angles. Finally, we will write our own program that uses the pre-trained neural network and a webcam, to authenticate the user sitting in front of the computer.

Specifically, these are the topics that we will cover in this chapter:

- The facial recognition problem
- Face detection and face recognition
- One-shot learning
- Siamese neural networks
- Contrastive loss
- Faces dataset
- Training a Siamese neural network in Keras
- Creating your own facial recognition system

Technical requirements

The following Python libraries are required for this chapter:

- Numpy 1.15.2
- Keras 2.2.4
- OpenCV 3.4.2
- PIL 5.4.1

The code for this chapter can be found in the GitHub repository for this book at `https://github.com/PacktPublishing/Neural-Network-Projects-with-Python/tree/master/Chapter07`.

To download the code onto your computer, you may run the following `git clone` command:

```
$ git clone
https://github.com/PacktPublishing/Neural-Network-Projects-with-Python.git
```

After the process is complete, there will be a folder entitled `Neural-Network-Projects-with-Python`. Enter the folder by running the following:

```
$ cd Neural-Network-Projects-with-Python
```

To install the required Python libraries in a virtual environment, run the following command:

```
$ conda env create -f environment.yml
```

Note that you should have installed Anaconda on your computer first before running this command. To enter the virtual environment, run the following command:

```
$ conda activate neural-network-projects-python
```

Navigate to the `Chapter07` folder by running the following command:

```
$ cd Chapter07
```

The following files are located in the folder:

- `face_detection.py` contains the Python code for face detection using OpenCV
- `siamese_nn.py` contains the Python code to create and train a Siamese neural network
- `onboarding.py` contains the Python code for the onboarding process of the face recognition system
- `face_recognition_system.py` contains the complete face recognition system program

Please run the Python files in this order:

1. `siamese_nn.py`: To train a Siamese neural network for face recognition
2. `onboarding.py`: To start the onboarding process for the face recognition system
3. `face_recognition_system.py`: The actual face recognition program that uses your webcam

To run each Python file, simply execute the files as follows:

```
$ python siamese_nn.py
```

Facial recognition systems

Facial recognition systems have become ubiquitous in our every lives. When the iPhone X was first unveiled in 2017, Apple boasted that their new state-of-the-art face ID system was able to instantaneously recognize and authenticate users with just a single glance. Driving this was the Apple A11 Bionic chip, which includes dedicated neural network hardware, allowing the iPhone to perform blazingly fast facial recognition and machine learning operations. Today, almost all smartphones have a facial recognition security system.

In 2016, Amazon started its first supermarket with advanced facial recognition capabilities, known as **Amazon Go**. Unlike traditional supermarkets, Amazon Go uses facial recognition to know when you first arrive at the supermarket and when you removed an item from the shelf. When you've finished shopping, you can simply walk out of the store, without waiting in line at the cashier, as all your purchases are captured by Amazon's AI systems. This allows busy shoppers to do their grocery shopping in person at the supermarket, without wasting time waiting in line for the cashier. No longer belonging to a dystopian future, facial recognition systems have already become an important part of our everyday lives.

Breaking down the face recognition problem

Let's break down the face recognition problem into smaller steps and subproblems. That way, we can better understand what's going on under the hood of a facial recognition system. A face recognition problem can be broken down into the following smaller subproblems:

- **Face detection**: Detect and isolate faces in the image. In an image with multiple faces, we need to detect each of them separately. In this step, we should also crop the detected faces from the original input image, to identify them separately.
- **Face recognition**: For each detected face in the image, we run it through a neural network to classify the subject. Note that we need to repeat this step for each detected face.

Intuitively, this process makes a lot of sense. If we think of how humans recognize faces, we see that it is very similar to the process that we described. Given an image, our eyes immediately zoom into each face (face detection), and we recognize the faces individually (face recognition).

The following diagram illustrates the subprocesses in face recognition:

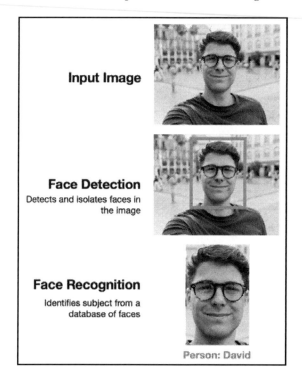

Face detection

First of all, let's take a look at face detection. The face detection problem is actually a rather interesting problem in computer vision that researchers have worked on for many years. In 2001, Viola and Jones demonstrated how real-time, large-scale face detection can be done with minimal computational resources. This was a significant discovery at the time, as researchers seek to do real-time, large-scale face detection (for example, to monitor a large crowd in real-time). Today, face detection algorithms can be run on simple hardware such as our personal computers with just a few lines of code. In fact, as we shall see shortly, we will use OpenCV in Python to construct a face detector, using your own webcam.

There are several approaches to face detection, including the following:

- Haar Cascades
- Eigenfaces
- **Histogram of Oriented Gradients (HOG)**

We'll explain how to do face detection using Haar Cascades (as presented by Viola and Jones in 2001), and we'll see the beautiful simplicity in this algorithm.

The key idea behind the Viola-Jones algorithm is that all human faces share certain properties, such as the following:

- The area of the eye is darker than the forehead and the cheeks
- The area of the nose is brighter than the eyes

In a frontal, non-occluded image of a human face, we can see features such as the eyes, the nose, and the lips. If we look closely at the area around the eyes, we see that there is a repeating pattern of dark and light pixels, as shown in the following diagram:

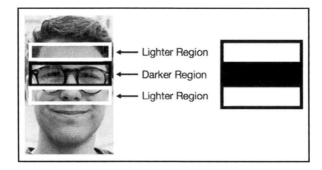

Of course, the preceding example is just one possible feature. We can also construct other features that capture other regions of the face, such as the nose, lips, chin, and so on. Some examples of other features are shown in the following diagram:

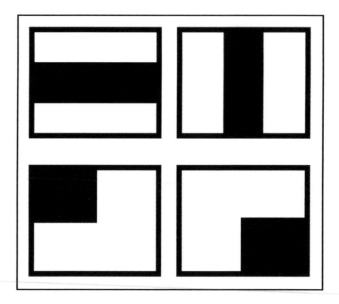

These features with alternating regions of dark and light pixels are known as Haar features. Depending on your imagination, you can construct an almost infinite number of features. In fact, in the final algorithm presented by Viola and Jones, there were more than 6,000 Haar features used!

Do you see the similarities between Haar features and convolutional filters? They both detect identifying geometric representations in images! The difference is that Haar features are handcrafted features that detect eyes, noses, lips, and so on, in human faces, based on what we know. On the other hand, convolutional filters are created during training, using a labeled dataset and are not handcrafted. However, they perform the same function: identifying geometric representation in images. The similarities between Haar features and convolutional filters show that many ideas in machine learning and AI are shared and improved iteratively over the years.

To use the Haar features, we slide them over every region in the image and compute the similarity of the pixels with the Haar features. However, since most areas in an image do not contain a face (think about the photos we take—faces are usually limited to a small area in the photo), it is computationally wasteful to test all the features. To overcome this, Viola and Jones introduced a cascade classifier. The idea is to start with the most simple Haar feature. If the candidate region fails, this simple Haar feature (that is, the prediction from this feature is that the region does not contain a face), we immediately move on to the next candidate region. This way, we do not waste computational resources on regions that do not contain a face. We progressively move on to more complex Haar features, and we repeat the process. Eventually, the regions in the image with a face are the regions that pass all the Haar features. This classifier is known as a **cascade classifier**.

The Viola-Jones algorithm using Haar features demonstrated remarkable accuracy and false positive rates in face detection, while being computationally efficient. In fact, when the algorithm was first presented in 2001, it was running on a 700 Mhz Pentium III processor!

Face detection in Python

Face detection can be implemented by the OpenCV library in Python. OpenCV is an open source computer vision library for computer vision tasks. Let's see how we can use OpenCV for face detection.

First, we import OpenCV:

```
import cv2
```

Next, let's load a pre-trained cascade classifier for face detection. This cascade classifier can be found in the accompanying GitHub repository and should have been downloaded to your computer (refer to the *Technical requirements* section):

```
face_cascades =
cv2.CascadeClassifier('haarcascade_frontalface_default.xml')
```

Next, we define a function that takes in an image, performs face detection on the image, and draws a bounding box around the image:

```
def detect_faces(img, draw_box=True):
    # convert image to grayscale
    grayscale_img = cv2.cvtColor(img, cv2.COLOR_BGR2GRAY)

    # detect faces
    faces = face_cascades.detectMultiScale(grayscale_img, scaleFactor=1.6)

    # draw bounding box around detected faces
```

```
for (x, y, width, height) in faces:
    if draw_box:
        cv2.rectangle(img, (x, y), (x+width, y+height), (0, 255, 0), 5)
face_box = img[y:y+height, x:x+width]
face_coords = [x,y,width,height]
return img, face_box, face_coords
```

Let's test our face detector on some sample images. The images can be found in the 'sample_faces' folder, and they look like this:

As we can see, there is a fair amount of noise (that is, non-face structures) in each image, which can potentially trip up our face detector. In the bottom-right image, we can also see that there are multiple faces.

We apply the detect_faces function that we defined earlier on these images:

```
import os
files = os.listdir('sample_faces')
images = [file for file in files if 'jpg' in file]
for image in images:
    img = cv2.imread('sample_faces/' + image)
    detected_faces, _, _ = detect_faces(img)
    cv2.imwrite('sample_faces/detected_faces/' + image, detected_faces)
```

We see the following output images saved in
the `'sample_faces/detected_faces'` folder:

Fantastic! Our face detector passed with flying colors. The speed of the detection was really impressive as well. We can see that face detection using OpenCV in Python is simple and takes no time at all.

Face recognition

With face detection complete, let's turn our attention to the next step: face recognition. You might have noticed that face detection had nothing to do with neural networks! Face detection using Haar features is an old but reliable algorithm that is still widely used today. However, face detection only extracts the region that contains a face. Our next step would be to perform face recognition using the extracted faces.

Face recognition using neural networks is the main topic in this chapter. For the rest of the chapter, we'll focus on training a neural network for face recognition.

Requirements of face recognition systems

At this point, you should be fairly familiar with using neural networks for image recognition tasks. In Chapter 4, *Cats Versus Dogs – Image Classification Using CNNs*, we built a CNN for classifying images of cats versus dogs. Can the same techniques be used in facial recognition? Sadly, CNNs fall short for this task. To understand why, we need to look at the requirements of facial recognition systems.

Speed

The first requirement of a facial recognition system is that they need to be fast. If we look at the onboarding process of the facial recognition systems in our smartphones, we usually need to use the front-facing camera in the phone to scan our face at various angles for a few seconds. During this short process, our phone captures images of our face, and uses an image to train a neural network to recognize us. This process needs to be fast.

The following picture shows the typical onboarding process for a facial recognition system in smartphones:

Can a CNN satisfy this speed requirement? From the project that we built in `Chapter 4`, *Cats Versus Dogs – Image Classification Using CNNs,* we saw how slow it is to train a CNN to identify images of cats and dogs. Even with powerful GPUs, training a CNN can sometimes take hours (or even days!). From a user experience point of view, it is not practical for the onboarding process of facial recognition systems to take this long. Therefore, CNNs do not satisfy the speed requirement of facial recognition systems.

Scalability

The second requirement of facial recognition systems is that it needs to be scalable. The model that we train must ultimately be able to scale to millions of different users, each with a unique face. Again, this is where CNNs fall short. Recall that in `Chapter 4`, *Cats Versus Dogs – Image Classification Using CNNs,* we trained a CNN to differentiate cats from dogs. This neural network is only able to identify and classify images of cats and dogs, and not of other animals, which it was not trained on. This means that if we were to use CNNs for facial recognition, we would have to train a separate neural network for each individual user. This would simply be unworkable from a scalability point of view! This would mean that Amazon would need to train an individual neural network for each of its millions of users, and to run through millions of different neural networks whenever a user walks through the doors of Amazon Go.

The following diagram illustrates the constraints faced by CNNs on facial recognition:

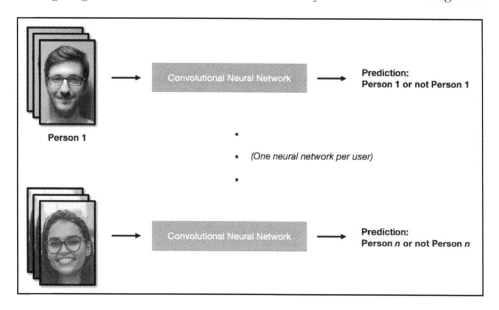

Given the constraints in memory, it is impractical to train a neural network for every user. Such a system would get bogged down very quickly as the number of users grew. Therefore, CNNs fail to provide a scalable solution for facial recognition.

High accuracy with small data

The third requirement of a facial recognition system is that it needs to be sufficiently accurate (hence secure) while working with a small amount of training data. In `Chapter 4, Cats Versus Dogs – Image Classification Using CNNs`, we used a huge dataset containing thousands of images of cats and dogs for training our CNN. By contrast, we almost never get this luxury when it comes to the dataset size for facial recognition. Going back to the example of the onboarding process for facial recognition in smartphones, we can see that only a handful of photos are taken, and we need to be able to train our model, using this limited dataset.

Once again, CNNs do not satisfy this requirement, because we need lots of images to train a CNN. While CNNs are fairly accurate at image classification tasks, this comes at the expense of requiring a huge training set. Imagine having to take thousands of selfies with our smartphones before we can start using the facial recognition systems in our phones! This would simply not work for most facial recognition systems.

One-shot learning

Given the unique requirements and constraints faced by facial recognition systems, it is clear that the paradigm of training a CNN for classification using a huge dataset (known as batch learning classification) is unsuitable for the facial recognition problem. Instead, our objective is to create a neural network that can learn to recognize any face using just a single training sample. This form of neural network training is known as **one-shot learning**.

One-shot learning brings about a new and interesting paradigm in machine learning problems. Thus far, we have thought of machine learning problems as mostly classification problems. In `Chapter 2`, *Predicting Diabetes, with Multilayer Perceptrons*, we used an MLP to classify patients at risk of diabetes. In `Chapter 4`, *Cats Versus Dogs – Image Classification Using CNNs*, we used a CNN to classify images of cats and dogs. In `Chapter 6`, *Sentiment Analysis of Movie Reviews Using LSTM*, we used an LSTM network to classify the sentiment of movie reviews. In this chapter, we need to approach facial recognition not simply as a classification problem, but also as an estimation of the similarity between two input images.

As an example, a one-shot learning facial recognition model should perform the following tasks when determining whether the presented face belongs to an arbitrary person (say, person A):

1. Retrieve the stored image of person A (obtained during the onboarding process). This is the *true* image of person A.
2. At testing time (for example, when someone is is trying to unlock the phone of person A), capture the image of the person. This is the *test* image.
3. Using the *true* photo and the *test* photo, the neural network should output a similarity score of the faces in the two photos.
4. If the similarity score output by the neural network is below a certain threshold (that is, the people in the two photos look dissimilar), we deny access, and if they are above the threshold, we grant access.

The following diagram illustrates this process:

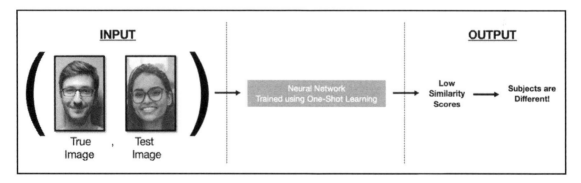

Naive one-shot prediction – Euclidean distance between two vectors

Before we dive into how neural networks can be used for one-shot learning, let's look at one naive approach.

Given the true image and a test image, one naive approach for a one-shot prediction is to simply measure the difference between the two images. As we have already seen, all images are simply three-dimensional vectors. We know that the Euclidean distance provides a mathematical formulation of the difference between two vectors. To refresh your memory, the Euclidean distance between two vectors is shown in the following diagram:

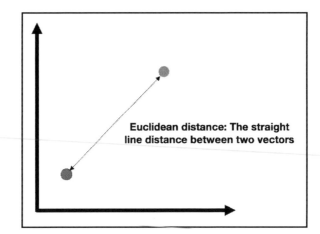

Measuring the Euclidean distance between two images provides us with a naive approach for a one-shot prediction. However, does it provide us with a satisfactory similar score for facial recognition? The answer is no. Although the Euclidean distance for facial recognition makes sense on paper, it has a poor practical value. In reality, photos can be different due to variations in angles and lighting, and also changes in the appearance of the subject, which can arise due to the wearing of accessories such as glasses. As you can imagine, a facial recognition system that uses the Euclidean distance alone would perform terribly in reality.

Siamese neural networks

So far, we have seen that a pure CNN and a pure Euclidean distance approach would not work well for facial recognition. However, we don't have to discard them entirely. Each of them provides something useful for us. Can we combine them together to form something better?

Intuitively, humans recognize faces by comparing their key features. For example, humans use features such as the shape of the eyes, the thickness of the eyebrows, the size of the nose, the overall shape of the face, and so on to recognize a person. This ability comes naturally to us, and we are seldom affected by variations in angles and lighting. Could we somehow teach a neural network to identify these features from images of faces, before using the Euclidean distance to measure the similarity between the identified features? This should sound familiar to you! As we have seen in the previous chapters, convolutional layers excel in finding such identifying features automatically. For facial recognition, researchers have found that when convolutional layers are applied to human faces, they extract spatial features, such as eyes and noses.

This insight forms the core of our algorithm for one-shot learning:

- Use convolutional layers to extract identifying features from faces. The output from the convolutional layers should be a mapping of the image to a lower-dimension feature space (for example, a 128 x 1 vector). The convolutional layers should map faces from the same subject close to one another in this lower-dimension feature space and vice versa, faces from different subjects should be as far away as possible in this lower-dimension feature space.
- Using the Euclidean distance, measure the difference of the two lower-dimension vectors output from the convolutional layers. Note that there are two vectors, because we are comparing two images (the true image and the test image). The Euclidean distance is inversely proportional to the similarity between the two images.

This works better than the naive Euclidean distance approach from the previous section (applied to raw-image pixels), because the output from the convolutional layers in the first step represents identifying features in faces (such as eyes and noses), which are invariant to angles and lighting.

One last thing to note is that, since we are feeding two images into our neural network simultaneously, we need two separate sets of convolutional layers. However, we require the two separate sets of convolutional layers to share the same weights, because we want similar faces to be mapped to the same point in the lower-dimension feature space. If the weights from the two sets of convolutional layers are different, similar faces would be mapped to different points, and the Euclidean distance would not be a useful metric at all!

We can thus think of these two sets of convolutional layers as twins, as they share the same weights. The following diagram provides an illustration of the neural network that we have just described:

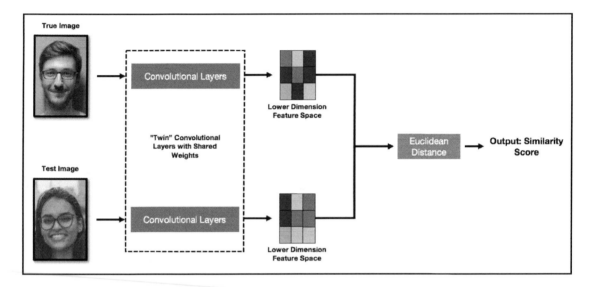

This neural network is known as a Siamese neural network, because just like a Siamese twin, it has a conjoined component at the convolutional layers.

Contrastive loss

This new paradigm of training a neural network for distance-based predictions instead of classification-based predictions requires a new loss function. Recall that in previous chapters, we used simple loss functions such as categorical cross-entropy to measure the accuracy of our predictions in classification problems.

In distance-based predictions, loss functions based on accuracy would not work. Therefore, we require a new distance-based loss function to train our Siamese neural network for facial recognition. The distance-based loss function that we will be using is called the **contrastive loss function**.

Take a look at the following variables:

- Y_{true}: Let Y_{true} be *1* if the two input images are from the same subject (same face) and *0* if the two input images are from different subjects (different faces)
- D: The predicted distance output from the neural network

So, the *Contrastive Loss* is defined as follows:

$$Contrastive\ Loss = Y_{true} * D^2 + (1 - Y_{true}) * max(margin - D, 0)$$

Here, the margin is simply a constant regularizing term. Don't worry if the preceding equation looks scary! All it does is simply produce a high loss (that is, a penalty) when the predicted distance is large when the faces are similar, and a low loss when the predicted distance is small, and vice versa for the case when the faces are different.

The following graph shows the loss for the increasing predicted distance, when the faces are similar (left) and when the faces are different (right):

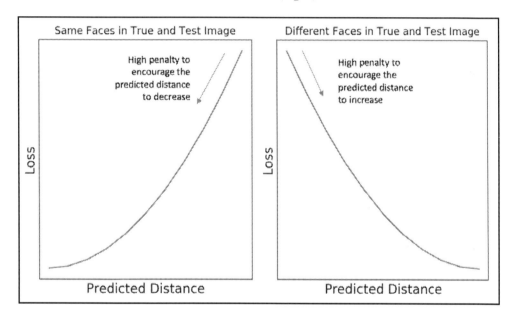

Simply put, the contrastive loss function ensures that our Siamese neural network learns to predict a small distance when the faces in the true and test images are the same, and a large distance when the faces in the true and test images are different.

The faces dataset

Let's now look at the faces dataset that we will be using for this project. There are numerous publicly available faces dataset for use, as consolidated at `http://www.face-rec.org/databases/`.

While there are many face datasets that we can use, the most appropriate dataset for training a facial recognition system should contain photos of different subjects, with each subject having multiple photos taken from different angles. It should also ideally contain photos of the subject wearing different expressions (eyes closed and so on), as such photos are commonly encountered by facial recognition systems.

With these considerations in mind, the dataset that we have chosen is the Database of Faces, created by AT&T Laboratories, Cambridge. The database contains photos of 40 subjects, with 10 photos of each subject. The photos of each subject were taken under different lighting and angles, and they have different facial expressions. For certain subjects, multiple photos were taken of people with and without glasses. You may visit the website at `https://www.cl.cam.ac.uk/research/dtg/attarchive/facedatabase.html` to learn more about the AT&T faces dataset.

The faces dataset is provided together with the code for this chapter. To download the dataset and the code from the GitHub repository, please follow the instructions in the *Technical requirements* section earlier in the chapter.

After downloading the GitHub repository, the dataset is located in the following path:

```
'Chapter07/att_faces/'
```

The images are stored in subfolders, with one subfolder per subject. Let's import the raw-image files as NumPy arrays in Python. We start by declaring a variable with the file path:

```
faces_dir = 'att_faces/'
```

Next, we want to iterate through each subfolder in the directory, and load each image in the subfolder as a NumPy array. To do that, we can import and use the `load_img` and `img_to_array` functions provided in `keras.preprocessing.image`:

```
from keras.preprocessing.image import load_img, img_to_array
```

Since there are 40 subjects, let's use images from the first 35 subjects as training samples and the remaining five subjects as testing samples. The following code iterates through each subfolder and loads the images into an `X_train` and an `X_test` array accordingly:

```
import numpy as np

X_train, Y_train = [], []
X_test, Y_test = [], []

# Get list of subfolders from faces_dir
# Each subfolder contains images from one subject
subfolders = sorted([f.path for f in os.scandir(faces_dir) if f.is_dir()])
```

```
# Iterate through the list of subfolders (subjects)
# Idx is the subject ID
for idx, folder in enumerate(subfolders):
    for file in sorted(os.listdir(folder)):
        img = load_img(folder+"/"+file, color_mode='grayscale')
        img = img_to_array(img).astype('float32')/255
        if idx < 35:
            X_train.append(img)
            Y_train.append(idx)
        else:
            X_test.append(img)
            Y_test.append(idx-35)
```

Note that the label in `Y_train` and `Y_test` is simply the index of the subfolders as we iterate through each of them (that is, the subject in the first subfolder is assigned label 1, the subject in the second subfolder is assigned label 2, and so on).

Finally, we convert `X_train`, `Y_train`, `X_test`, and `X_test` into NumPy arrays:

```
X_train = np.array(X_train)
X_test  = np.array(X_test)
Y_train = np.array(Y_train)
Y_test  = np.array(Y_test)
```

Good! We now have our training-and-testing dataset. We'll train our Siamese neural network using the training set and test it using the photos in the testing dataset.

Now, let's plot out some images from a subject to better understand the kind of data we are working with. The following code plots nine of the images from a particular subject (as entered in the `subject_idx` variable):

```
from matplotlib import pyplot as plt

subject_idx = 4
fig, ((ax1,ax2,ax3),(ax4,ax5,ax6),
      (ax7,ax8,ax9)) = plt.subplots(3,3,figsize=(10,10))
subject_img_idx = np.where(Y_train==subject_idx)[0].tolist()

for i, ax in enumerate([ax1,ax2,ax3,ax4,ax5,ax6,ax7,ax8,ax9]):
    img = X_train[subject_img_idx[i]]
    img = np.squeeze(img)
    ax.imshow(img, cmap='gray')
    ax.grid(False)
    ax.set_xticks([])
    ax.set_yticks([])
plt.tight_layout()
plt.show()
```

We see the following output:

As we can see, each photo of the subject was taken at a different angle, and the subject had different facial expressions. In some photos, we can also see that the subject removed his glasses. There's certainly a lot of variation from image to image.

We can also plot a single image from the first nine subjects, using the following code:

```
# Plot the first 9 subjects
subjects = range(10)

fig, ((ax1,ax2,ax3),(ax4,ax5,ax6),
      (ax7,ax8,ax9)) = plt.subplots(3,3,figsize=(10,12))
subject_img_idx = [np.where(Y_train==i)[0].tolist()[0] for i in subjects]

for i, ax in enumerate([ax1,ax2,ax3,ax4,ax5,ax6,ax7,ax8,ax9]):
    img = X_train[subject_img_idx[i]]
    img = np.squeeze(img)
    ax.imshow(img, cmap='gray')
    ax.grid(False)
    ax.set_xticks([])
    ax.set_yticks([])
    ax.set_title("Subject {}".format(i))
plt.show()
plt.tight_layout()
```

We'll get the following output:

Cool! It looks as though we have a diverse bunch of subjects to work with.

Creating a Siamese neural network in Keras

We are finally ready to start creating a Siamese neural network in Keras. In the previous sections, we looked at the theory and the high-level structure of a Siamese neural network. Let's now look at the architecture of a Siamese neural network in greater detail.

The following diagram shows the detailed architecture of the Siamese neural network we'll build in this chapter:

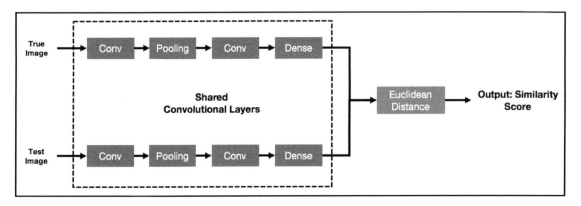

Let's start by creating the shared convolutional network (boxed in the preceding diagram) in Keras. By now, you should be familiar with the **Conv** layer, **Pooling** layer, and **Dense** layer. If you need a refresher, feel free to refer to Chapter 4, *Cats Versus Dogs – Image Classification Using CNNs*, for their definitions.

Let's define a function that builds this shared convolutional network using the Sequential class in Keras:

```
from keras.models import Sequential, Input
from keras.layers import Conv2D, MaxPooling2D, Flatten, Dense

def create_shared_network(input_shape):
    model = Sequential()
    model.add(Conv2D(filters=128, kernel_size=(3,3), activation='relu',
                     input_shape=input_shape))
    model.add(MaxPooling2D())
    model.add(Conv2D(filters=64, kernel_size=(3,3), activation='relu'))
    model.add(Flatten())
    model.add(Dense(units=128, activation='sigmoid'))
    return model
```

We can see that this function creates a convolutional network according to the architecture in the preceding diagram. At this point, you might be wondering, *how do we actually share weights across two twin networks in Keras?* Well, the short answer is that we don't actually need to create two different networks. We only need a single instance of the shared network to be declared in Keras. We can create the top and bottom convolutional network using this single instance. Because we are reusing this single instance, Keras will automatically understand that the weights are to be shared.

This is how we can do it. First, let's create a single instance of the shared network, using the function that we defined previously:

```
input_shape = X_train.shape[1:]
shared_network = create_shared_network(input_shape)
```

We specify the input for the top and bottom layers using the `Input` class:

```
input_top = Input(shape=input_shape)
input_bottom = Input(shape=input_shape)
```

Next, we stack the shared network to the right of the input layers, using the `functional` method in Keras. The syntax to do this is as follows:

```
output_top = shared_network(input_top)
output_bottom = shared_network(input_bottom)
```

Now, this syntax may not be familiar to you, because we have been using the more user-friendly `Sequential` method for building models so far. Although it is simpler, it tends to lose a bit of flexibility, and there are certain things that we cannot do using the `Sequential` method alone, including building such a network, as shown. Therefore, we use the `functional` method for building such a model.

At this point, this is what our model looks like:

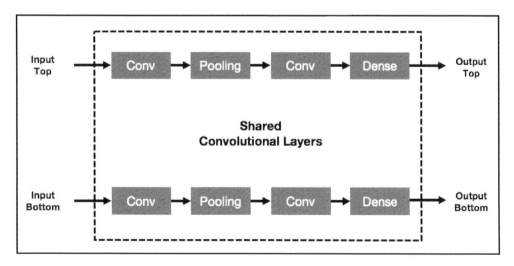

Great! All that's left is to combine the output from the top and bottom, and to measure the Euclidean distance between the two outputs. Remember, the outputs from the top and bottom at this point are 128 x 1-dimensional vectors, representing the lower-dimensional feature space.

Since there is no layer in Keras that can readily compute the Euclidean distance between two arrays, we would have to define our own layer. The `Lambda` layer in Keras allows us to do exactly that by wrapping an arbitrary function as a `Layer` object.

Let's create a `euclidean_distance` function to compute the Euclidean distance between two vectors:

```python
from keras import backend as K
def euclidean_distance(vectors):
    vector1, vector2 = vectors
    sum_square = K.sum(K.square(vector1 - vector2), axis=1, keepdims=True)
    return K.sqrt(K.maximum(sum_square, K.epsilon()))
```

We can then wrap this `euclidean_distance` function inside a `Lambda` layer:

```python
from keras.layers import Lambda
distance = Lambda(euclidean_distance, output_shape=(1,))([output_top,
                  output_bottom])
```

Finally, we combine the `distance` layer defined in the previous line with our inputs to complete our model:

```python
from keras.models import Model
model = Model(inputs=[input_top, input_bottom], outputs=distance)
```

We can verify the structure of our model by calling the `summary()` function:

```python
print(model.summary())
```

We'll see the following output:

```
Layer (type)                    Output Shape          Param #    Connected to
=====================================================================================
input_1 (InputLayer)            (None, 112, 92, 1)    0

input_2 (InputLayer)            (None, 112, 92, 1)    0

Shared_Conv_Network (Sequential (None, 128)           18707264   input_1[0][0]
                                                                  input_2[0][0]

Euclidean_Distance (Lambda)     (None, 1)             0          Shared_Conv_Network[1][0]
                                                                  Shared_Conv_Network[2][0]
=====================================================================================
Total params: 18,707,264
Trainable params: 18,707,264
Non-trainable params: 0
```

If we take a look at the summary in the previous screenshot, we can see that there are two input layers in our model, each of 112 x 92 x 1 in shape (because our images are 112 x 92 x 1). The two input layers are connected to a single shared convolutional network. The two outputs (each a 128-dimensional array) from the shared convolutional network are then combined into a `Lambda` layer, which calculates the Euclidean distance of the two 128-dimensional arrays. Finally, this Euclidean distance is output from our model.

That's it! We have successfully created our Siamese neural network. We can see that most of the complexity in the network comes from the shared convolutional network. With this basic framework in place, we can easily tune and increase the complexity of the shared convolutional network as required.

Model training in Keras

Now that we have created our Siamese neural network, we can start to train our model. Training a Siamese neural network is slightly different than training a regular CNN. Recall that when training a CNN, the training samples are arrays of images, along with the corresponding class label for each image. In contrast, to train a Siamese neural network we need to use pairs of arrays of images, along with the corresponding class label for the pairs of images (that is, 1 if the pairs of images are from the same subject, and 0 if the pairs of images are from different subjects).

The following diagram illustrates the differences between training a CNN and a Siamese neural network:

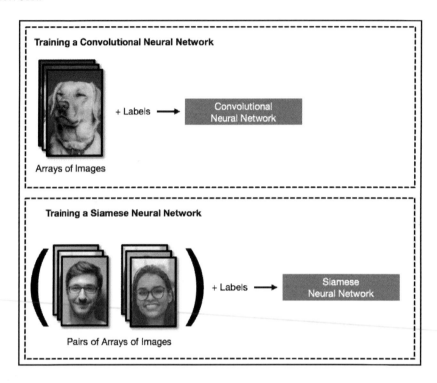

So far, we have loaded the raw image into an X_train NumPy array, along with an array with the Y_train class labels. We need to write a function that creates these pairs of arrays of images from X_train and Y_train. An important point we need to note is that in the pair of arrays of images, the number of classes should be equal (that is, an equal number of positive and negative pairs, where *positive* refers to images from the same subject and *negative* refers to images from different subjects), and that we should alternate between positive and negative pairs. This prevents our model from being biased, and ensures that it learns both positive and negative pairs of images equally well.

The following function creates pairs of arrays of images and their labels from X_train and Y_train:

```
import random
def create_pairs(X,Y, num_classes):
    pairs, labels = [], []
    # index of images in X and Y for each class
    class_idx = [np.where(Y==i)[0] for i in range(num_classes)]
    # The minimum number of images across all classes
```

```
        min_images = min(len(class_idx[i]) for i in range(num_classes)) - 1
        for c in range(num_classes):
            for n in range(min_images):
                # create positive pair
                img1 = X[class_idx[c][n]]
                img2 = X[class_idx[c][n+1]]
                pairs.append((img1, img2))
                labels.append(1)
                # create negative pair
                # list of classes that are different from the current class
                neg_list = list(range(num_classes))
                neg_list.remove(c)
                # select a random class from the negative list.
                # This class will be used to form the negative pair.
                neg_c = random.sample(neg_list,1)[0]
                img1 = X[class_idx[c][n]]
                img2 = X[class_idx[neg_c][n]]
                pairs.append((img1,img2))
                labels.append(0)
        return np.array(pairs), np.array(labels)

num_classes = len(np.unique(Y_train))
training_pairs, training_labels = create_pairs(X_train, Y_train,
                                        len(np.unique(Y_train)))
test_pairs, test_labels = create_pairs(X_test, Y_test,
                                    len(np.unique(Y_test)))
```

There is one more thing to do before we can start training our model. We need to define a function for the contrastive loss, since contrastive loss is not a default loss function in Keras.

To recap, this is the formula for *Contrastive Loss*:

$$Contrastive\ Loss = Y_{true} * D^2 + (1 - Y_{true}) * max(margin - D, 0)$$

Where Y_{true} is the true label of the training pairs and D is the predicted distance output from the neural network.

We define the following function for calculating the contrastive loss:

```
def contrastive_loss(Y_true, D):
    margin = 1
    return K.mean(Y_true*K.square(D)+(1 - Y_true)*K.maximum((margin-D),0))
```

Notice that the function includes K.mean, K.square, and K.maximum. These are simply Keras's backend functions to simplify array calculations such as the mean, max, and square.

Alright, we have all the necessary functions to train our Siamese neural network. As usual, we define the parameters of the training using the `compile` function:

```
model.compile(loss=contrastive_loss, optimizer='adam')
```

And we train our model for 10 epochs by calling the `fit` function:

```
model.fit([training_pairs[:, 0], training_pairs[:, 1]], training_labels,
          batch_size=64, epochs=10)
```

Once the training is complete, we'll see the following output:

```
Epoch 1/10
630/630 [==============================] - 2s 3ms/step - loss: 0.2505 - accuracy: 0.7619
Epoch 2/10
630/630 [==============================] - 1s 2ms/step - loss: 0.1344 - accuracy: 0.8937
Epoch 3/10
630/630 [==============================] - 1s 2ms/step - loss: 0.0932 - accuracy: 0.9413
Epoch 4/10
630/630 [==============================] - 1s 2ms/step - loss: 0.0612 - accuracy: 0.9730
Epoch 5/10
630/630 [==============================] - 1s 2ms/step - loss: 0.0404 - accuracy: 0.9921
Epoch 6/10
630/630 [==============================] - 1s 2ms/step - loss: 0.0283 - accuracy: 0.9984
Epoch 7/10
630/630 [==============================] - 1s 2ms/step - loss: 0.0208 - accuracy: 1.0000
Epoch 8/10
630/630 [==============================] - 1s 2ms/step - loss: 0.0155 - accuracy: 1.0000
Epoch 9/10
630/630 [==============================] - 1s 2ms/step - loss: 0.0123 - accuracy: 1.0000
Epoch 10/10
630/630 [==============================] - 1s 2ms/step - loss: 0.0091 - accuracy: 1.0000
```

Analyzing the results

Let's apply our model on the withheld testing set to see how well it does. Remember, our model has never seen the images and subjects from the testing set, so this is a good measurement of its real-world performance.

First, we pick two images from the same subject, plot them out side by side, and apply the model to this pair of images:

```
idx1, idx2 = 21, 29
img1 = np.expand_dims(X_test[idx1], axis=0)
img2 = np.expand_dims(X_test[idx2], axis=0)
```

```
fig, (ax1, ax2) = plt.subplots(1, 2, figsize=(10,7))
ax1.imshow(np.squeeze(img1), cmap='gray')
ax2.imshow(np.squeeze(img2), cmap='gray')

for ax in [ax1, ax2]:
    ax.grid(False)
    ax.set_xticks([])
    ax.set_yticks([])

dissimilarity = model.predict([img1, img2])[0][0]
fig.suptitle("Dissimilarity Score = {:.3f}".format(dissimilarity), size=30)
plt.tight_layout()
plt.show()
```

We'll see the following output:

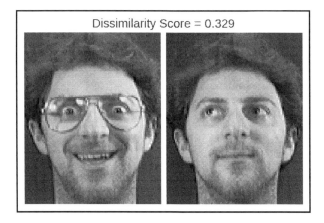

Note that the **Dissimilarity Score** is just the distance output by the model. The greater the distance, the greater the dissimilarity between the two faces.

Our model works well! We can clearly see that the subjects in the photos are the same. In the first image, the subject is wearing glasses, looking into the camera, and smiling. In the second image, the same subject is not wearing glasses, not looking into the camera, and not smiling. Our face recognition model is still able to recognize that the two faces in this pair of photos belong to the same person, as we can see from the low dissimilarity score.

Next, we pick a pair of faces from different subjects and see how well our model performs:

```
idx1, idx2 = 1, 39
img1 = np.expand_dims(X_test[idx1], axis=0)
img2 = np.expand_dims(X_test[idx2], axis=0)

fig, (ax1, ax2) = plt.subplots(1, 2, figsize=(10,7))
```

```
ax1.imshow(np.squeeze(img1), cmap='gray')
ax2.imshow(np.squeeze(img2), cmap='gray')

for ax in [ax1, ax2]:
    ax.grid(False)
    ax.set_xticks([])
    ax.set_yticks([])

dissimilarity = model.predict([img1, img2])[0][0]
fig.suptitle("Dissimilarity Score = {:.3f}".format(dissimilarity), size=30)
plt.tight_layout()
plt.show()
```

We'll see the following output:

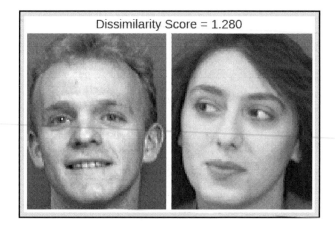

Our model performs well for negative pairs (pairs of images where the subjects are different) as well. In this case, the **Dissimilarity Score** is **1.28**. We know that positive pairs have a low dissimilarity score and that negative pairs have a high dissimilarity score. But what is the threshold score that separates them? Let's do more tests on positive and negative pairs to find out:

```
for i in range(5):
    for n in range(0,2):
        fig, (ax1, ax2) = plt.subplots(1,2, figsize=(7,5))
        img1 = np.expand_dims(test_pairs[i*20+n, 0], axis=0)
        img2 = np.expand_dims(test_pairs[i*20+n, 1], axis=0)
        dissimilarity = model.predict([img1, img2])[0][0]
        img1, img2 = np.squeeze(img1), np.squeeze(img2)
        ax1.imshow(img1, cmap='gray')
        ax2.imshow(img2, cmap='gray')

        for ax in [ax1, ax2]:
```

```
        ax.grid(False)
        ax.set_xticks([])
        ax.set_yticks([])

    plt.tight_layout()
    fig.suptitle("Dissimilarity Score = {:.3f}".format(dissimilarity),
                 size=20)
plt.show()
```

The following screenshot shows the results for certain pairs of subjects. Note that positive pairs are on the left, while negative pairs are on the right:

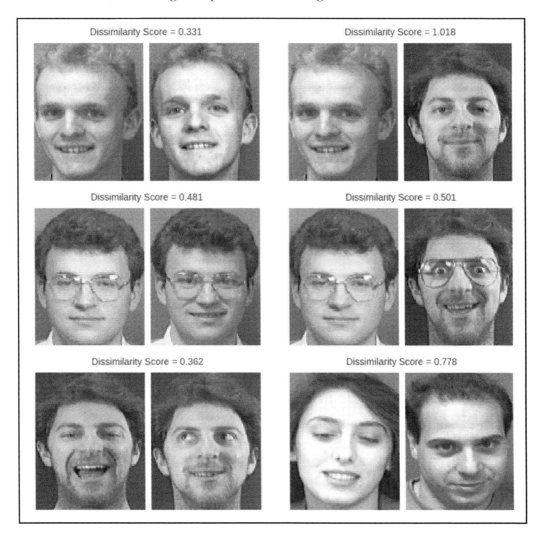

Did you spot anything interesting? Judging from the preceding results, the threshold score seems to be around 0.5. Anything below 0.5 should be classified as a positive pair (that is, faces match), and anything above 0.5 should be classified as a negative pair. Note that the negative pair on the second-row-to-the-right column is really near the threshold, with a score of 0.501. Interestingly, the two subjects do look alike, with similar glasses and hairstyles!

Consolidating our code

At this point, it would be useful to consolidate our code. We have written a lot of code so far, including helper functions. Let's consolidate the helper functions into a `utils.py` file as follows.

First, we import the necessary libraries:

```
import numpy as np
import random
import os
import cv2
from keras.models import Sequential
from keras.layers import Flatten, Dense, Conv2D, MaxPooling2D
from keras import backend as K
from keras.preprocessing.image import load_img, img_to_array
```

We include the `euclidean_distance`, `contrastive_loss`, and `accuracy` functions needed to train a Siamese neural network in the `utils.py` file:

```
def euclidean_distance(vectors):
    vector1, vector2 = vectors
    sum_square = K.sum(K.square(vector1 - vector2), axis=1, keepdims=True)
    return K.sqrt(K.maximum(sum_square, K.epsilon()))

def contrastive_loss(Y_true, D):
    margin = 1
    return K.mean(Y_true*K.square(D)+(1 - Y_true)*K.maximum((margin-D),0))

def accuracy(y_true, y_pred):
    return K.mean(K.equal(y_true, K.cast(y_pred < 0.5, y_true.dtype)))
```

We include the `create_pairs` function in the `utils.py` file. Recall that this helper function is used to generate negative and positive pairs of images for training a Siamese neural network:

```
def create_pairs(X,Y, num_classes):
    pairs, labels = [], []
    # index of images in X and Y for each class
    class_idx = [np.where(Y==i)[0] for i in range(num_classes)]
    # The minimum number of images across all classes
    min_images = min(len(class_idx[i]) for i in range(num_classes)) - 1
    for c in range(num_classes):
        for n in range(min_images):
            # create positive pair
            img1 = X[class_idx[c][n]]
            img2 = X[class_idx[c][n+1]]
            pairs.append((img1, img2))
            labels.append(1)
            # create negative pair
            neg_list = list(range(num_classes))
            neg_list.remove(c)
            # select a random class from the negative list.
            # this class will be used to form the negative pair
            neg_c = random.sample(neg_list,1)[0]
            img1 = X[class_idx[c][n]]
            img2 = X[class_idx[neg_c][n]]
            pairs.append((img1,img2))
            labels.append(0)

    return np.array(pairs), np.array(labels)
```

We also include the `create_shared_network` helper function in our `utils.py` file, which is used to create a Siamese neural network in Keras:

```
def create_shared_network(input_shape):
    model = Sequential(name='Shared_Conv_Network')
    model.add(Conv2D(filters=64, kernel_size=(3,3), activation='relu',
                      input_shape=input_shape))
    model.add(MaxPooling2D())
    model.add(Conv2D(filters=64, kernel_size=(3,3), activation='relu'))
    model.add(Flatten())
    model.add(Dense(units=128, activation='sigmoid'))
    return model
```

The last helper function in our `utils.py` file is the `get_data` function. This function helps us to load the respective raw images into NumPy arrays:

```
def get_data(dir):
    X_train, Y_train = [], []
    X_test, Y_test = [], []
    subfolders = sorted([file.path for file in os.scandir(dir) if
                         file.is_dir()])
    for idx, folder in enumerate(subfolders):
        for file in sorted(os.listdir(folder)):
            img = load_img(folder+"/"+file, color_mode='grayscale')
            img = img_to_array(img).astype('float32')/255
            img = img.reshape(img.shape[0], img.shape[1],1)
            if idx < 35:
                X_train.append(img)
                Y_train.append(idx)
            else:
                X_test.append(img)
                Y_test.append(idx-35)

    X_train = np.array(X_train)
    X_test = np.array(X_test)
    Y_train = np.array(Y_train)
    Y_test = np.array(Y_test)
    return (X_train, Y_train), (X_test, Y_test)
```

You can see the `utils.py` file in the code we provided.

Similarly, we can create a `siamese_nn.py` file. This Python file will hold the main code to create and train our Siamese neural network:

```
'''
Main code for training a Siamese neural network for face recognition
'''
import utils
import numpy as np
from keras.layers import Input, Lambda
from keras.models import Model

faces_dir = 'att_faces/'

# Import Training and Testing Data
(X_train, Y_train), (X_test, Y_test) = utils.get_data(faces_dir)
num_classes = len(np.unique(Y_train))

# Create Siamese Neural Network
input_shape = X_train.shape[1:]
shared_network = utils.create_shared_network(input_shape)
```

```
input_top = Input(shape=input_shape)
input_bottom = Input(shape=input_shape)
output_top = shared_network(input_top)
output_bottom = shared_network(input_bottom)
distance = Lambda(utils.euclidean_distance, output_shape=(1,))([output_top,
output_bottom])
model = Model(inputs=[input_top, input_bottom], outputs=distance)

# Train the model
training_pairs, training_labels = utils.create_pairs(X_train, Y_train,
                        num_classes=num_classes)
model.compile(loss=utils.contrastive_loss, optimizer='adam',
            metrics=[utils.accuracy])
model.fit([training_pairs[:, 0], training_pairs[:, 1]], training_labels,
        batch_size=128,
        epochs=10)

# Save the model
model.save('siamese_nn.h5')
```

This Python file is saved as `'Chapter07/siamese_nn.py'` in the code we provided. Notice how the code is a lot shorter than before, as we have refactored our code to call the helper functions in the `utils.py`.

Note that the last line in the preceding code saves the trained model at the `Chapter07/siamese_nn.h5` location. This allows us to easily import the trained model for face recognition, without retraining a model from scratch.

Creating a real-time face recognition program

We have finally come to the most important part of the project. We are going to put together the code that we have written so far to create a real-time face recognition program. This program will use the webcam in our computer for facial recognition, and to authenticate whether the person sitting in front of the webcam is indeed you.

To do so, the program needs to do the following:

1. Train a Siamese neural network for facial recognition (this has already been done in the previous section).
2. Use the webcam to capture a true image of the authorized user. This is the onboarding process of the facial recognition system.
3. Subsequently, when a user wants to unlock the program, use the pre-trained Siamese neural network from *Step 1* and the true image from *Step 2* to authenticate the user.

This part of the project requires a webcam (either the one in your laptop or an external webcam attached to your computer). If you do not have a webcam in your computer, you may skip this part of the project.

The onboarding process

Let's write the code for the onboarding process. During the onboarding process, we need to activate the webcam to capture a true image of the authorized user. OpenCV has a function called `VideoCapture` that allows us to activate and capture the image from the computer's webcam:

```
import cv2
video_capture = cv2.VideoCapture(0)
```

Let's give the user five seconds to prepare before taking a photo using the webcam. We start a `counter` variable with an initial value of 5 and snap a photo using the webcam once the counter reaches 0. Note that we use the code in the `face_detection.py` file that we have written earlier in the chapter to detect faces in front of the webcam. The photo will be saved as `'true_img.png'` in the same folder as the code:

```
import math
import utils
import face_detection

counter = 5

while True:
    _, frame = video_capture.read()
    frame, face_box, face_coords = face_detection.detect_faces(frame)
    text = 'Image will be taken in {}..'.format(math.ceil(counter))
    if face_box is not None:
        frame = utils.write_on_frame(frame, text, face_coords[0],
```

```
                                         face_coords[1]-10)
    cv2.imshow('Video', frame)
    cv2.waitKey(1)
    counter -= 0.1
    if counter <= 0:
        cv2.imwrite('true_img.png', face_box)
        break

# When everything is done, release the capture
video_capture.release()
cv2.destroyAllWindows()
print("Onboarding Image Captured")
```

The onboarding process looks like this:

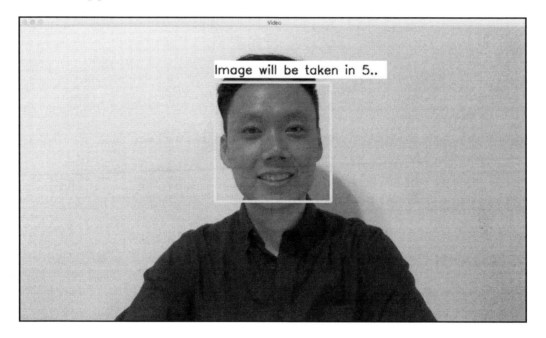

This code is saved as `Chapter07/onboarding.py` in the files we provided. To run the onboarding process for yourself, simply execute the Python file from a command prompt (in Windows) or a Terminal (macOS/Linux) by calling the following:

```
$ python onboarding.py
```

Face recognition process

With the onboarding process complete, we can now move on to the actual face recognition process. We start by asking the user for their name. The name will be displayed above the detected face, as we shall see later. The input function in Python allows the user to enter their name:

```
name = input("What is your name?")
```

The user will then enter a name on the command line when prompted.

Next, let's import our pre-trained Siamese neural network from earlier in the chapter:

```
from keras.models import load_model
model = load_model('siamese_nn.h5',
                   custom_objects={'contrastive_loss':
                   utils.contrastive_loss,
                   'euclidean_distance':utils.euclidean_distance})
```

Next, we load the true image of the user captured during the onboarding process and preprocess it by normalizing, resizing, and reshaping the image for our Siamese neural network:

```
true_img = cv2.imread('true_img.png', 0)
true_img = true_img.astype('float32')/255
true_img = cv2.resize(true_img, (92, 112))
true_img = true_img.reshape(1, true_img.shape[0], true_img.shape[1], 1)
```

The rest of the code uses the VideoCapture function in OpenCV to capture a video from the user's webcam, and passes each frame from the video to our face_detection instance. We use a fixed-length list (implemented by Python's collections.deque class) of 15 to collect the 15 most recent predictions (one prediction per frame). We average the scores from the 15 most recent predictions, and we authenticate the user if the average similarity scores is over a certain threshold. The rest of the code is shown as follows:

```
video_capture = cv2.VideoCapture(0)
preds = collections.deque(maxlen=15)

while True:
    # Capture frame-by-frame
    _, frame = video_capture.read()

    # Detect Faces
    frame, face_img, face_coords = face_detection.detect_faces(frame,
                                        draw_box=False)
```

```
        if face_img is not None:
            face_img = cv2.cvtColor(face_img, cv2.COLOR_BGR2GRAY)
            face_img = face_img.astype('float32')/255
            face_img = cv2.resize(face_img, (92, 112))
            face_img = face_img.reshape(1, face_img.shape[0],
                        face_img.shape[1], 1)
            preds.append(1-model.predict([true_img, face_img])[0][0])
            x,y,w,h = face_coords
            if len(preds) == 15 and sum(preds)/15 >= 0.3:
                text = "Identity: {}".format(name)
                cv2.rectangle(frame, (x, y), (x+w, y+h), (0, 255, 0), 5)
            elif len(preds) < 15:
                text = "Identifying ..."
                cv2.rectangle(frame, (x, y), (x+w, y+h), (0, 165, 255), 5)
            else:
                text = "Identity Unknown!"
                cv2.rectangle(frame, (x, y), (x+w, y+h), (0, 0, 255), 5)
            frame = utils.write_on_frame(frame, text, face_coords[0],
                                    face_coords[1]-10)
        else:
            # clear existing predictions if no face detected
            preds = collections.deque(maxlen=15)

        # Display the resulting frame
        cv2.imshow('Video', frame)

        if cv2.waitKey(1) & 0xFF == ord('q'):
            break

    # When everything is done, release the capture
    video_capture.release()
    cv2.destroyAllWindows()
```

This code is saved as `'Chapter07/face_recognition_system.py'` in the files we
provided. To run the program for yourself, simply execute the Python file from a command
prompt (in Windows) or a Terminal (macOS/Linux) by calling the following:

```
$ python face_recognition_system.py
```

Make sure that you run the onboarding program first (to capture a true image) before
running the face recognition program.

This is what it looks like when the program is trying to identify your face initially:

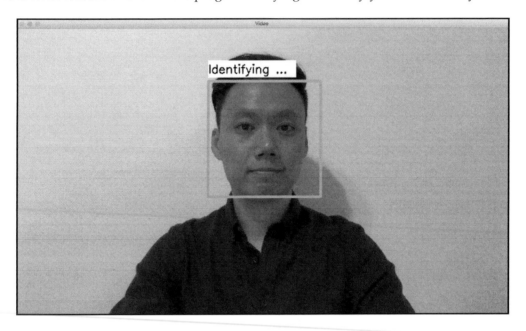

After a few seconds, the program should recognize you:

Future work

As we saw, our face recognition system certainly works well under simple conditions. However, it is definitely not fool-proof, and certainly not secure enough to be implemented in important applications. For one, the face detection system can be fooled by a static photo (try it yourself!). Theoretically, that means we can bypass the authentication by placing a static photo of an authorized user in front of the webcam.

Techniques to solve this problem are known as **anti-spoofing techniques**. Anti-spoofing techniques are a keenly studied area in face recognition. In general, there are two main anti-spoofing techniques used today:

- **Liveness detection**: Since a photo is a static two-dimensional image and a real face is dynamic and three-dimensional, we can check for the *liveness* of the detected face. Ways to perform liveness detection include checking the optic flow of the detected face, and checking the lighting and texture of the detected face in contrast to the surroundings.
- **Machine learning**: We can also differentiate a real face from an image by using machine learning! We can train a CNN to classify whether the detected face belongs to a real face or a static image. However, you would need plenty of labeled data (face versus non-face) to accomplish this.

Here's a video from Andrew Ng, showing how face recognition (with liveness detection) is implemented in Baidu's headquarters in China:

```
https://www.youtube.com/watch?v=wr4rx0Spihs
```

If you would like to understand how Apple implements its face ID system in iPhones, you can refer to the paper at `https://www.apple.com/business/site/docs/FaceID_Security_Guide.pdf` published by Apple.

Apple's implementation of face ID is more secure than the system that we used in this chapter. Apple uses a TrueDepth camera to project infrared dots on your face, creating a depth map, which is then used for facial recognition.

Summary

In this chapter, we created a face recognition system based on a Siamese neural network. The face recognition system uses a webcam to stream frames from a live video to a pre-trained Siamese neural network, and using a true image of the user, the system is able to authenticate the user in front of the webcam.

We first dissected the face recognition problem into smaller subproblems, and we saw how a face recognition system first performs a face detection step to isolate the face from the rest of the image, before the actual face recognition step. We saw how face detection is commonly done by the Viola-Jones algorithm, which uses Haar features to detect faces in real time. Face detection using Haar filters is implemented in Python via the OpenCV library, which allows us to perform face detection in just a few lines of code.

We then focused on face recognition, and we discussed how the requirements of face recognition systems (speed, scalability, high accuracy with small data) makes CNNs unsuitable for this problem. We introduced the architecture of Siamese neural networks, and how distance-based predictions in Siamese neural networks can be used for face recognition. We trained a Siamese neural network from scratch in Keras, using the AT&T faces dataset.

Lastly, using the pre-trained Siamese neural network, we created our own face recognition system in Python. The face recognition system consists of two steps. In the first step (the onboarding process), we used OpenCV's face detection API to capture an image of the user using a webcam, as the true image for the Siamese neural network. In the second step, the system uses the true image to recognize and authenticate users of the program.

In the next and final chapter, Chapter 8, *What's Next?*, we'll consolidate and recap the different projects that we've completed so far in this book. We'll also peer into the future, and see what neural networks and AI will look like in the next few years.

Questions

1. How is face detection different than face recognition?

   The objective of face detection is to locate human faces in an image. The output from the face detection process is a bounding box around detected faces. On the other hand, the objective of face recognition is to classify faces (that is, identify subjects). Face detection and face recognition are the two key steps in every facial recognition system, and the output from the face detection step is passed as input to the face recognition step.

2. What is the Viola-Jones algorithm for face detection?

The Viola-Jones algorithm uses Haar features for face detection. Haar features are filters with alternating dark and bright areas that represents the contrast in pixel intensity in human faces. For example, the eye area in an image of a human face has a darker pixel value than the forehead and the cheeks areas. These Haar filters are used to localize areas in an image that may contain faces.

3. What is one-shot learning, and how is it different than batch learning?

In one-shot learning, the objective is to train a machine learning model with very little data. In contrast, batch learning uses a big dataset to train a machine learning model. One-shot learning is often used in image recognition tasks, as the quantity of training samples can be very sparse.

4. Describe the architecture of a Siamese neural network.

Siamese neural networks consist of two conjoined convolutional layers with shared weights, accepting a pair of input images. The conjoined convolutional layers project the two input images to a lower-dimension feature space. Using a Euclidean distance layer, we compute and output the distance of the two lower-dimension vectors, which is inversely proportional to the similarity of the two images.

5. When training a Siamese neural network for face recognition, what is the loss function used?

We use a contrastive loss function to train a Siamese neural network for face recognition. The contrastive loss function encourages a neural network to output a small distance when the pair of input images are similar, and vice versa, it encourages a large output distance when the pair of input images are different.

8
What's Next?

We did it! We have created six different neural network projects, each with their own unique architecture. In this final chapter, let's recap on what we have accomplished. We will also look at some of the recent advancements in neural networks and deep learning that were not covered in previous chapters. Finally, we will peer ahead and see what the future holds for neural networks and AI in general.

Specifically, these are the topics that we'll cover in this chapter:

- A recap of the different neural networks that we used in this book
- A recap of key neural network concepts
- Cutting edge advancements in neural networks
- The limitations of neural networks
- The future of AI and machine learning
- Keeping up with machine learning
- Favorite machine learning tools
- What will you create?

Putting it all together

We have accomplished a lot in this book. Let's do a quick recap of the projects that we have built in each chapter, as well as the neural network architecture enabling them. This section also serves as a quick refresher for the key neural network concepts that we have covered in this book.

Machine Learning and Neural Networks 101

In `Chapter 1`, *Machine Learning and Neural Networks 101,* we started off by building the simplest, one-layer neural network, known as the **perceptron**. At its core, the perceptron is simply a mathematical function that takes in a set of input, performs some mathematical computation, and outputs the result of the computation. For the perceptron, the mathematical computation is simply the multiplication of the weights with the inputs.

Therefore, the right set of weights dictates how well our neural network performs. At the start, the weights of the neural network are initialized randomly. The process of tuning the weights of our neural network to maximize model performance is called **model training**. During training, the weights of the neural network are continuously tuned to minimize the **loss function**. The loss function is simply a mathematical function that allows us to quantify how well our neural networks are doing. The algorithm that we use to adjust our weights to minimize the loss function is known as **gradient descent**.

We created our very first neural network from scratch, without using machine learning libraries such as Keras or scikit-learn. We applied our simple neural network on a toy example, where the neural network had to learn binary (that is, 1 or 0) predictions. We used a sum-of-squares error as the loss function to train our neural network, where the error is 1 if the prediction is wrong and the error is 0 if the prediction is correct. We then summed up the error across each individual point, giving us the sum-of-squares error. We saw that our neural network was able to learn from the training examples, producing accurate predictions for the testing data.

Having understood the concepts of a neural network, we then discussed the most important libraries in Python for neural networks and machine learning in general. We saw how pandas is essential when we are working with tabular data (that is, from CSV files) and how it can also be used for data visualization. More importantly, we talked about Keras, the essential library in Python for working with neural networks and deep learning.

We talked about the fundamental building blocks in Keras, which are the `layers`. There are several types of `layers` in Keras, but the most important ones are the `convolutional` and `dense` layers, which are the building blocks of all neural networks that we covered in the book.

Predicting Diabetes with Multilayer Perceptrons

In `Chapter 2`, *Predicting Diabetes with Multilayer Perceptrons*, we kicked off our first project by creating a neural network that can predict whether a patient is at risk of diabetes. Specifically, we used a neural network known as the MLP to perform this classification prediction. We used the Pima Indians Diabetes dataset for this problem. The dataset consists of 768 different data points, with eight measurements (that is, features) and one label for each data point.

As part of the machine learning workflow, we had to do data preprocessing before using this dataset with our neural network. We had to impute missing values, perform data standardization, and split our dataset into a training and testing dataset.

We also built our very first neural network using Keras in this chapter. We saw how we can use the `Sequential` class in Keras to construct a neural network layer by layer, just like stacking Lego blocks on top of one another. We also looked at the **ReLU** and **sigmoid activation** functions, which are the two commonly used activation functions.

We evaluated the performance of our neural network by using metrics such as the **confusion matrix** and the **ROC curve**, which are important tools to help us understand the performance of our neural network.

Predicting Taxi Fares with Deep Feedforward Nets

In `Chapter 3`, *Predicting Taxi Fares with Deep Feedforward Nets*, we used a **deep feedforward neural network** in a **regression prediction** problem, where the task was to predict the dollar amount of a NYC taxi fare, based on features such as pick-up and drop-off locations. In this project, we had to work with a noisy dataset that included missing data and data anomalies. We saw how data visualization is essential to help us identify outliers in the dataset, and to discover important trends in the dataset.

This project was also the first project where feature engineering was done. Using the existing features, we created other features that improved the accuracy of our neural network. Finally, we created and trained a deep feedforward neural network in Keras by using our dataset, which produced an impressive mean square error of 3.50.

Cats Versus Dogs – Image Classification Using CNNs

In `Chapter 4`, *Cats Versus Dogs – Image Classification Using CNNs*, we started our first neural network project in the domain of image recognition and computer vision. Specifically, we created a CNN that is able to classify images of cats and dogs.

We saw how digital images are essentially two-dimensional arrays (for grayscale images), with each array value representing the intensity of each pixel. CNNs are the go-to neural network architecture for most image recognition problems. The **filtering** and **convolution** operation in the CNN is used to identify important spatial features in the images, which makes it suitable for image recognition problems. CNNs have gone through several iterations and improvements over the years. LeNet first came to the scene in 1998, before more sophisticated neural networks such as the VGG16 and ResNet were developed in the 2010s.

We created our own CNN in Keras, and we used Keras's `ImageDataGenerator` and the `flow_from_directory` method to train a neural network when the dataset (images of cats and dogs) was too large to fit into memory in one go. The simple CNN that we created achieved an accuracy of 80%. We also used **transfer learning** to leverage on a pre-trained VGG16 neural network for the cats-and-dogs classification problem. This method showed the sophistication of the VGG16 model, achieving an accuracy of 90%.

Removing Noise from Images Using Autoencoders

In `Chapter 5`, *Removing Noise from Images Using Autoencoders*, we looked at **autoencoders**, a special class of neural networks that learns a **latent representation** of the input. Autoencoders have an **encoder** component that compresses the input into a latent representation, and a **decoder** component that reconstructs the input using the latent representation.

In an autoencoder, the size of the hidden layer that's used for the latent representation is an important hyperparameter that needs to be tuned carefully. The size of the latent representation should be sufficiently small enough to represent a compressed representation of the input features, and also sufficiently *large* enough for the decoder to reconstruct the input without too much loss. We trained an autoencoder to compress MNIST images. We showed that by using a hidden layer size of 32 × 1, and we achieved a compression rate of 24.5, while ensuring that the reproduced images were similar to the original input images.

We also looked at using autoencoders for **image denoising**. By using a noisy image as the input and a clean image as the output, we can train an autoencoder to identify features of the image that do not belong to noise. Thus, we can apply the autoencoder to remove noise from images. Such autoencoders are known as **denoising autoencoders**. We trained and applied a denoising autoencoder to the noisy office documents dataset, which consists of scanned images of dirty office documents. Using deep convolutional layers within the denoising autoencoder, we managed to remove noise almost entirely from the office documents.

Sentiment Analysis of Movie Reviews Using LSTM

In `Chapter 6`, *Sentiment Analysis of Movie Reviews Using LSTM*, we looked at sentiment analysis, which is a sequential problem in the domain of **Natural Language Processing (NLP)**. We saw that sentiment analysis is a challenging problem even for humans, because words convey different meanings in different contexts. RNNs are thought to be the best form of neural networks for tackling sequential problems such as sentiment analysis. However, conventional recurrent neural networks suffer from a long-term dependency problem, which makes it unsuitable for lengthy bodies of text.

A variation of recurrent neural networks, known as the LSTM network, was designed to overcome the long-term dependency problem. The intuition behind LSTMs is that because of its ability to assign weights to certain words, we can selectively forget words that are less important and remember words that are more important.

We also looked at how we can represent words as vectors using word embeddings. Word embeddings transform words into a lower-dimensional feature space, placing words that are similar near to one another, while words that are dissimilar are placed further away.

We created and trained an LSTM network in Keras for sentiment analysis on the IMDB movie reviews dataset, and we looked at some of the important hyperparameters to tune while training an LSTM net. In particular, we saw how the optimizer makes a significant difference in the performance of the LSTM network. Our final LSTM network achieves 85% accuracy in classifying the sentiment of IMDB movie reviews.

Implementing a Facial Recognition System with Neural Networks

In Chapter 7, *Implementing a Facial Recognition System with Neural Networks*, we created a facial recognition system using Siamese neural networks. Siamese neural networks are a special class of neural networks, with a shared, conjoined component. Siamese neural networks accept a pair of images as input, and can be trained to output a distance that is inversely proportional to the similarity of the two images. This forms the idea behind using Siamese neural networks for facial recognition. If the two faces in the input pair of images belong to the same subject, then the distance output should be small, and vice versa. By training a Siamese neural network on positive pairs (faces that belong to the same subject) and negative pairs (faces that belong to different subjects), using contrastive loss, it will eventually learn to output an appropriate distance for positive and negative pairs.

We also looked at face detection, which is an important precursor to facial recognition. Face detection is used to isolate and extract faces from raw images, which is then passed to our neural network for face recognition. Face detection is commonly done using the Viola-Jones algorithm, which uses Haar features to detect facial features in images. To create our facial recognition system, we combined OpenCV, which uses the video stream from a computer's webcam for face detection, and the Siamese neural network that we trained for face recognition.

Cutting edge advancements in neural networks

As we saw in the previous section, we covered a lot of material in this book. However, the possibilities of neural networks are truly boundless. There are other important types of neural networks that we have not yet discussed in this book. For completeness, we shall discuss them in this section. As you shall see, these neural networks are very different than what we have seen so far, and it should provide you with a new perspective.

Generative adversarial networks

Generative adversarial networks (**GANs**) are a class of generative neural networks. To understand generative models, it's important to contrast them against discriminative models. So far in this book, we have focused only on discriminative models. Discriminative models are concerned with learning the mapping of features to a label. For example, when we created a CNN to classify images of cats and dogs, the CNN is a discriminative model that learns the mapping of features (images) to a label (a cat or a dog).

On the other hand, generative models are concerned with generating appropriate features, given the label. For example, given labeled images of cats and dogs, a generative model would learn to create the appropriate features for each label. In other words, a generative model learns to synthesize images of cats and dogs!

GANs are one of the most exciting developments in AI in recent years. In fact, Yann LeCun called GANs *the most interesting idea in machine learning in the past 10 years.* So, how do GANs work? Intuitively, GANs consist of two components—the generator and the discriminator. The role of the generator is to generate features (such as images), and the role of the discriminator is to evaluate how well the generated features represent the original features. When we train the GAN, we pit the generator against the discriminator (hence the term *adversarial* in GAN). Eventually, the generator will become so good that the discriminator can no longer differentiate the generated features from the original features and the GAN can now generate lifelike images.

To have a sense of how good GANs have become, check out the following paper, which was released by researchers from NVIDIA:

`https://arxiv.org/pdf/1812.04948.pdf`

Within the paper, you'll see some samples of faces generated by GANs that are indistinguishable from real human faces. GANs have improved at such a frightening pace that we can now generate hyper-realistic human faces.

GANs have been applied to several interesting use cases. For example, researchers have found a way to use GANs in style transfer. In style transfer, GANs learn the artistic style of a given image, and apply it to another image. For example, we can use GANs to learn the artistic style of Vincent van Gough's famous *The Starry Night* painting, and apply it to any arbitrary image. Check out the GitHub repository at `https://github.com/jcjohnson/neural-style` for examples of style transfer.

Deep reinforcement learning

Reinforcement learning is a branch of machine learning that learns the best action to take in any given state to maximize future rewards. Reinforcement learning has been applied to games such as chess. In chess, the position of the pieces on the chessboard represents the state that we are in. The role of reinforcement learning in this case is to learn the best action to take (that is, the pieces to move) in any given state.

If we think of the best action to take in any arbitrary state being represented by a mathematical function (call it the action-value function), then we can use neural networks to learn this action-value function. Once the function has been learned, our neural network can be used to predict the best action to take in any given state—essentially, our neural network becomes an unbeatable chess player! The application of deep neural networks to reinforcement learning is known as deep reinforcement learning.

Deep reinforcement learning has found much success in game-playing. In 2017, AlphaGo, an AI game-playing agent trained using deep reinforcement learning, managed to beat Ke Jie, one of the best Go players in the world. AlphaGo's victory sparked much fanfare and discussion over the future of AI.

In 2018, deep reinforcement learning took another leap when OpenAI Five (a team of five neural networks) managed to beat amateur human players at Dota 2. Dota 2 is a multiplayer online game once thought to be beyond the realm of AI, due to the immense complexity and dynamism of the game. Professional Dota 2 players are celebrities in their own right, with legions of fans admiring the speed of thought and lighting-fast reactions possessed by the best Dota 2 players in the world. Today, OpenAI Five continuously pushes the boundary of what it can do in Dota 2. OpenAI Five trains itself by playing 180 years' worth of games against itself every day. OpenAI Five views the the state of the game as an array of 20,000 numbers, and from there, it decides on the best action to take.

To learn more about OpenAI Five, as well as to try out an interactive demo, do visit OpenAI's website:

```
https://blog.openai.com/openai-five/
```

Beyond game-playing, deep reinforcement learning has made important contributions to autonomous vehicles as well. Autonomous vehicles abstract the world around them using computer vision algorithms. This abstraction represents the state that the vehicle is in. From there, deep reinforcement learning selects the best action to take (for example, accelerate, brake), according to its state.

Limitations of neural networks

The possibilities of a neural network may seem boundless, but there are in fact limitations as to what neural networks and machine learning in general can achieve.

First of all, neural networks have poor interpretability. In other words, neural networks often function as black-box algorithms, and it is difficult to *interpret* the results produced by a neural network. Take for example our project in `Chapter 2`, *Predicting Diabetes with Multilayer Perceptrons*, where we used a neural network to predict patients at risk of developing diabetes. The neural network takes in input, such as blood glucose level, blood pressure, age, and so on, and outputs a prediction of whether the patient is at risk of developing diabetes. Even though the neural network is able to make such a prediction with high accuracy, we do not actually know what are the factors that influence the predictions. This may be insufficient for a doctor, who may wish to create an intervention plan for the patient.

When applied in a real-world setting, this lack of interpretability is a real concern for business users, who may be uncomfortable with deploying a black-box algorithm. Beyond model performance, business users would also like to know why the model works, and what factors influence a target variable that the business is concerned with.

Improving the interpretability of neural networks is one of the areas that researchers are working on. In particular, researchers are working on producing interpretable results when deep neural networks are applied to computer vision problems. To that end, some researchers have proposed to reduce the convolutional layers of a CNN to a graphical model, which represents the semantic hierarchy hidden inside the neural network.

The second limitation of neural networks is that they can be easily fooled when applied to image recognition. In `Chapter 4`, *Cats Versus Dogs – Image Classification Using CNNs*, we achieved a high accuracy (90%) when CNNs were used to classify images of cats and dogs. While CNNs are considered state-of-the-art for image recognition, their Achilles' heel is that they can be easily fooled by a malicious agent.

A recent study by Nguyen and others showed that because neural networks perceive images differently than humans, an image that is completely unrecognizable to humans can be used to fool neural networks, leading neural networks to produce erroneous predictions. For examples of these synthetic images that are unrecognizable to humans, but can be used to fool neural networks, check out the paper from Nguyen and others:

```
https://arxiv.org/pdf/1412.1897.pdf
```

Furthermore, researchers showed that by combining these synthetic images with an existing image in an imperceptible way to humans, neural networks can be fooled to produce a wrong prediction.

This finding has a significant impact on the feasibility of using neural networks in computer vision based security systems. A malicious agent could possibly provide a carefully handcrafted input image to the neural network, fooling it, and bypassing the security system.

It is clear that neural networks are far from perfect, and they are certainly not the magic solution to all our problems. However, there are reasons to be optimistic, as new breakthroughs are constantly being discovered every day that improve our understanding of neural networks.

The future of artificial intelligence and machine learning

Next, let's discuss the future of AI and machine learning in general. In my opinion, we will see the rise of the following key developments over the next few decades:

- Artificial general intelligence
- Automated machine learning

Artificial general intelligence

Artificial general intelligence (**AGI**) is defined as *an artificial intelligence agent with the ability to perform any intellectual task that a human being can*. Some researchers have made the distinction of weak AI versus strong AI, with weak AI being used to describe the level of AI today. AI agents today are mostly concerned with performing a single task. For example, we train AI agents to predict whether a patient is at risk of diabetes, and another AI agent to classify images of cats and dogs. These AI agents are separate entities, and an AI agent that is trained to perform a certain task cannot be used to perform other tasks. This narrow view of AI is termed weak AI.

On the other hand, strong AI refers to generalized AI agents that can perform any task. A strong AI agent could be something like a self-conscious, human-like AI assistant. At the moment, strong AI belongs to the realm of science fiction. In my opinion, the current machine learning algorithms at our disposal (for example, neural networks, decision trees) will not be sufficient to achieve AGI. In the words of Francois Chollet (the developer of Keras):

> *"You cannot achieve general intelligence simply by scaling up today's deep learning techniques."*
>
> *- Francois Chollet*

It will take a significant breakthrough to attain AGI—the kind of breakthrough that once saw neural networks and deep learning define the *weak AI* that we know today.

Automated machine learning

Even though a data scientist has been termed *the sexiest job of the 21st century*, the reality is that most data scientists spend a disproportionate amount of time on time-consuming tasks such as data preprocessing and hyperparameter tuning. To address this issue, companies such as Google are developing tools to automate the machine learning process. Google has recently launched **AutoML**, a solution that uses neural nets to design neural nets. Google believes that AutoML can package the expertise that is currently possessed by data scientists and provide that expertise on demand as a service on the cloud.

Of course, some data scientists have taken offense at the thought that they could one day be replaced by AI, and they claim that automated machine learning would never become a reality. My personal opinion is that the truth is somewhere in-between. Today, there are already libraries in Python that can help us automate some of the more time-consuming tasks, such as hyperparameter tuning. Such libraries can brute-force their way through a range of hyperparameters, selecting the set of hyperparameters that maximizes our results. There are even libraries in Python that can visualize a dataset automatically, plotting the most relevant graphs automatically. As such libraries become more mainstream, I believe that data scientists will spend less time on such time-consuming activities, and more time on other impactful tasks, such as model design and feature engineering.

Keeping up with machine learning

The field of machine learning and AI is constantly evolving, and new knowledge is constantly being discovered. How do we keep ourselves updated in this ever-changing field? Personally, I keep myself updated by reading books, scientific journals, and practicing on real datasets.

Books

The fact that you are reading this book shows that you are committed to improving your knowledge! Unfortunately, we cannot cover every single topic of machine learning in this book. If you enjoyed this book, you may wish to refer to the catalog of books that Packt has. You will find that Packt has books on nearly every single topic in machine learning. The Packt team also ensures that the reader stays up to date with the latest developments by continuously publishing books on the latest technologies in machine learning.

Packt's catalog can be found at `https://www.packtpub.com/all`.

Scientific journals

AI researchers have always believed in openness. They believe that knowledge should be freely shared and that the best way to grow as a community is by sharing. Therefore, most of the cutting-edge scientific papers in AI and machine learning can be found freely online. In particular, most AI researchers share their findings on the following website:

`https://arxiv.org`

Arxiv is an open-access depository for scientific journals. Most of the cutting-edge findings are shared freely on arxiv as soon as they are available. This results in rapid development, with ideas being built on top of one another iteratively.

Practicing on real-world datasets

Lastly, as machine learning practitioners, it is important to keep our skills sharp by practicing often. **Kaggle** is a website that hosts data science competitions by using real-world datasets. There are different levels of competitions, so beginners and experts can find something suitable for their level of ability. The type of dataset also varies from tabular data, images (computer vision problems), and text (NLP problems).

Kernels are perhaps one of the most useful features of Kaggle. Through Kaggle kernels, users can share their code and methods openly. This ensures reproducible results, and, often, you will learn a technique that you did not know about. Kaggle also provides a free cloud environment to run your code, including GPU support. If you would like to put your skills to the test, after reading this book Kaggle is a great place to start.

Favorite machine learning tools

In this book, I have used a lot of Python and Keras. Beyond that, there are also several machine learning tools that I consider to be useful:

- **Jupyter Notebook**: Jupyter notebooks are interactive notebooks that are often used during the early stages of machine learning projects. The advantage of using Jupyter Notebooks is that it allows us to write interactive code iteratively. Unlike a `.py` Python file, code can be executed in chunks, and output (for example, graphs) can be displayed in line with the code.
- **Google Colab**: Google Colab is a free cloud platform that allows us to write Jupyter Notebook code in the cloud. All changes are synced automatically, and teams can work collaboratively on the same notebook. The greatest advantage of Google Colab is that you can run code with GPU instances in the cloud, which are provided for free by Google! This means that we can train a deep neural network efficiently from anywhere in the world, even if we do not own a powerful GPU.

Summary

In this chapter, we did a quick recap of all the different neural networks and key concepts that were covered in this book. We then looked at some cutting-edge developments in neural networks, including generative adversarial networks and deep reinforcement learning. Even though the potential of neural networks may seem boundless at times, it is important for us to remember that there are limitations to what the current state of neural networks can accomplish. Next, we surveyed the landscape of machine learning and AI in general, and we saw what AI could look like in the near future. We also offered some tips to readers on keeping up with the constantly evolving field of machine learning.

Finally, I would like to conclude this book by asking the following question—what will you create? We live in an age of highly advanced technology, where access to information is freely available. Whatever your current level, whether you are a seasoned machine learning veteran or a beginner in this field, you have all the resources that you need to succeed. I would like to encourage you to always be curious, and to always have a thirst for knowledge. Many of the discoveries in this field came from curious people like you and me. We can all contribute. What will you create?

Other Books You May Enjoy

If you enjoyed this book, you may be interested in these other books by Packt:

Generative Adversarial Networks Cookbook
Josh Kalin

ISBN: 978-1-78913-990-7

- Structure a GAN architecture in pseudocode
- Understand the common architecture for each of the GAN models you will build
- Implement different GAN architectures in TensorFlow and Keras
- Use different datasets to enable neural network functionality in GAN models
- Combine different GAN models and learn how to fine-tune them

Deep Learning with PyTorch
Vishnu Subramanian

ISBN: 978-1-78862-433-6

- Use PyTorch for GPU-accelerated tensor computations
- Build custom datasets and data loaders for images and test the models using torchvision and torchtext
- Build an image classifier by implementing CNN architectures using PyTorch
- Build systems that do text classification and language modeling using RNN, LSTM, and GRU
- Learn advanced CNN architectures such as ResNet, Inception, Densenet, and learn how to use them for transfer learning

Leave a review - let other readers know what you think

Please share your thoughts on this book with others by leaving a review on the site that you bought it from. If you purchased the book from Amazon, please leave us an honest review on this book's Amazon page. This is vital so that other potential readers can see and use your unbiased opinion to make purchasing decisions, we can understand what our customers think about our products, and our authors can see your feedback on the title that they have worked with Packt to create. It will only take a few minutes of your time, but is valuable to other potential customers, our authors, and Packt. Thank you!

Index

Made in the USA
Lexington, KY
04 July 2019